MOVING AROUND THE WINDOW

These keyboard shortcuts work the same way as the Money windows, except where noted.

TO	PRESS
Move to next transaction	↓
Move to previous transaction	↑
Move down one screen; in the Checks & Forms window, Move to next transaction	Pg Dn
Move up one screen; in the Checks & Forms window, Move to previous transaction	Pg Up
Move to the first transaction	Home
End a transaction entry and move to the first transaction	Ctrl-Home
Move to the first blank entry	End
End a transaction entry and move to the first blank entry	Ctrl-End

ENTERING TRANSACTIONS

TO	PRESS
Split a transaction	Ctrl-S
Open a drop-down list box in a field which contains an arrow	F4, Alt-↑, or Alt-↓
Insert the current date in date field	Ctrl-D
Increase number or date by one	+
Decrease number or date by one	–
Copy information from same field in the last-entered transaction	Shift-"
Mark transaction as cleared	Ctrl-M
Mark transaction as reconciled	Shift-Ctrl-M
Cancel changes	Esc

SYBEX **LEARN FAST!** BOOKS

The SYBEX *Learn Fast!* series offers busy, computer-literate people two books in one: a quick, hands-on tutorial guide to program essentials, and a comprehensive reference to commands and features.

The first half of each *Learn Fast!* book teaches the basic operations and underlying concepts of the topic software. These lessons feature trademark SYBEX characteristics: step-by-step procedures; thoughtful, well-chosen examples; an engaging writing style; valuable margin notes; and plenty of practical insights.

Once you've learned the basics, you're ready to start working on your own. That's where the second half of each *Learn Fast!* book comes in. This alphabetical reference offers concise instructions for using program commands, dialog boxes, and menu options. With dictionary-style organization and headings, this half of the book is designed to give you fast access to information.

SYBEX is very interested in your reactions to the *Learn Fast!* series. Your opinions and suggestions will help all of our readers, including yourself. Please send your comments to: SYBEX Editorial Department, 2021 Challenger Dr. Alameda, CA 94501.

LEARN *Microsoft Money* **FAST!**

LEARN *Microsoft®* *Money* FAST!

PETER KENT

San Francisco · *Paris* · *Düsseldorf* · *Soest*

Acquisitions Editor: David Clark
Developmental Editor: James A. Compton
Editors: Jeff Kapellas and David Krassner
Technical Editor: Rebecca Moore Lyles
Word Processors: Ann Dunn and Susan Trybull
Book Series Designer: Claudia Smelser
Chapter Art: Claudia Smelser
Screen Graphics: Richard Green
Desktop Publishing Production: Len Gilbert
Proofreader/Production Assistant: Catherine Mahoney
Indexer: Ted Laux
Cover Designer: Ingalls + Associates
Cover Photographer: Mark Johann
Screen reproductions produced with Collage Plus.

Library of Congress Card Number: 91-68341
ISBN: 0-7821-1044-4

Manufactured in the United States of America
10 9 8 7 6 5 4 3 2 1

To Debbie, Nicholas, and Christopher

ACKNOWLEDGMENTS

Thanks to Jim Compton and Jeff Kapellas of SYBEX for editing my manuscript into shape, and to the SYBEX production people who made it look so good.

TABLE*of*CONTENTS

Preface xvii

PART I TUTORIAL

LESSON 1 *Getting Ready* 3

Installing Microsoft Money 4

Opening Money 4

The Money Window and Its Components 6

- The Account Book Window 8

Working with Files 10

- Do You Need More Files? 10
- Creating a New File 11
- Opening Files 12

Creating Accounts 12

- The Types of Accounts 13
- Editing an Account 13
- Creating a Credit Card Account 14
- The Delete and Rename Options 15

Closing Money 15

For More Information 16

LESSON 2 *Entering Transactions* 17

Starting Microsoft Money 18

Opening an Account Book Window 19

- Selecting the Top Line View 20
- Selecting the Correct Account 21

Entering Transactions 21

Using the Keyboard 22
Using Categories 23
SmartFill, SuperSmartFill, and Other Neat Tricks 24
Working with More Than One Account 26
Selecting Multiple Accounts 26
Editing Transactions 28
Creating New Accounts and Categories 28
Transferring Money 29
For More Information 30

LESSON 3 *Working with Categories, Classifications, and Payee Lists* **31**

Displaying the Category List 32
Renaming Categories 34
Editing Category Information 35
Deleting Categories 35
Creating New Categories 36
Creating Subcategories 37
Printing Category Lists 38
Working with Classifications 38
Creating a New Classification 39
Working with the Payee List 41
For More Information 43

LESSON 4 *Viewing Different Accounts and Transactions* **45**

Selecting Transaction Types 46
Selecting a Payee 47
Selecting a Category or Classification 47
Creating Detailed Specifications Using View ➤ Other 48
Using the Checks & Forms Window 50
The Check Form 51
The Deposit Form 53
The Payment Form 53

The Transfer Form 54
The Different Forms 54

LESSON 5 *Assigning Transactions to Several Categories* 57
Splitting a Transaction Before Entering a Total 58
Splitting a Transaction After Entering a Total 59
Using the Calculator 61
For More Information 63

LESSON 6 *Entering Future Transactions and Paying Bills* 65
Scheduling an Existing Transaction as a Future Payment 67
Scheduling a Payment with the Future Transactions Window 68
Setting Reminders 69
Using Scheduled Transactions 70
For More Information 72

LESSON 7 *Printing Checks* 73
Preparing the Checks 74
Preparing the Information 74
Preparing the Printer 75
Printing Your Checks 76
For More Information 78

LESSON 8 *Producing Reports* 79
Displaying the Summary Report 83
Customizing the Report 84
Selecting the Row 84
Selecting the Column 84
Selecting the Date Range 85
Selecting Accounts 85
Selecting Transactions 85
Viewing the Report 86
Adjusting the Report Width 87

Selecting the Font 88
Printing the Report 89
Exporting Your Reports 90
Now the Bad Part! 91
Opening the Windows Recorder 91
Preparing Recorder 92
Recording the Macro 93
Displaying a Report Using Recorder 95
For More Information 95

LESSON 9 *Balancing Your Checkbook* **97**
The First Steps 98
Checking the Starting Balance 99
Marking the Transactions 100
Finishing the Operation 102
Avoiding Problems 104
For More Information 105

LESSON 10 *Creating a Budget* **107**
Defining Budget Amounts 108
Displaying a Budget Report 110
Modifying the Budget Report 111
For More Information 113

PART II REFERENCE

Account Types 117
Customizing Money 121
Edit ➤ Copy 127
Edit ➤ Cut 127
Edit ➤ Delete Transaction 127

Edit ➤ Enter from Schedule 127
Edit ➤ Find 128
Edit ➤ Mark as Cleared 129
Edit ➤ Mark as Uncleared 130
Edit ➤ Mark as Unreconciled 130
Edit ➤ Paste 130
Edit ➤ Schedule in Future 131
Edit ➤ Split Transaction 131
Edit ➤ Undo 132
Edit ➤ Unvoid Transaction 132
Edit ➤ Void Transaction 133
Editing Transactions 133
Entering Transactions 134
File ➤ Archive 142
File ➤ Backup 143
File ➤ Exit 145
File ➤ Export 146
File ➤ Import 148
File ➤ New 150
File ➤ Open 150
File ➤ Print Checks 151
File ➤ Print Setup 151
Help Menu Options 153
List ➤ Account List 154
List ➤ Category List 158
List ➤ Other Classification 162
List ➤ Payee List 163
Options ➤ Balance Accounts 167
Options ➤ Calculator 167
Options ➤ Entire Transaction View 170
Options ➤ Password 171
Options ➤ Pay Bills 172
Options ➤ Settings 173
Options ➤ Top Line View 173
Reports 175
Report ➤ Budget Report 183

Report ➤ Income and Expense Report 184
Report ➤ Net Worth Report 186
Report ➤ Register Report 187
Report ➤ Summary Report 190
Report ➤ Tax Report 192
Starting Money 195
Toolbar Icon Buttons 197
View Drop-Down List Box 198
Window ➤ Account Book 199
Window ➤ Checks & Forms 201
Window ➤ Future Transactions 202

APPENDIX A *Setting Up Your Payroll* **205**

Creating the Categories 206
Entering the First Payment 206
Creating the Future Payments 207
Paying Your Employees 207
Paying the Government 208
Creating a Payroll Report 209

APPENDIX B *Questions and Answers* **211**

Index 219

PREFACE

Microsoft Money is the first low-cost personal finance software designed for Microsoft Windows. Along with Microsoft Publisher and Microsoft Works for Windows, it is one of three intial programs in the "Microsoft Solution Series." Money is designed for tracking personal finances or small business accounts.

This book describes how to use Microsoft Money version 1.0. We have assumed that you are already familiar with Microsoft Windows. If you are not, we suggest you learn the Windows basics first—how to use menus and dialog boxes; how to size, move, and swap windows; and so on. See your Windows documentation for detailed information on Windows.

CONVENTIONS USED IN THIS BOOK

The following conventions are used throughout this book.

Menu option names As a form of shorthand we will often refer to a menu option by preceding its name with the name of the menu on which it is found. For example, "select File ➤ Save As" means "select the Save As option in the File menu."

Clicking with the mouse Again, as a form of shorthand, we will often use the term "click on" instead of saying "use the mouse to move the pointer to the button and press the mouse button."

Mouse instructions Text references to "the mouse button" generally mean the primary button. Although most programs assign the left button as the primary one, Windows lets you swap the buttons, so the right button is primary. This helps left-handed people use the mouse with more dexterity. If you would like to change buttons before you begin, see Customizing Money in the Reference section of this book.

Keyboard instructions The average Windows user navigates around Windows applications with a mouse; it's the most efficient, comfortable way to work with Windows. However, you can do everything *without* the use of a mouse, by using a variety of keystrokes. We assume in this book that you will be using a mouse, though we do occasionally describe the keyboard operations. If you understand the use of the keyboard in Microsoft Windows, though, you will already understand how to use it in Money.

Keyboard shortcuts The Keyboard shortcuts on the inside covers of this book include not only those keyboard commands that are required by users without mice, but also include shortcuts that even mouse users may want to use. You can use these shortcuts to select commands quicker than you could using the menus. Some of these shortcuts are included in the main text, but see the inside covers for the complete list.

Key notations Most special keys are referred to by the name printed on the key. Sometimes, we will call the four cursor-movement keys on the right side of the keyboard (↑, ↓, →, and ←) the arrow keys. The key labeled Enter or Return is referred to as the ↵ key. The Backspace key will appear as the Backspace key (note that this key is situated in the upper-right corner of the main part of the keyboard; don't confuse it with the arrow key labeled ←).

Margin notes and icons Throughout the book, you will see notes, tips, and warnings in the margin, and icons when we refer to specific icons and icon buttons.

PART ONE

TUTORIAL

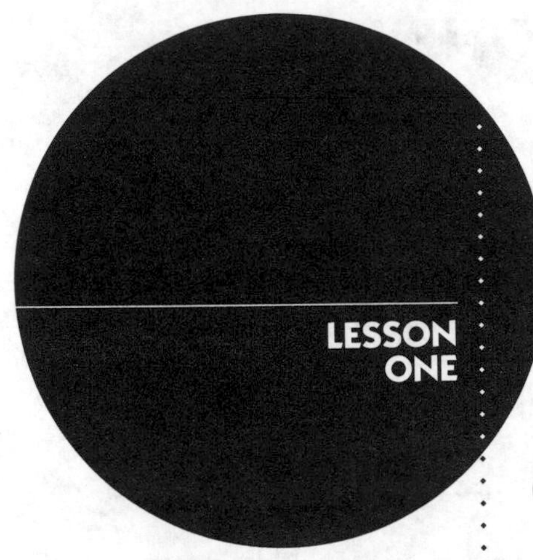

GETTING READY

INTRODUCING

Installing Money
Opening Money
The Money Window
Creating Files
Opening Files
Creating Accounts
Editing Accounts
Deleting and Renaming Accounts

Microsoft Money's installation program takes about five minutes to load Money onto your hard disk. When the installation is completed, you have the option of starting Money immediately. We will begin this chapter by installing Money, so if you have already done this, you can skip the next section.

For the discussions on installing and entering the program, we will assume you have already started Windows, and have the Program Manager displayed on your screen. (If you are not familiar with Windows, refer to your Windows documentation.)

INSTALLING MICROSOFT MONEY

Place the Microsoft Money disk in the appropriate floppy-disk drive. Then select File ➤ Run. The Run dialog box appears. Type the name of the disk drive followed by **setup** (**a:setup** or **b:setup**). Click the OK button and the Microsoft Money Setup screen appears. Enter your name and your company name, and then click on the Continue button.

We will use a shorthand method to describe commands. Instead of saying "Select the Run option from the File menu," we will say "Select File ➤ Run."

The Destination Path dialog box appears. You can instruct Money to install its files in a directory other than the default C:\MSMONEY directory by entering the new path name in the box provided. Click Continue. Microsoft Money will load its files into the specified directory, create an *MS Solution Series* program group in the Program Manager, and display a dialog box telling you that the installation is complete. The box has two buttons: Return to Windows and Run Microsoft Money.

OPENING MONEY

1. In the dialog box, click on the Run Microsoft Money button. A blank Microsoft Money window appears along with the Setup New File dialog box (see Figure 1.1). This box lets you choose the categories you want to use for your accounts: Home (Investment Income, Food, Gifts, and so on), Business (Advertising, Office Expenses, Payroll, and so on), a mixture of the two types, or no categories at all. Assigning transactions to categories enables you to track your income and expenses. No matter what you select right now, you will be able to add, edit, or delete categories later. For the purpose of these lessons, we will assume you select the Both Home And Business option.
2. Click OK and the Create New Account dialog box and Create First Account message box will appear (see Figure 1.2).
3. Click on the message box's OK button to close the box and then select an account type.

We are going to create a checking account. The Bank Account option button is already selected, and Checking is displayed in the Account Name text box. You can either click on the OK button to accept the name or enter a new name (Business Checking, for example). The name can be up to 32 characters long, but it cannot include these characters: \ [ ] ? * ". Click OK. The Opening Balance dialog box appears.

4. Find your last checking account statement and enter the ending balance in the Opening Balance dialog box. (If the statement isn't available, you can enter an estimate or simply leave the box blank.) If you recently opened the account, enter 0 and later enter all the transactions into the account— including the initial deposit. You can always change later anything you enter now. Click OK and a dialog box appears, asking if you want to see a demonstration of Money's features. This demonstration is about 2 minutes long. It gives a *very* basic overview of Money. (There are also 4 other previews of Money's features; these are available from the Help menu.)

For information on other ways of opening Money, see File ➤ Open in the Reference section.

Do you have absolutely no idea what your account balance is? You haven't balanced your check book in months? Or years? Enter 0 as the starting balance. Later, when

FIGURE 1.1:

The Setup New File dialog box

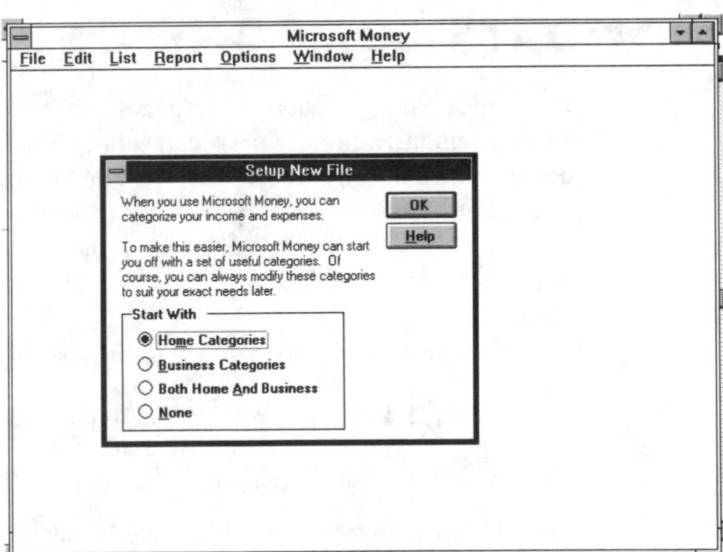

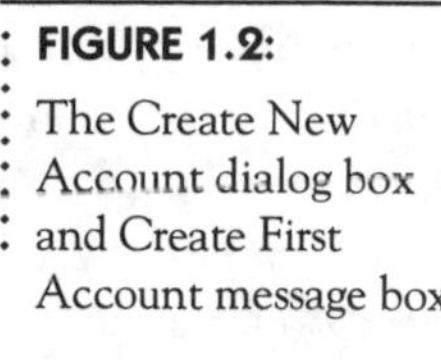

FIGURE 1.2:
The Create New Account dialog box and Create First Account message box

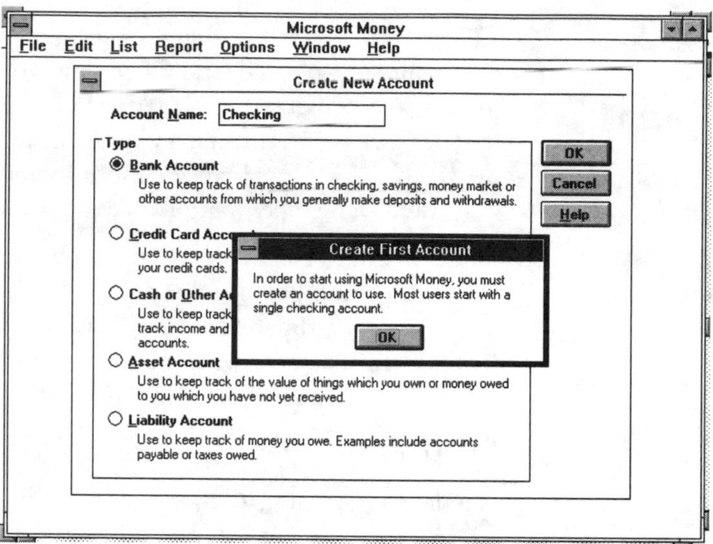

you reconcile the checking account against your next account statement, you can let Money adjust the balance for you. Then future balances will be correct—as long as you enter all future transactions, of course! You can also enter the final balance from your last bank statement, and later enter all the transactions that have yet to appear on your statement.

THE MONEY WINDOW AND ITS COMPONENTS

If you click No when Money asks if you want to see a demonstration—or when the Money demonstration is over—you will see a blank Money window with a smaller document window inside (Figure 1.3). The Money window always appears the same as the last time you closed it, so if this is not the first time you have used Money, the window may look a little different. If the Account Book window is not currently displayed, select Window ➤ Account Book and the Account Book window will appear.

These are the components of the Money window:

Title bar: The title bar displays the name of the program. Once you have opened a file other than the default file (MSMONEY.MNY), the title bar will also show the path and file name.

Control menu: This is the usual Windows control menu, which allows you to size and move the windows using the keyboard. Double-click on the menu to close a window.

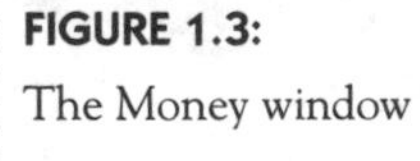

FIGURE 1.3:
The Money window

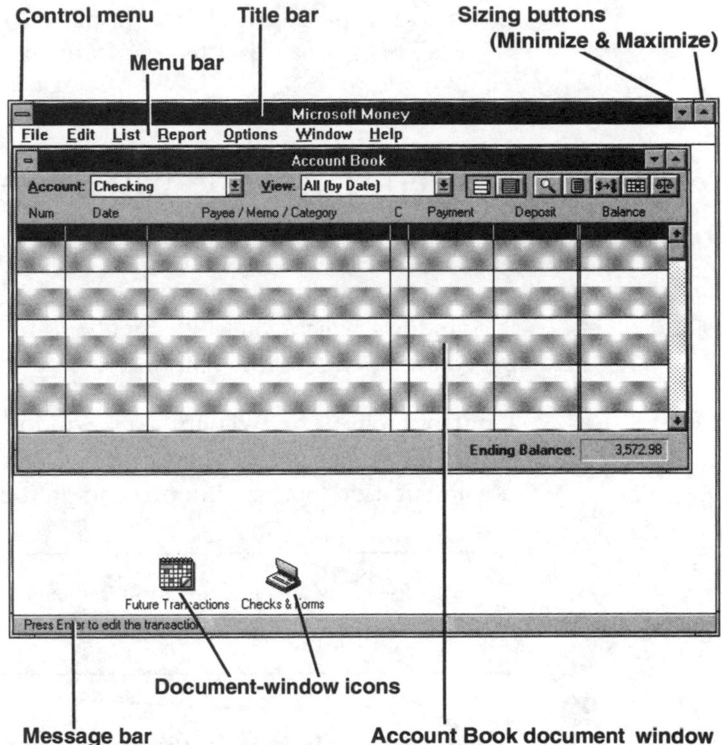

See your Windows documentation for more information on such Windows components as the Control menu and sizing buttons.

Maximize and minimize buttons: Clicking on the maximize and minimize buttons enlarges or reduces the window. You can make the Money window fill the entire screen, or shrink it to icon size.

Menu bar: The menu bar contains seven menus, from which you can select various commands: File, Edit, List, Report, Options, Window, and Help. For more information on the various menus and commands, see the menu or command name in the Reference section.

Document-window icons: The small icons inside the application window are known as document-window icons. Double-clicking on an icon displays the window. Figure 1.3 shows the Future Transactions and Checks & Forms windows.

Message bar: This bar displays messages about the current operation. If you have turned off the Show Message Bar option in the Settings dialog box, the message bar will not be displayed. (See Customizing Money in the Reference section.) It tells you what a dialog box does or how a command works.

THE ACCOUNT BOOK WINDOW

The Account Book window (Figure 1.4) is one of the three windows you use to modify account information—the others are the Future Transactions and Checks & Forms windows, which you will learn about in later chapters. For now, let's look at the Account Book window components.

Control menu: The Account Book window has its own Control menu, which enables you to move, size, and close the window. See your Windows documentation for more information on these commands.

If you don't have a mouse, you can select the Control menu on the document window by pressing Alt-spacebar and pressing →.

Maximize and Minimize buttons: Clicking on these buttons enlarges the window to full-screen size or reduces it to icon size.

FIGURE 1.4:

The Account Book window

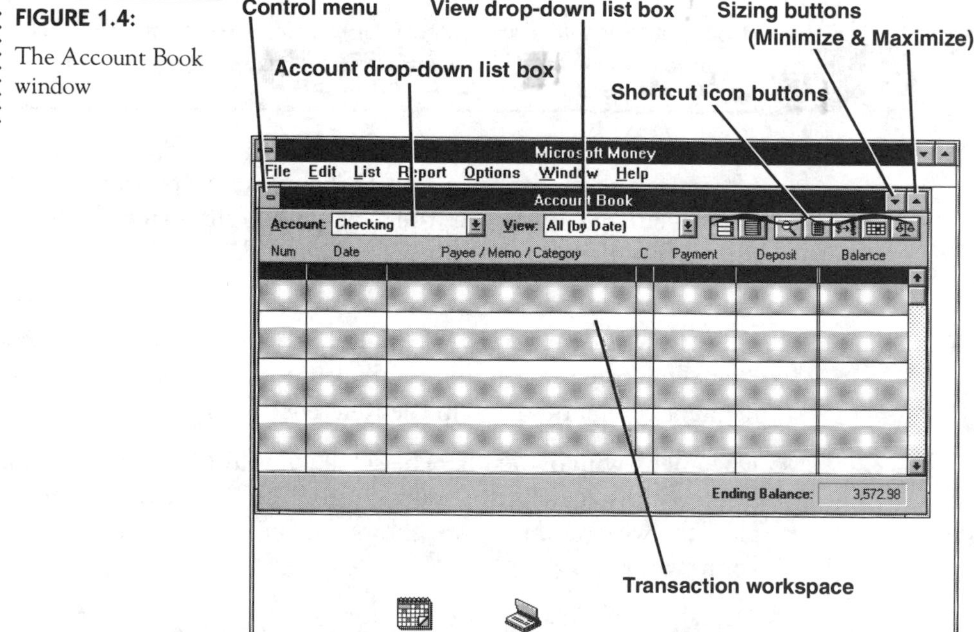

Toolbar: The Toolbar is the gray area below the Account Book window title bar. It contains the Account and View drop-down list boxes, as well as several icon buttons for selecting commands.

Account drop-down list: This list contains the names of all the accounts you have created, enabling you to select which accounts you want to work with by selecting from this list.

View drop-down list: This list enables you to select the types of transactions you want to see: all transactions, only those related to a particular payee, all unreconciled checks, and so on.

Icon buttons: Clicking on an icon button invokes a command. For example, clicking on the small magnifying glass displays the Find dialog box, which is the same result as selecting the Find command from the Edit menu. Table 1.1 lists the icon buttons and the menu commands that they duplicate.

Transaction workspace: This area is where you enter your transactions: checks written, deposits made, automatic deposits and withdrawals, and so on.

TABLE 1.1: Icon buttons and their associated menu commands

ICON	MENU COMMAND
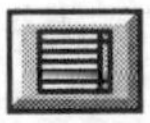	Options ➤ Top Line View
	Options ➤ Entire Transaction View
	Edit ➤ Find
	Options ➤ Calculator
 $→$	Edit ➤ Split Transactions
	Edit ➤ Schedule in Future
	Options ➤ Balance Account

WORKING WITH FILES

Microsoft Money handles your information in a very convenient way. In most cases you don't need to open or close a file, nor do you need to save your information—Money does those things for you automatically. You can treat the program like a checkbook. You open the programs, make your changes, and close the program.

See the File ➤ Backup and File ➤ Archive entries in the Reference section for information about keeping backup copies of your work.

When you first started Money, the program automatically created a file called MSMONEY.MNY. Money automatically opens this file at start-up and saves each transaction you enter in it. For most people's personal accounts and for many small businesses, the MSMONEY.MNY file works well. Each Money file can contain up to 63 accounts, more than enough for most cases. However, Money also allows you to create other files to allow more flexibility in managing your data.

DO YOU NEED MORE FILES?

If you have a small business, you don't need to set up separate files to handle your personal and business accounts. For example, while many small-business owners have business checking accounts, they also make business purchases using their personal credit cards. They also write *personal* checks that are business related. If your accounts are mixed up like this, it is much easier to keep *all* your accounts—business and personal—in MSMONEY.MNY.

However, there may be situations in which you want to keep information totally separate: Perhaps you are keeping your accounts as well as those of a relative on the computer, or maybe you have two separate businesses. You could still work with the MSMONEY.MNY file and keep individual accounts separate—as you will discover as you learn more about the program—but you may find it more convenient to keep them separate. Or maybe several people in your company or family want to keep their accounts in Money. Each person could create a new file and assign a password to the file to keep everyone else out or store the file on a floppy disk.

The next two sections deal with creating and opening files. If you don't need to create additional files, you may want to skip to "Creating Accounts."

CREATING A NEW FILE

Select File ➤ New. The New dialog box appears (see Figure 1.5). The default MSMONEY directory is automatically displayed in the Directories list box when you open the New dialog box.

See File ➤ New and File ➤ Backup in the Reference section for more information on creating and protecting files.

If you want to create the new file on a drive other than the one displayed in the Drives box, click on the down arrow on the right side of that box and then click on the drive name. (But first make sure there is a disk in the drive you select!) Then, select the directory; if you want to place the file in a directory other than the one displayed in the Directories list, double-click on the directory names to navigate through the list until you find the one you want, and then double-click on the directory you want to use.

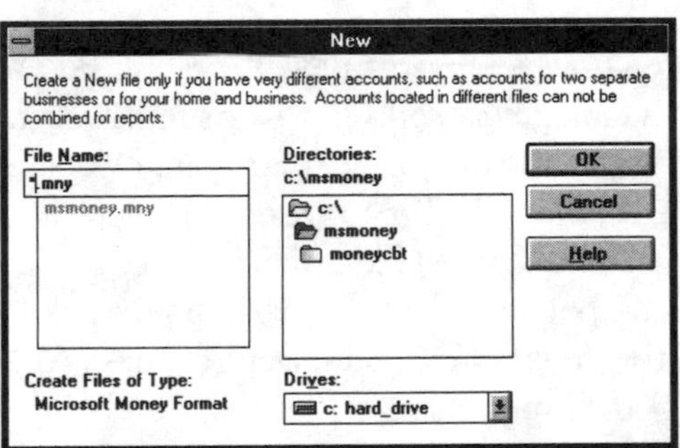

FIGURE 1.5:
The New dialog box

Next, position the cursor between the asterisk and the period in the name in the File Name list box, like this: * | .mny. Press the Backspace key to delete the asterisk, and type the new file's name. You can use up to eight letters, numbers, or special characters in the name but you cannot use a period, asterisk, or question mark.

Now click OK and the Backup dialog box appears (Figure 1.6). This box appears even if you haven't entered any information into the MSMONEY.MNY file. However, if you have turned off the Reminder to Backup option in the Settings dialog box, the Backup dialog box will *not* appear. (See Customizing Money in the Reference section.)

If you want to make a backup copy of the file, place a formatted disk in one of your floppy-disk drives, make sure the disk drive indicated in the Backup dialog box is correct (Figure 1.6 shows a backup to drive A:), and click Yes. If you don't want to make a backup, click No.

FIGURE 1.6:
The Backup dialog box

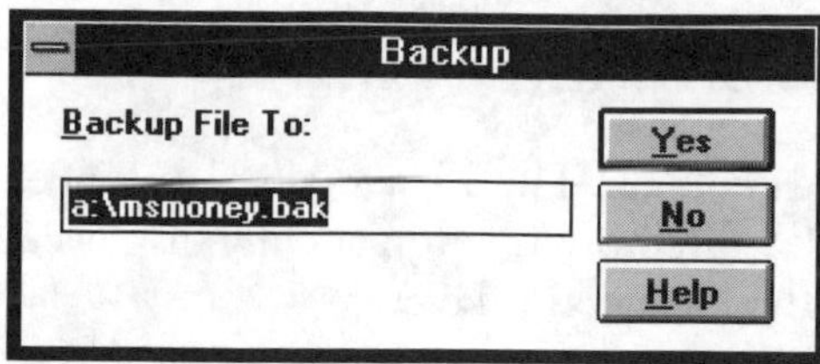

Money now creates the new file; notice that the title bar displays the path and file name of the file you specified. Money then displays the Setup New File dialog box and leads you through the procedure used for creating an account, the same procedure as when you installed Money (see steps 1–4 under "Opening Money," earlier in this chapter).

OPENING FILES

If you have several different files, how do you change from one to the other? You simply replace one open file with another. Money will not allow you to remain in the program without an open account file, and you never have to *close* a file to enter another.

Here's how you open a new file: Select File ➤ Open. The Open dialog box appears. This dialog box works in a way similar to the New dialog box. Select the drive and directory of the file you want to open. Double-click on the name of the file in the File Name list box. The Backup dialog box appears. Back up the current file if you wish or click No. The selected file is then opened.

At the bottom, the Open dialog box is a list box labeled List Files of Type. Click on the down arrow and select Backups (*.BAK) to display backup files, or All Files (*.*) to display Money files that you have renamed with an extension other than .MNY in the list box.

If you decide that you would like to merge two files, or split one file into multiple files, you can use the File ➤ Import and File ➤ Export commands to do so. See those topics in the Reference section for more information.

CREATING ACCOUNTS

The basic unit in Microsoft Money is the *account*. An account can be many things. It could be a checking or savings account, a brokerage account, an account recording credit card purchases, a car loan, or an IRA or other type of pension account. But an account may also be something you would never think of as such: a stamp collection, an inventory of computer equipment, or even a box of valuable Batman comics. Anything that can be given a monetary value can be recorded in a Money account.

See List ➤ Account List in the Reference section for more information on creating accounts.

THE TYPES OF ACCOUNTS

There are several different types of accounts used by Money:

Bank Account	Used for most types of bank accounts: checking, money market, savings, and so on
Credit Card Account	Lets you keep track of your credit card balances
Cash or Other Account	Let's you track personal expenses paid with cash, or a business' petty cash account
Asset Account	Tracks any kind of asset, such as money owed by clients, gold coin collection
Liability Account	Tracks any kind of debt, such as a loan or mortgage

You already created one account when you first opened Money. In the next section, we will add information about that account and create a credit card account.

EDITING AN ACCOUNT

When you created the first account, Money didn't prompt you for all of the account information, so let's start by entering the additional information. Select List ➤ Account List. The Account List dialog box appears (see Figure 1.7). Notice that the list already contains one account—the account you created earlier. Enter the opening balance, bank name, account number, and any comments on the right side of the dialog box. For the opening balance, enter the final balance from your last bank statement—you will then need to enter all outstanding checks and deposits as transactions. If you are sure that your current checkbook is correctly balanced, you could use your current balance. You can put anything you want in the comment box: telephone numbers, your bank manager's name, notes about other accounts, and so on. The box can hold between seven and ten lines of information. You may also add a keyboard shortcut of up to six characters, which you may use when entering transactions instead of typing the full account name.

FIGURE 1.7:

The Account List dialog box

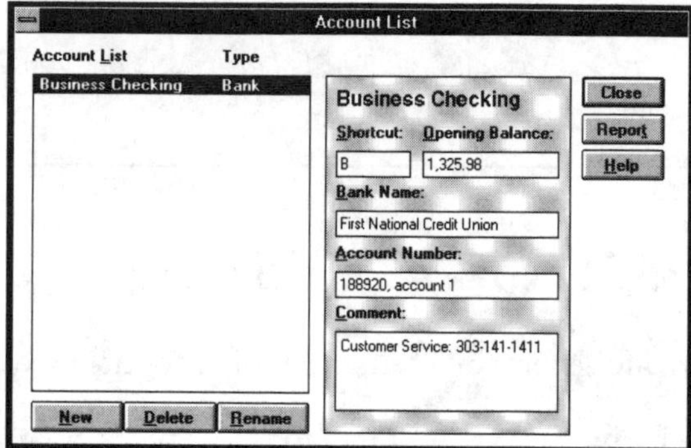

CREATING A CREDIT CARD ACCOUNT

Now let's create a credit card account.

1. Click on the New button below the list. The Create First Account dialog box appears. You have used this dialog box before, when you created your first Money account.
2. Enter a credit card name (Mastercard, Visa, Penney's, or whatever).
3. Click on the Credit Card Account option, and then click OK. The Opening Balance dialog box appears.
4. You can click OK to get the opening balance to 0, or enter an opening balance and then click on OK.
5. Now enter the account information: the keyboard shortcut, bank name, account number, and comments.

If you always pay off the card's balance as soon as you receive the bill, you might want to set the balance to 0 and then enter all your outstanding credit card charges later. If you maintain a credit-card balance, paying only a portion of what you owe each month, you should probably enter the balance you had after your last payment.
To maintain your credit card account, you will enter into the account all new credit card charges, finance charges (from your monthly statement), and payments.

THE DELETE AND RENAME OPTIONS

Notice that the Account List box includes two buttons labeled Delete and Rename. As their names indicate, you can use these to remove an account from the list or change an account's list. Simply click on the account name and then click on the appropriate button. If the account that you are trying to delete contains transactions, a warning message will appear, giving you a chance to change your mind.

Before you continue to the next chapter, you may want to create all the accounts you think you will need. Of course, you can always add or rename accounts later.

CLOSING MONEY

You can use one of several methods to close Money:

- Select File ➤ Exit
- Press Alt-F4
- Select Close from the Control menu
- Double-click on the Control menu

When you issue the Close command, the Backup dialog box appears—the same dialog box you see when you open a file. If you want to backup your data to a floppy disk, type the name of the backup disk and file, place a disk in the appropriate disk drive, and click Yes. Otherwise, just click No.

If the Backup dialog box does not appear when you issue the Close command, the Reminder to Backup option in the Settings dialog box, is turned off. You can display the Settings dialog box displayed by selecting Options ➤ Settings.

Now that you have created your first accounts, you are ready to begin entering transactions into those accounts. Move on to Lesson 2 to learn how to enter transaction information.

FOR MORE INFORMATION

See the following entries in the Reference section:

File ➤ New

File ➤ Open

List ➤ Account List

Starting Money

Window ➤ Account Book

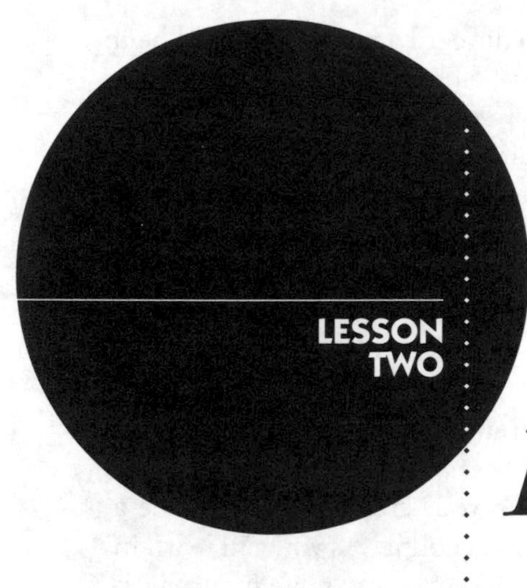

*E*NTERING TRANSACTIONS

INTRODUCING

Starting Money from Windows
The Account Book Window
Selecting Accounts
Top Line View
Keyboard Operations
Using Categories
SmartFill and SuperSmartFill
Money's Shortcuts
Viewing Multiple Accounts
Editing Transactions
Creating New Accounts and Categories
Transferring between Accounts

Microsoft Money provides several ways to enter transactions and has some special features that help you enter information quickly, with a minimum of keystrokes. Money actually "learns" the types of transactions that you regularly enter and then—when you enter each transaction—"guesses" the transaction type and enters it for you.

What do we mean by transaction? Well, that depends on what type of account you are working with. In a bank account, it could be a check you write (or are going to print) or a deposit. It might be a cash withdrawal, interest earned by your account, or a charge for new checks. For a credit card account, it could be a charge or credit, a cash withdrawal, a finance charge, a check sent by you to make your monthly payment, or the yearly fee.

Transactions in a cash account are usually quite simple: either cash spent or cash received. Asset and liability accounts could be all sorts of things. Perhaps you are tracking a car loan in a liability account: the transactions will mostly be payments to the loan, though you may also need to add late-payment charges to the account. Or maybe you are keeping track of your stamp collection's value in an asset account; transactions would mostly indicate increases and decreases to the value of the collection as you buy and sell stamps.

Notice that many transactions are really transfers from one account to another. A cash withdrawal may be a transfer from a checking account to a petty cash account. A check written to the bank holding your credit card would be a transfer from the checking account to the credit card account. As you will learn in this chapter, Money allows you to enter the transaction *once* and have it appear in both the accounts at the same time.

At the end of the last chapter, we closed Money, so before we begin, let's find out how to open Money from the Windows Program Manager.

STARTING MICROSOFT MONEY

When you installed Money, it created a "MS Solution Series" program group.

Money will run only in Windows' Standard or 386 Enhanced mode. See your Windows documentation for information on Windows memory modes.

The MS Solution Series group window may appear as either a small icon, as shown at left, or as an open window. If the MS Solution Series window appears as an icon, double-click on it to open the group window.

The Series Info icon displays information about other applications in the series, such as Microsoft Works for Windows and Microsoft Publisher.

Program groups contain a number of icons, each representing a program that can be run. To open Money, simply double-click on the Microsoft Money icon, shown at left, or click once on the icon and press ↵.

OPENING AN ACCOUNT BOOK WINDOW

Before we begin entering transactions, let's select the correct window and account.

You can use one of the three following methods to display the Account Book window if it isn't displayed already:

- Select Account Book from the Window menu
- Double-click on the Account Book icon (shown at left) at the bottom of the Money window (if you can't see it, it may be hidden behind another document window)
- Press Ctrl-Esc until "Account Book" appears in the title bar

You can maximize this window by clicking on the up arrow in the top right corner of the window or by selecting Maximize from the Control menu. Figure 2.1 shows a maximized Account Book Window.

As you can see, this window looks much like a checkbook register. It has a number of columns:

Num: This number contains the check number of the transaction. For non-checking transactions, you can use notations such as dep (deposit), int (interest), auto (automatic withdrawal), phone (phone-service transaction), or chrg (bank charge).

Date: The date of the transaction.

FIGURE 2.1:
The Account Book window (Entire Transaction view)

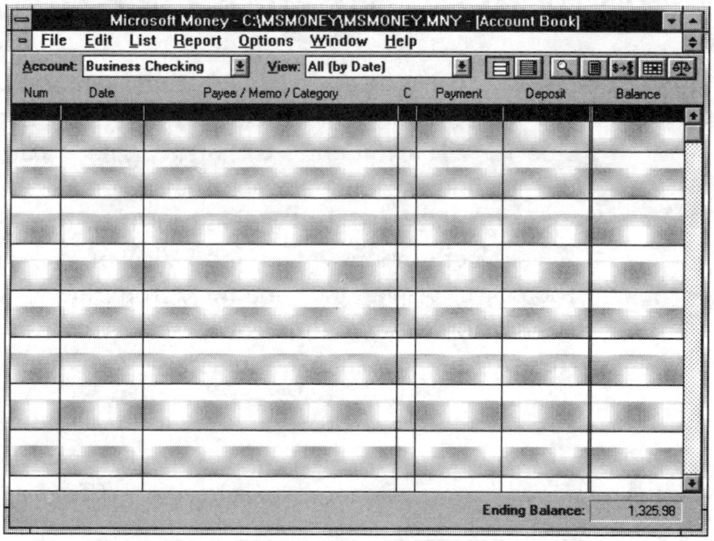

The date format is M/D/Y. You use the Windows Control Panel to change this format—to D/M/Y or D-M-Y, for example. See Customizing Money in the Reference section.

Payee/Memo/Category: The payee is the person or company the payment is made to, or from whom money is received. *Payee* means "one to whom money is paid." But as far as Money is concerned, it means the other party in the transaction, whether giving or receiving money. The second line of each transaction is a memo field for describing the transaction. The third line is the transaction category.

C: This column indicates whether the transaction has cleared your bank. You will learn more about this in Chapter 10, when you compare your account with your bank statement.

Payment: The amount of a check, bank charge, automatic payment, or cash withdrawal.

Deposit: The amount deposited in the account.

Balance: The current balance of the account. This total is calculated by Money.

SELECTING THE TOP LINE VIEW

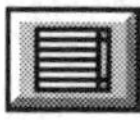

You have two ways to view the Account Book window: the Entire Transaction view and the Top Line view (Figure 2.1 shows the Entire Transaction view). The Top Line view lets you enter the number, date, payee, whether the transaction has cleared, and the value of each transaction. The Entire Transaction view lets you enter this information as well as categorize the transaction.

Select Options ➤ Top Line View or click on the second icon button in the Toolbar, to display the window in Top Line view. Whereas each entry in Entire Transaction view has three rows, each has only one row in Top Line view. Since we are going to enter simple transactions, we don't need all three rows.

If the window is already displayed in Top Line view, the Options menu will contain the Entire Transaction View command instead of Top Line View command.

SELECTING THE CORRECT ACCOUNT

The next step before entering transactions is to make sure the window is displaying your checking account. Select the account from the Account drop-down list box in the Toolbar. To display the list, click on the down arrow next to the Account text box, or press Alt-A. Then scroll through the list box with the mouse and click on the desired account, or use the up and down arrows to move the highlight to the account you are going to use and press ↵. You can display a single account, all the accounts, or two or more selected accounts in the Account Book window. For now, just select one account.

ENTERING TRANSACTIONS

Now let's enter some simple transactions into the Account Book window. For this exercise, you can find your checkbook and enter the payments and deposits that have yet to appear on a bank statement. The Account Book window looks like a checkbook register, and for each transaction you can enter the same information you would enter into a register.

1. Point to the first blank entry in the account book and click the mouse, or press End to move the highlight to the first blank entry.
2. Type the first check number and press Tab. When you begin typing, Money automatically places the cursor in the first field. If the first transaction is not a check, either leave the cell empty and press Tab twice to move to the date field, or enter a code such as Dep or Auto, and then press Tab. Or, if the first entry is a check that you want to print later, just type the word **print** and press Tab.
3. Type the date and press Tab. Enter the date in U.S. date format, that is, month, day, year. Separate the elements using / (for example, 9/3/92). (If you want to change the date format, see Customizing Money in the Reference section.)

As a shortcut, you can type just part of the date before moving to the next field. Type the day of the month and press Tab, and Money completes the date for you, using the current month setting in your computer. Or, enter the month and day (for example, 9/3), press Tab, and Money adds the year. You can also simply press Ctrl-D to enter the current date. If a transaction is more than four months old, however, Money will change its year. If, for example, the current date is 10/1/92, and you enter a transaction date of 5/31, Money will enter the transaction date as 5/31/93, not 5/31/92.

---

4. Glance at the date and make sure it is correct. If you made a mistake, you may "lose" the entry because Money places transactions in chronological order in the account book.
5. Type the name of the person or company to whom you are writing the check (or from whom the deposit comes). Press Tab. You can use any characters in this field *except* \ [ ] ? * or ″.
6. If the transaction is a payment, enter the check value and then press Tab. If the transaction is a *deposit*, just press Tab. The cursor then moves to the Deposit field.
7. If the transaction is a deposit, enter the deposit amount and press Tab. If the transaction is a payment, just press Tab. You will hear a beep; Money will save the transaction and move the highlight to the next line.
8. Repeat steps 1–7 to enter your other transactions.

By the way, although we used the Tab key here, you can also use the mouse or one of the keyboard operations explained below to move to other fields. If Money carries out a particular operation when you move to another field (such as completing a date), it will do so no matter which method you use to move.

USING THE KEYBOARD

While you are entering transactions, you can use the following keystrokes to move around the Account Book window:

TO	PRESS
Start entering information in a transaction	Tab or ↵, or simply start typing
Move ahead one field	Tab, or ↵ if the Alternate Register Navigation option is selected in the Settings dialog box
Move back one field	Shift-Tab, or Shift-↵ if the Alternate Register Navigation option is selected in the Settings dialog box
Move up one field	↑
Move down one field	↓

TO	PRESS
Move to the first field	Home
Move to the last field	End
Complete a transaction at any point	↵ (if the Alternate Register Navigation option is *not* selected in the Settings dialog box)
Complete a transaction while in the last field in the entry	Tab or ↵
Complete a transaction and move to the first blank entry in the account	Ctrl-End
Complete a transaction and move to the first transaction in the account	Ctrl-Home
Cancel changes made to a transaction	Esc

Be careful in your use of ↵. You may have a tendency to press ↵ to select items from the list boxes (which you will learn about in the next section) but doing so will end the entry. Instead, highlight the item and press the Tab key to move to the next field. However, you can modify the way the ↵ key works by selecting Alternate Register Navigation in the Settings dialog box; the ↵ key will then work just like the Tab key, moving the cursor to the next entry. See Customizing Money in the Reference section for information about Alternate Register Navigation.

USING CATEGORIES

Microsoft Money is not simply a nifty program for balancing your checkbook. The real power of Money lies in its ability to assign transactions to categories. This enables you to create and track budgets, and assign transactions to taxable and tax-deductible classifications (making tax time much easier). To assign transactions to categories, you must use the Entire Transaction view of the Account Book window.

Select Options ➤ Entire Transaction View, click on Entire Transaction View icon button in the Toolbar (shown at left), or press Ctrl-T. Each entry will display three lines. Select the first blank entry and you will see that the second line is labeled Memo and the third is Category. Enter the information on the first line in the same way you did for previous transactions. When you have finished entering information on the first line, press the Tab key to move the cursor to the memo field. You can type a descriptive note about the transaction, and then tab to the Category field.

As the cursor lands in the Category field, a list box drops down below it.

If a list box doesn't drop down, the Automatically Drop Lists option in the Settings dialog box is turned off. To open the list, click on the arrow button in the Category field, or press F4, Alt-↑, or Alt-↓. If you want to change the setting, see Customizing Money in the Reference section.

Type the name of the category to which you want to assign this transaction, or select one from the list box. For example, if you wrote a check to a grocery store, you might want to assign the transaction to Food category. Tab to the next field. Again, type a subcategory for the transaction, or select one from the list. In our example, you might want to assign the transaction to the subcategory Groceries (Money also includes a "Dining Out" subcategory). Press Tab to move to the next entry. Continue in this manner until you have finished entering the transactions.

Don't press ↵ when you select an option from a list box unless it's the last piece of information you need for the transaction. Pressing ↵ ends the entry. Instead, press Tab to continue to the next field.

Each of the predefined Money categories has its own shortcut. For example, you can type Wear if you want to assign a transaction to the Clothing category, or School if you want to assign it to Education. Money will then enter the full category name for you. You can also assign shortcuts to Payee names, such as S for Smith, or Jo for Johnson. You will find out how to assign these shortcuts in the next chapter.

SMARTFILL, SUPERSMARTFILL, AND OTHER NEAT TRICKS

Each time you enter a name into the Payee field, Money stores that name. This list is the backbone of what Microsoft calls *SmartFill*. Each time you enter information into the Payee field, Money compares the characters you type with the entries in the Payee list. If the first character you type is "S," Money checks to see if any entries on the list start with "S." If the next character is "m," Money looks at all the entries that begin with "Sm." If the next letter is "y," it checks to see if it has an entry matching "Smy." If only one name on the list starts with those first three characters, Money enters that name into the Payee field. Money continues to monitor your typing until there is only one possible option.

If you want to see the list of Payees, select List ➤ Payee List. For more information on payee lists, see Lesson 3.

Of course, if the name that Money enters is not the one you want to use, you can simply continue typing, and Money removes the name it entered. However, if Money got it right, you can just press Tab and Money uses *SuperSmartFill* to enter all the information it has stored from the last time you entered a transaction for that payee: the amount, the memo notes, and the transaction categories. In many cases, you can simply press ↵ and complete the entry. For example, if you are paying your rent, the information is unlikely to change from month to month. In other cases, though, some of the information will have changed and need to be corrected. No problem: just press Tab, enter the new information, and press ↵ to finish.

SmartFill helps you with all the fields that have drop-down list boxes. Just type the first few characters of a category name, for example, and SmartFill fills in the rest.

You may also have noticed that Money automatically inserts check dates and numbers. If you enter a transaction with a check number of 132 and a date of 9/1/93, the next time you enter a transaction, Money will enter a check number of 133 and a date of 9/1/93 for you. Of course, you can correct this information if necessary, but you will find that Money often gets it right, and this can save you a lot of time.

Here are some other tricks you can use while entering transactions:

Insert the current date in the date field	Ctrl-D
Increase a number or date by one	+
Decrease a number or date by one	–
Copy information from the same field in the last entered transaction	Shift-" (quotation mark)
Esc	Cancel the entry

The Shift-" shortcut is especially useful when you are entering a number of similar transactions. If, for example, you have several checks to different payees that share the same category and subcategory, you can enter the information once, and then just press Shift-" in the subsequent category and subcategory fields to copy the original information.

WORKING WITH MORE THAN ONE ACCOUNT

You can work with more than one account at a time, if you wish. For example, if you enter your checks and credit card bills into Money once a week, you may want to display your credit card account and bank account at the same time. What will this look like? Much the same, except that each entry will have an extra field to the left side of the middle line to show to which account the transaction belongs (Figure 2.2). This may be confusing at first, but there's no need for it to be; Money keeps track of where everything belongs, as long as you indicate where you want each transaction to go.

FIGURE 2.2:
Account Book Window with an extra field

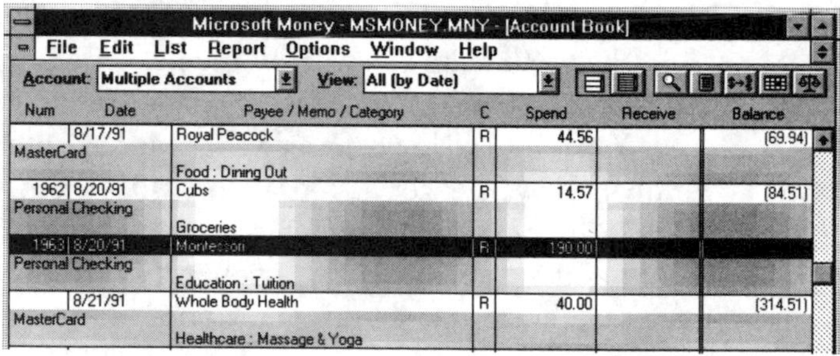

SELECTING MULTIPLE ACCOUNTS

To access multiple accounts, you must first open the Account drop-down list by clicking on the down arrow next to the Account box in the Toolbar, or by pressing Alt-A. The first part of the list displays the names of all the accounts you have created. At the bottom of the list box, you will see three more options:

All Accounts: Selecting this option instructs Money to include transactions from all your accounts.

Multiple Accounts: This option lets you select several accounts from which the transactions should come.

New Account: This option lets you create a new account; it is the same as selecting List ➤ Account List and clicking on the New button.

When you select the Multiple Accounts option, the Select Accounts dialog box appears (see Figure 2.3). Click Select All and then *deselect* the accounts you don't

FIGURE 2.3:
The Select Accounts dialog box

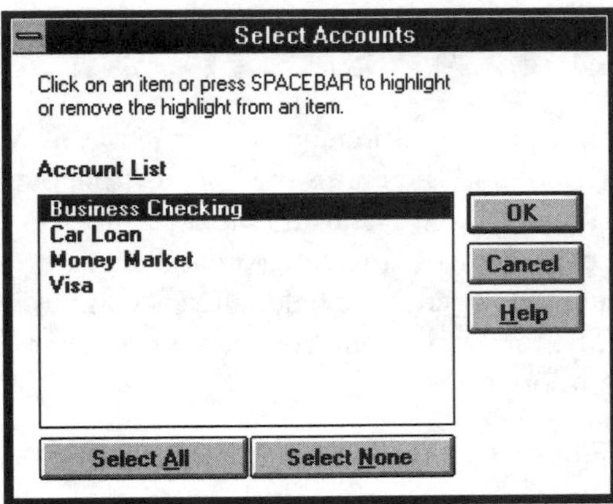

want to use, or click Select None and *select* the ones you do want. Select each account by clicking on it or by using the arrow keys to move to an entry and pressing the spacebar. When you click OK, transactions from the selected accounts are displayed in the Account Book window.

The Ending Balance shows the balance of all accounts listed in the Select Accounts dialog box.

Each entry now has a note on the second line showing the account affected by the transaction. You can enter transactions in the same way as before, with one exception: after you enter the date, payee name, and amount, the cursor will jump to the account field. You then need to type the name of the account, type the shortcut you specified when you created the account, or select an account from the list.

You can create a new account by typing the new name in the Account field and pressing Tab. The Create New Account dialog box appears. When you have finished entering the new account information, the cursor moves to the next field.

Remember that unlike the category lists, which normally open automatically when the cursor lands on the field, the Account list won't appear until you open it. You must press F4, Alt-↑, or Alt-↓ to display the list. Money won't let you proceed until you enter or select an account name for the transaction.

EDITING TRANSACTIONS

You edit transactions in much the same way as you enter them. You can click on a transaction, and then press the Tab key to move to the field you want to change. Or you can click on a field and Money will select the text in that field. There is one difference, though—the category and subcategory drop-down list boxes will not automatically open if the fields already contain text.

The following menu commands can assist you in entering and editing transaction information.

Edit ➤ Cut (Ctrl-X or Shift-Del): Highlight text—a date, payee, amount, or whatever—and select this command to remove the text and place it in the clipboard.

Edit ➤ Copy (Ctrl-C or Ctrl-Ins): Similar to Edit ➤ Cut, this command copies the highlighted text to the clipboard—the original text remains untouched.

Edit ➤ Paste (Ctrl-V or Shift-Ins): This command inserts text from the clipboard into a field.

Edit ➤ Undo (Ctrl-Z or Alt-Backspace): This command removes text inserted using Edit ➤ Paste—or undoes the most recent typing—so long as you have not moved out of the field.

Edit ➤ Delete Transaction (Del): Select a transaction and then select Edit ➤ Delete Transaction to remove the transaction from the account. You can also press Ctrl-Del to remove the transaction without seeing the confirmation message.

Edit ➤ Void Transaction: You may want to void a transaction rather than delete it—if, for example, you wrote a check incorrectly and want to record that the check was destroyed. Enter the check number and date as you would for any other transaction, and select Edit ➤ Void Transaction. A "**VOID**" message will be placed in the Balance column next to that entry.

CREATING NEW ACCOUNTS AND CATEGORIES

If you enter a name that Money does not recognize into the Account, Category, or Subcategory field, Money will ask you if you want to create a new account, category, or subcategory. You will be able to cancel—and replace the name you typed—or go through the normal procedure for creating accounts or categories, and then return to the transaction.

TRANSFERRING MONEY

If you delete an account that includes transfers, Money creates a new category: either Xfer To Deleted Account or Xfer From Deleted Account.

Money always displays a special Transfer category at the top of the category list when you enter a transaction. This category can't be removed for the list or renamed. It lets you shift money from one account to another. For example, if you write a check and send it to your money market account, you wouldn't want that to appear as an expense; you haven't *spent* the money, you just transferred it to another place. Or if you have a credit card account and you send a check to the bank to pay off your monthly balance, you wouldn't want to categorize the check as an expense. After all, you have already categorized each charge when you entered them into the credit card account. Instead, you would show the check as a transfer to your credit card account, where it will show up as a credit, offsetting the charges that you are paying off.

When you want to transfer money to another account, just select the Transfer category or type **transfer**, and press Tab. A list box with the names of all the other accounts will appear (see Figure 2.4). Select the account to which the money is being transferred, and press Tab again. When you finish the entry, Money will automatically create a new entry in the account to which you just transferred money. For example, suppose you entered a check to the bank issuing your credit card. You select the Transfer category and then select your credit card account, as the Transfer To account. If you now display your credit card account you will find a new entry, with the category line indicating "Transfer From: Checking."

You can also transfer money into the current account *from* another account by entering the transaction as a *deposit*.

FIGURE 2.4:

Entering a Transfer

Account: Business Checking View: All (by Date)

Num	Date	Payee / Memo / Category	C	Payment	Deposit	Balance
132	9/30/93	First National Credit Union		332.93		
	Memo:	Payment to credit card				
	Category:	Transfer				

Business Checking
Car Loan
Money Market
Visa

Now that you have seen how to enter information into the Account Book, turn to the next chapter and take a look at how to work with categories, classifications, and payee lists.

FOR MORE INFORMATION

For additional information on the topics covered in this chapter, see the following entries in the Reference section:

Account drop-down list box

Editing Transactions

Entering Transactions

Keyboard Shortcuts

List ➤ Account List

List ➤ Category List

Options ➤ Top Line View

Starting Money

View drop-down list box

Window ➤ Account Book

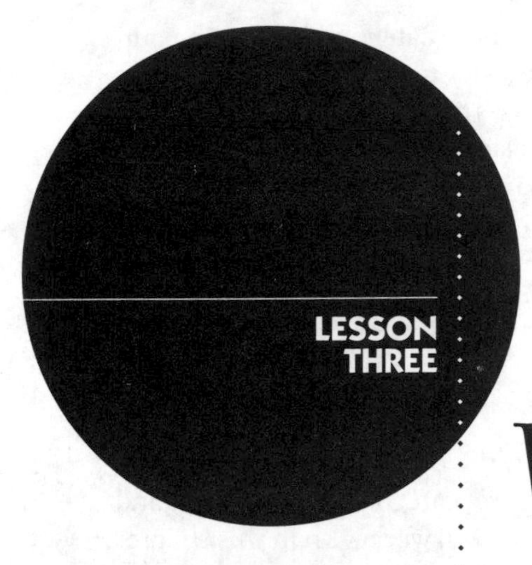

Working with Categories, Classifications, and Payee Lists

INTRODUCING

The Category List
Renaming and Adding Categories
Deleting Categories and Transferring Transactions
Adding and Editing Information
Printing Category Lists
Creating Classifications
The Payee List

As you've already seen, Microsoft Money has a number of predefined categories. However, these categories probably won't satisfy all your needs. That's not the fault of Money—it's just that everyone has different priorities and lifestyles and the predefined categories can't satisfy everyone. Fortunately, you can change them. You may want to rename some categories, delete others, and even create a few of your own. You can also create, delete, and rename subcategories.

In this chapter you will learn how to work with the category list. For the purpose of illustration, we will set up some new categories for a small business—the categories required for the Internal Revenue Service's Schedule C (Business Profit and Loss). If you don't need these categories, you should follow along and create some categories that you *do* want.

See also List ➤ Category List in the Reference section for more information on the material presented in this chapter.

By the way, the Category list you have depends on the option you selected when you created the current file: Home categories, Business categories, both Home and Business categories, or no categories at all. The list we will work with in this chapter contains both Home and Business categories.

DISPLAYING THE CATEGORY LIST

To display the Category List dialog box (Figure 3.1), select List ➤ Category List or press Alt-L C.

The Category List dialog box contains list boxes for categories and subcategories. The Subcategory list displays the subcategories of the currently selected item in the Category list. The items in the Category list are divided into two groups: INCOME and EXPENSES.

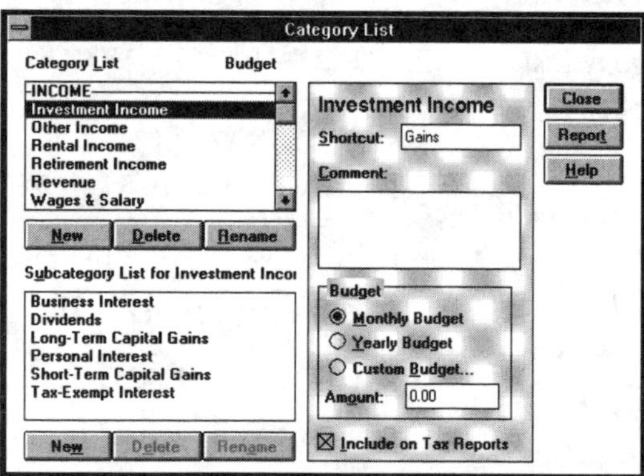

FIGURE 3.1: The Category List dialog box

The Home and Business categories are mixed together, and some categories have both personal and business subcategories. These categories, however, have business applications:

INCOME

Rental Income

Revenue

EXPENSES

Advertising

Bus. Automobile

Bus. Entertainment

Bus. Insurance

Bus. Miscellaneous

Bus. Purchases

Bus. Services

Bus. Taxes

Bus. Travel

Bus. Utilities

Freight

Office Expenses

Payroll

Returns & Allowances

If you selected Business Categories when you created a new file, the categories would be slightly different.

If you run a small business and file Schedule C with your income taxes, you will need these categories:

Gross receipt or sales

Returns and allowances

Other income

Advertising

Bad debts

Car and truck expenses
Commissions and fees
Depletion
Depreciation and section 179
Employee benefit programs
Insurance (other than health benefits)
Interest: Mortgage
Interest: Other
Legal and professional service fees
Office expenses
Pension and profit-sharing plans
Rent or lease: Vehicles, machinery, and equipment
Rent or lease: Other business property
Repairs and maintenance
Supplies
Taxes and licence fees
Travel
Meals and entertainment
Utilities
Wages
Other expenses

Of course, some of these categories may not apply to your business. For example, if you don't employ anyone, you won't need an Employee benefit programs category.

RENAMING CATEGORIES

Some of the Money categories are close to what we want, so lets just rename them. Since we included both home and business categories when we created the account, we should organize the category list to keep business categories separate from home categories. For example, you may want to rename the Advertising category B-Advertising, so you can keep all the business categories in one place in the list. Or, since Money organizes the list alphabetically, you may want to use a designation such as "Z-" to move all the business categories to the bottom of the list.

To rename the Advertising category as B-Advertising, select Advertising and click Rename. When the Rename Category dialog box appears, just press Home to move the cursor to the beginning of the New Name text box, type **B-,** and click OK.

EDITING CATEGORY INFORMATION

Next to the list boxes in the Category List dialog box is a grey area that displays information about the currently selected category. You can enter this information when you create a category, or add it later if you wish. This information includes:

Shortcut: Enter up to six characters to be used to select a category when entering a transaction.

Comment: Enter a description of other information about the category you have created in this area.

Budget: If you want to create a budget, you can use this box to assign a total to each category. You will learn more about this function in Chapter 11.

Include on Tax Reports: If you select this check box, all transactions assigned to the category will be included in the Tax Report. This report will help you with your taxes by showing your taxable and tax-deductible transactions. You will learn more about producing reports in Chapter 8.

If you plan to export information to a tax package, you could use the tax package's category codes as category shortcuts. See Report ➤ Tax Report in the Reference section.

DELETING CATEGORIES

You may simply want to remove those categories that you don't need; in our example, there is no Freight category on Schedule C, so we can remove this category. Just select the category you want to remove and click on Delete. The category is immediately removed if it has no subcategories and if you haven't used it in any transactions. If it *does* have subcategories, Money will ask you to confirm the deletion of the category and its associated subcategories. And if you *have* used the category for a transaction, you will see the Delete Category dialog box (Figure 3.2).

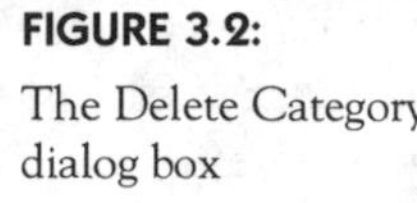

FIGURE 3.2:
The Delete Category dialog box

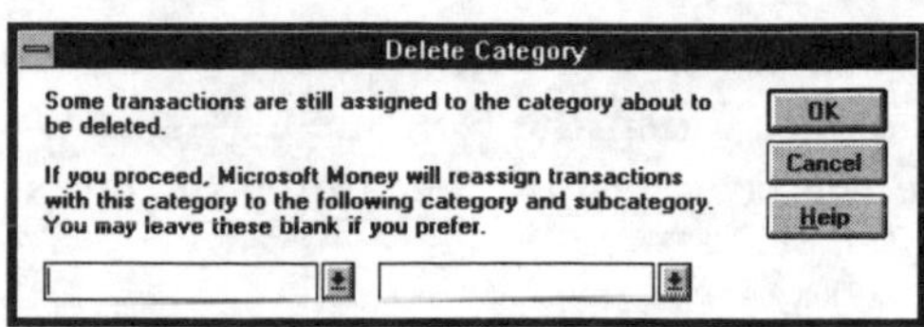

The Delete Transaction dialog box lets you assign the transactions in a deleted category to another category and subcategory. Just select a category from the drop-down list boxes and click on OK, and Money will automatically replace the deleted category with the new category in the relevant transactions.

CREATING NEW CATEGORIES

Although Money already contains many of the categories we need for Schedule C, it does not contain them all. The following categories appear in Schedule C, but don't appear in Money's category list:

Gross receipts or sales

Bad debts

Other income (Money's Other Income category contains *personal* income subcategories)

Commissions and fees

Depletion

Depreciation and section 179

Interest: Mortgage

Interest: Other

Legal and professional services

Pension and profit-sharing plans

Rent or lease: Vehicles, machinery, and equipment

Rent or lease: Other business property

Repairs and maintenance

Supplies

To create a new category, click on the New button below the Category list. The Create New Category dialog box appears (Figure 3.3). Type the name of the new category ("B-Insurance," for example), and then click on one of the option buttons. These buttons determine whether the category is an income or expense transaction. If you

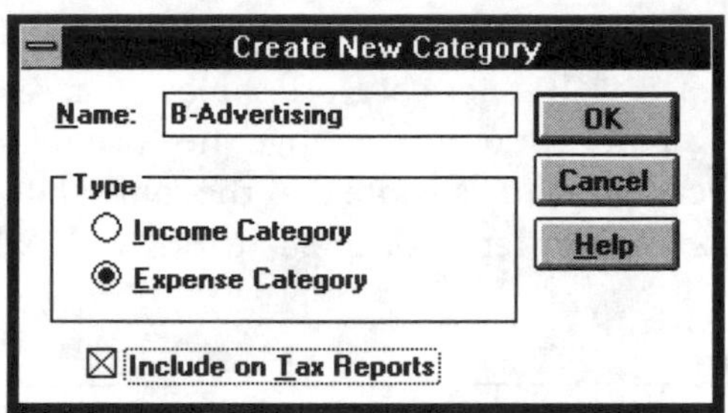

FIGURE 3.3:
The Create New Category dialog box

would like to include the new category in tax reports, make sure that the Include on Tax Reports check box is marked.

For more information on tax reports, see Report ➤ Tax Report in the Reference section.

As a quick way to create a category while entering a transaction, type the new category name into the Category field of the Account Book window and press Tab. The Create New Category dialog box will appear with the new name already entered into the Name text box. Make your option button and check box selections and click on OK. The category is added to the list and the cursor moves to the next field. You can also use this method to create new subcategories.

CREATING SUBCATEGORIES

You can also assign subcategories to categories. Why would you want to do that? Well, for example, Schedule C has a category called Other Expenses, which includes several blank lines for specific expenses. So you may want to create a category called "B-Other Expenses," and then create subcategories for each miscellaneous expense—Freight, On-line Database Charges, and so on. Or you may want more information in your records than the IRS requires. Schedule C includes a category called Advertising, but perhaps you want to track how much you spend on direct mail advertising, the yellow pages, newspaper advertising, and so on. You could create a subcategory for each one.

To work with a subcategory, first select the appropriate category. The subcategories associated with that category appear in the Subcategory List at the bottom of the dialog box. You can now create, remove, or rename these subcategories in the same way you did with the categories: Just click on the New button below the list to create a new subcategory, or select an existing subcategory and click on Delete or Rename.

Shortcut, comment, and budget amount information can be included for subcategories as well as for categories. However, selecting or deselecting the Include on Tax Reports option will change the option for the *parent* category and all of its *other* subcategories. Also note that the sum of budget amounts for subcategories can *exceed* the total entered for the category itself, which you wouldn't want to do, of course.

Assigning shortcuts to subcategories can make entering transactions even faster. You can tab past the category field, type the subcategory shortcut, and press Tab again. Money will fill both the category and subcategory fields for you. Of course, this won't work if you have more than one subcategory assigned the same shortcut.

PRINTING CATEGORY LISTS

If you want to view, print, or export a list of all categories and subcategories, click the Report button in the Category List dialog box. The Category List Report dialog box appears. Click the Customize button and you will see a dialog box that lets you change the title of the report and select several report options:

Shortcuts: Select this to include the assigned shortcuts for a category.

Tax Flags: Select this to include whether the Include on Tax Reports check box is selected for each category.

Basic Budgets: Select this to include the budget amount entered in the Category List dialog box.

Detailed Budgets: Select this to separate the budgeted amount for each category into columns for each month of the year.

You will learn more about reports in Lesson 8.

WORKING WITH CLASSIFICATIONS

As we've seen, categories are simply a way of classifying transactions according to expenditure or income type. Money also allows you to classify transactions in one or two other ways that *you* define. For example, if you own more than one business, you could create a classification called Business to enable you to classify transactions according to their related businesses. Say you operate both a pet grooming business and a computer programming consultancy. You can assign a transaction to, say, the B-Office Expenses category, and then select the correct Business classification (either the Pet Grooming Business or Computer Programming Consultancy) to indicate the purpose of the purchase. You could further categorize the transaction by creating a second classification—such as Employee—so that a transaction might be assigned to B-Office Expenses, Computer Programming Consultancy, *and* the name of the employee making the purchase.

You can customize these classifications in any way to fit your needs. Perhaps you work in construction; you could classify transactions according to work site. If you have a consulting business, you could classify transactions by client. Or perhaps you live in two different places, traveling from one location to the other several times a year; you could create a classification to track your expenses in each location.

What's the purpose of all this? Well, it allows you to define *exactly* what information you want to appear in your reports. Classifications enable you to create a report showing the expenses for one particular project, one particular client, or one particular construction site. Similarly, you can create reports showing purchases by a particular employee, or transactions made by one of your businesses.

CREATING A NEW CLASSIFICATION

Select List ➤ Other Classification to see the Other Classification dialog box. Then click on one of the New buttons to see the New Classification dialog box (see Figure 3.4).

The New Classification dialog box has a number of option buttons. These let you select a name for the type of classification that you will create: Client, Department, Job, Project, Property, or Work Order. If you prefer, you can type a different name (such as Location or Business) in the text box next to the bottom option button. You can even use the restricted characters \ [ ] ? * and " for classification names.

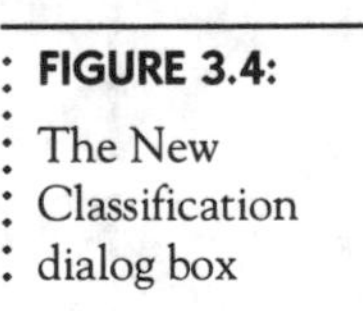

FIGURE 3.4:

The New Classification dialog box

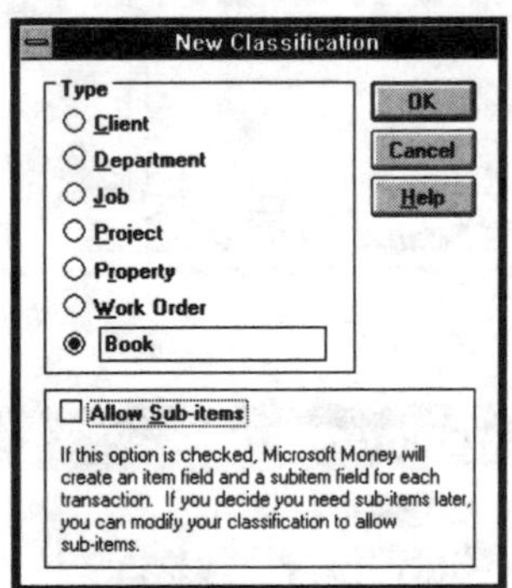

Checking the Allow Sub-items box enables you to subclassify transactions. Not only will you be able to show that the transaction is related to Client B, but also that it is related to Project X for that client.

When you click on OK, you see the Classification List dialog box (the title bar actually shows the name of the classification you created). The box shown in Figure 3.5 includes a Sub-item list, because we selected the Allow Sub-items option in the New Classification box.

You already know how to use this dialog box, of course—it's much the same as the Account List and Category List boxes. You can create, rename, and delete classifications, and add shortcuts and comments. You can also use the Report button to view and print a list of the assigned classifications.

Once you have created a classification, it is added to the List menu (see Figure 3.6), so you can always return and modify the lists. You can also rename the classification, or delete it entirely. Simply select List ➤ Other Classification and you will see a modified Other Classification dialog box (Figure 3.7). Click on the Delete button to remove the classification, or click the Modify button to change the classification's name or to modify the Allow Sub-items option.

See List ➤ Classification List in the Reference section for more information on classifications.

FIGURE 3.5:

The Classification List dialog box

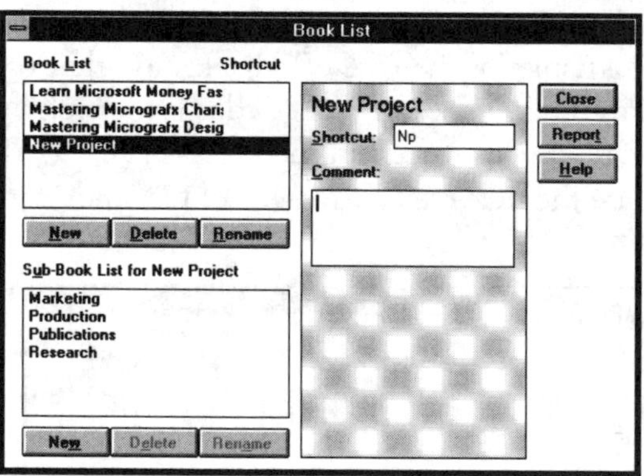

FIGURE 3.6:

The List menu

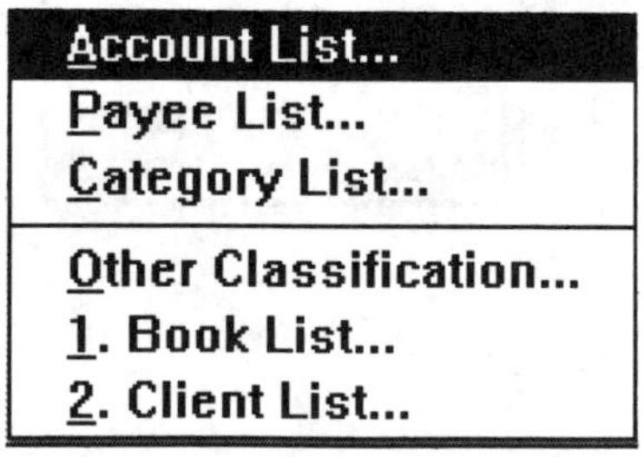

Account List...
Payee List...
Category List...
Other Classification...
1. Book List...
2. Client List...

FIGURE 3.7:
The Other Classification dialog box

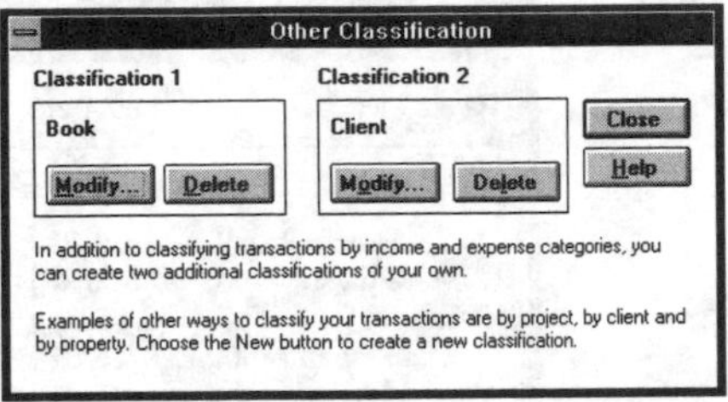

Remember also that you can enter a shortcut and comment for each item and sub-item. A comment could include vehicle identification and mileage numbers, client phone numbers, work order numbers—anything that provides useful information. Finally, click on the Close button to remove the dialog box.

Now that you have created your classifications, the Account Book and Checks & Forms windows have changed. They now have classification fields named according to whatever you entered or selected in the New Classification dialog box. Each time you enter a transaction, you can select the appropriate classification (see Figure 3.8).

FIGURE 3.8:
Classifying a transaction

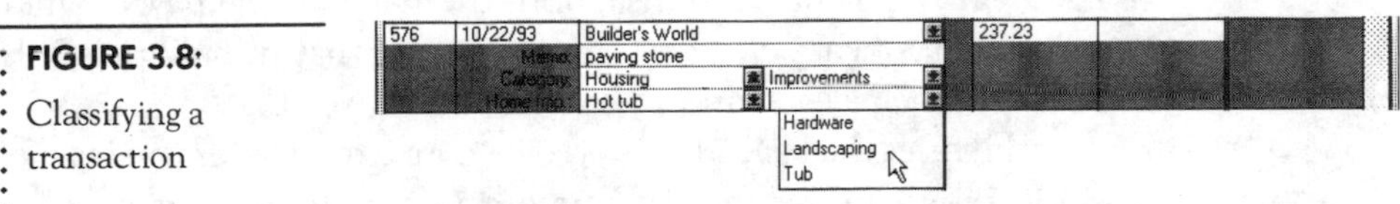

How do you use these classifications? You can use the View drop-down list box and the reports to provide information about specific projects. Do you want to see how much you have spent on a specific home-improvement project this year? Select Home Imp. from the View drop-down list box, select the project from the dialog box that appears, and click on OK. The window will only display transactions related to that project, and will show the total at the bottom.

Do you want to print a report of all your business transactions according to the client and project? Select Report ➤ Summary Report, click on the Customize Button, and select Sub-Client from the Row for Every drop-down list box. You can customize any of the reports except the Net Worth report to show you information related to a specific classification that you have created.

WORKING WITH THE PAYEE LIST

We've seen the Account List and the Category List, so let's take a look at the Payee List before we move on. Select List ➤ Payee List to see the Payee List dialog box (Figure 3.9).

FIGURE 3.9:
The Payee List dialog box

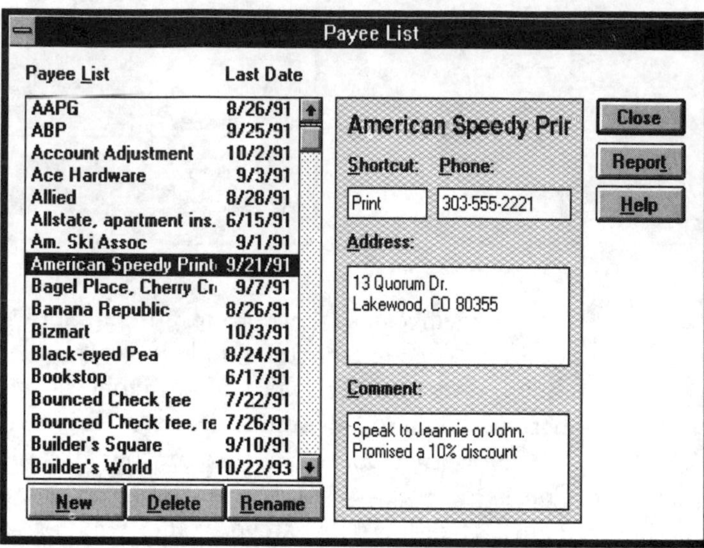

The Payee List is created automatically by Money when you enter transactions. Each time you enter a transaction, the name of the payee, amount, memo, category, and classification are recorded. Most of that information is hidden from the user—only the payee name is shown in the Payee List.

SmartFill uses the Payee List to retrieve information, as you learned in the last chapter. But you can use the list to store information about payees and to add shortcuts by entering the following information in the Payee List dialog box:

Shortcut: Shortcut keys for the payee's name, similar to account and category shortcuts. For example, if you write a check to King Soopers once a week, you could create a shortcut called Soop. Typing Soop into the Payee field and pressing Tab will enter the payee name King Soopers.

Phone: The phone number of the payee.

Address: The payee's address. This information is not only for your reference, but will also be printed on any checks that you print for that payee.

Comment: Any comments related to the payee: type of business, contact name, etc.

You can also add new payees, delete existing ones, or change payee names. In fact, this list can quickly fill up with a lot of useless names. Each time you enter a transaction, the payee's name is added to the list. There is no way to prevent Money from adding the information, even if you will never use that payee name again. Therefore, you may want to periodically remove these excess names from the list, particularly since too many names will cause problems for SmartFill.

You now know how to enter information into Money, and how to set up all the accounts, categories, and classifications you need. But there are other uses for Money, and in the next lesson you will learn how to view account and transaction information in different ways, and how to enter information in different windows.

FOR MORE INFORMATION

See the following entries in the Reference section:

File ➤ Print Setup

List ➤ Category List

List ➤ Classification List

List ➤ Payee List

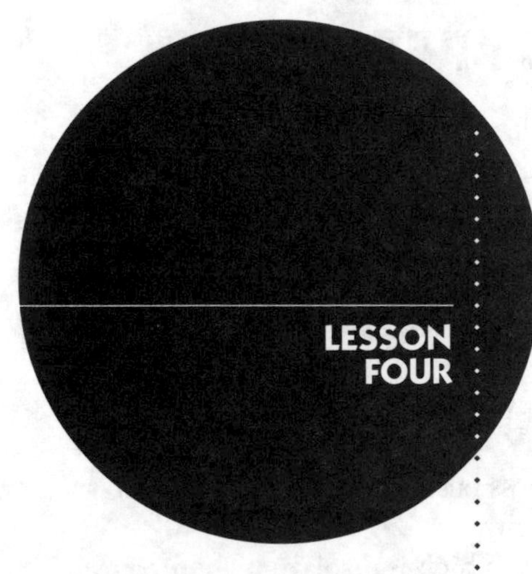

VIEWING DIFFERENT ACCOUNTS AND TRANSACTIONS

INTRODUCING

Selecting Transaction Types
Selecting Payees
Selecting Categories and Classifications
Selecting Other Transactions
Selecting Multiple Categories and Classifications
The Checks & Forms Window
The Different Forms

You have already learned how to enter transactions into accounts, and how to categorize and classify them. But Money lets you view information in different ways, and even enter transactions into a different window.

SELECTING TRANSACTION TYPES

Microsoft Money is extremely flexible. It lets you select exactly which accounts you want to view in the Account Book window (as you learned in Chapter 2) and exactly which *types* of categories you want to see from those accounts. For example, you might want to look at your business checking, personal checking, and credit card accounts at the same time. And you might want to see only those checks and charges that have not yet been reconciled against a bank statement, or only those transactions for a particular payee.

Money is a powerful analytical tool. It enables you to categorize your transactions to view the data in whatever form you wish. You can use it to find out your entertainment expenses for the last month, your gross business income for the last three months, or your interest income for the current year.

Figure 4.1 shows the View drop-down list box, which is displayed when you click on the arrow adjacent to the View text box or press Alt-V. The list box selections display specific transactions from the accounts selected in the Account drop-down list box:

All (by Date): Displays all transactions in chronological order.

All (by Num): Displays all transactions in numerical order.

Unprinted Checks: Displays only the checks that have "Print" entered in the Num column.

Unreconciled (by Date): Displays in chronological order only those transactions that have not yet been reconciled against a bank statement (i.e., those that don't have R in the C column).

Unreconciled (by Num): Displays in numerical order only the transactions that have not yet been reconciled against a bank statement.

A Payee: Lets you select from a list of payees; only transactions related to the selected payees will be displayed, in chronological order.

A Category: Lets you select from a list of categories; only transactions assigned to the selected categories will be displayed, in chronological order.

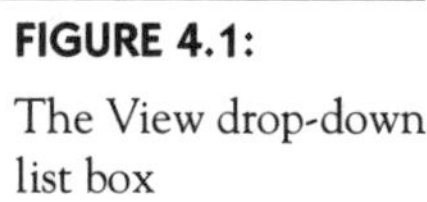

FIGURE 4.1:
The View drop-down list box

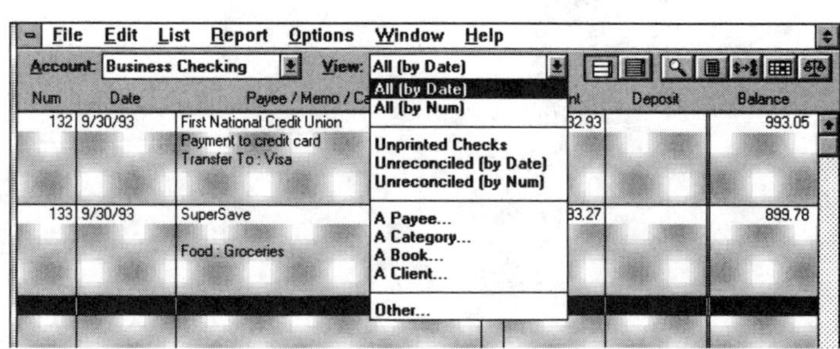

A Classification (this entry shows the name of the classification you have created): If you have created a classification group, select this to display only those transactions assigned to a particular classification.

Other: This option enables you to enter a combination of criteria for determining the transactions you want to view, specifying type, payee, category, reconciliation status, classification, date, check number, and amount.

The first five of these options are quite straightforward, but let's take a look at the others.

SELECTING A PAYEE

If you select A Payee from the View drop-down list box, the Select Payee dialog box will appear (Figure 4.2). Double-click on the name of the payee or payor you want to view, or click once and click on OK. (You can select only one payee.) You can use this method to display, for example, all the checks written to your grocery store, or all payments from a specific client.

Names deleted from the Payee List will not appear in the Select Payee box, even though the name remains in the transactions.

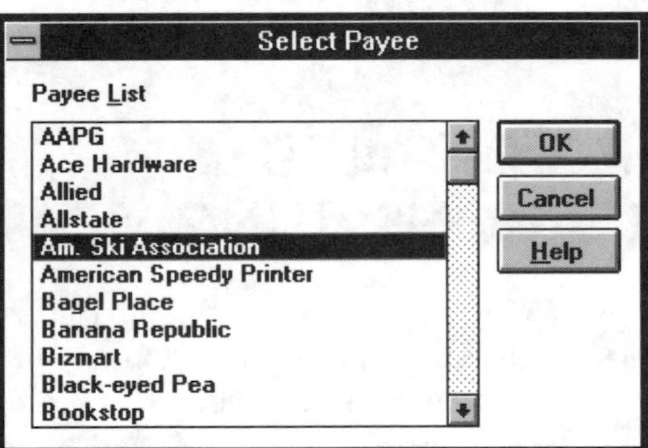

FIGURE 4.2: The Select Payee dialog box

SELECTING A CATEGORY OR CLASSIFICATION

If you select A Category from the View drop-down list box, you will see the Select Category dialog box (Figure 4.3). You can select the category of the transactions you want to view, or if you click on the Show Subcategory, you can even select the specific subcategory in which you are interested. This option enables you to find out how much you spent on clothing or the amount of your gross business income. Unlike the Select Payee box, you can select more than one category at a time. To select a contiguous group, click on the first category, press and hold the Shift key, and click on the last category. To select a non-contiguous group of categories, press the Ctrl key while you click on the different names. If you are using the keyboard, press and hold Shift while you press an arrow key to select a group—you cannot select a non-contiguous group.

If you have created a new classification, the View drop-down list box contains an extra option (or two, if you created two classifications). The menu displays the classification names: A Project or A Client, for example. The Select Classification dialog box works in the same manner as the Select Category dialog box; it enables you to view just those transactions related to a specific classification.

FIGURE 4.3:
The Select Category dialog box

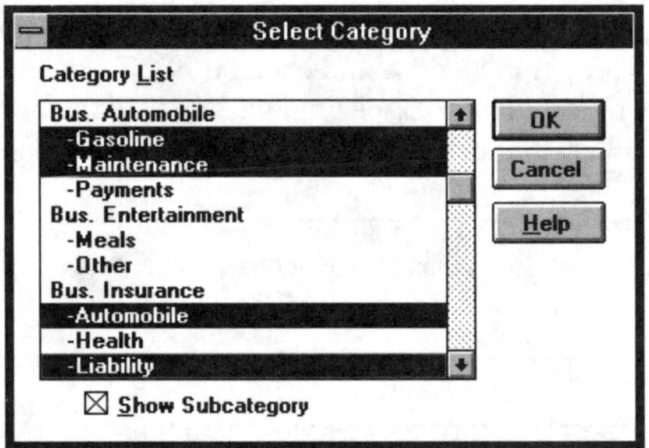

CREATING DETAILED SPECIFICATIONS USING VIEW ➤ OTHER

If you really want to get down to the nitty-gritty and specify *exactly* what you are looking for, select the Other option from the View list. The Other View dialog box (Figure 4.4) lets you specify eight different sets of display criteria and pick from six different sorting methods.

You can bypass the View drop-down list box by pressing Ctrl-O to display the Other View dialog box.

The settings in this box are combined, of course, to create an overall display criterion. For example, if you select a Payee, and then select the Food category, only

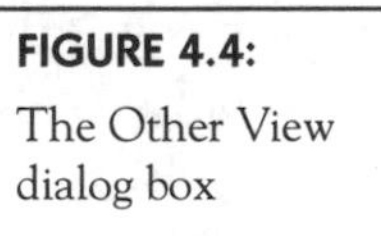

FIGURE 4.4:

The Other View dialog box

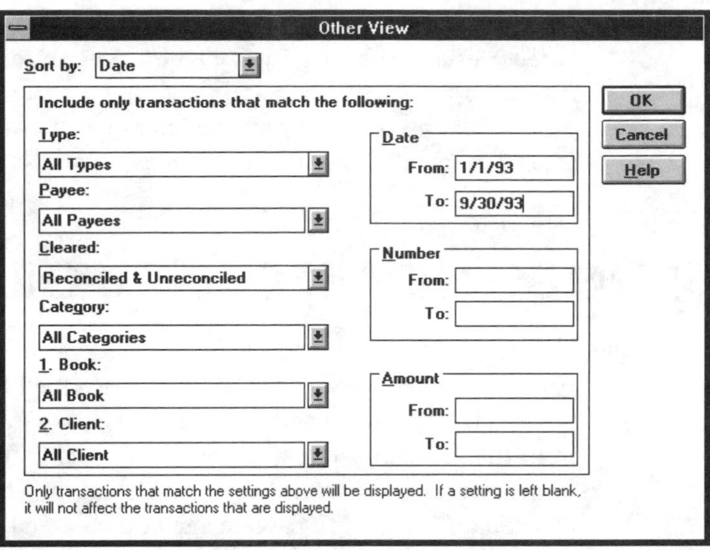

transactions that are related to the named Payee *and* assigned to the Food category will be displayed. Or you could select all the payments to a particular payee that have not yet been reconciled, or all deposits related to a particular category and payee (such as investment-income deposits from your broker.)

Selecting Multiple Categories and Classifications

You can select multiple categories and classifications. This would let you select all the business-related categories, for example, or all the classifications related to current clients. When you select the Select Multiple Categories option from the Category list box, you see another version of the Select Category dialog box (see Figure 4.5).

FIGURE 4.5:

The Select Category dialog box—multiple selections

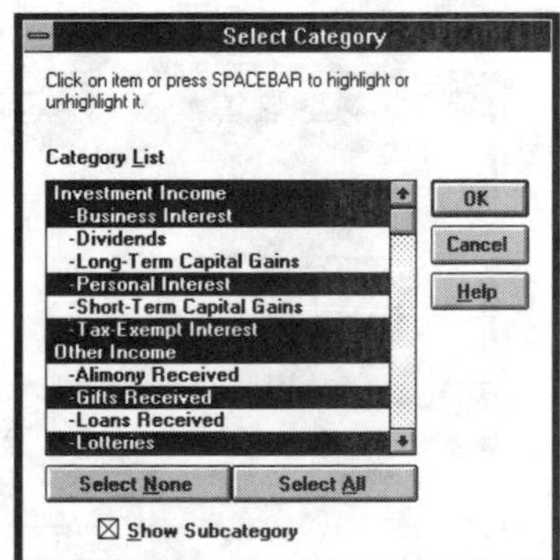

If you select the Show Subcategory check box, the list box will display all the categories and subcategories, enabling you to select individual subcategories. You can click on Select None and then click on the few you want to view, or click on Select All and then click on the few you *don't* want to see.

The Select Classification dialog box works in the same way.

USING THE CHECKS & FORMS WINDOW

The Account Book window is designed to look just like your check register or account book. The Checks & Forms window is designed to look just like a check. You may never have a need to use the Checks & Forms window; you can do almost everything from the Account Book window. The only extra thing you can do in the Checks & Forms window is address checks, which can then be used in window envelopes. (You can add an address to a payee name in the Payee List, so you don't even *have* to go to Checks & Forms to do that.) The only reason to use the Checks & Forms window is because you simply like working with it more than the Account Book.

Use one of these methods to display the Checks & Forms window:

- Select Window ➤ Checks & Forms
- Double-click on the Checks & Forms icon at the bottom of the window (if it isn't obscured by one of the other windows)
- Press Ctrl-Tab once or twice, until the window appears

Figure 4.6 shows the Checks & Forms window, as it looks when it first appears. (We are going to use a bank account; the form looks slightly different with different types of accounts.) Notice that the Toolbar looks much the same as it does in the Account Book window. The first two icons—Top Line View and Entire Transaction View—are missing because you don't need them in this window.

FIGURE 4.6:
The Checks & Forms window

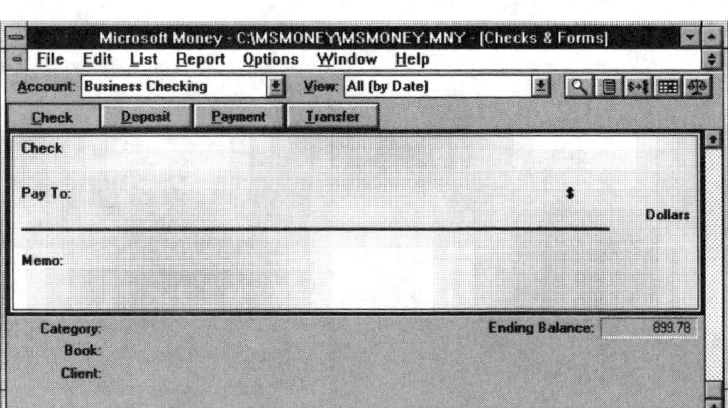

You must click on one of the four form buttons to begin a transaction—Check, Deposit, Payment, or Transfer. Clicking on a button displays the form you need. Once the form is displayed, the keyboard works in the same way that it does in the Account Book window, moving the cursor from field to field. In fact most of the keystrokes used to move around in the Account Book window—↑, ↓, Home, and so on—operate in the same way in the Checks & Forms window. (The only difference is that the Pg Up and Pg Dn keys move to the previous and next transactions, respectively.) To cancel a transaction while entering information in a form, press the Esc key.

Let's start by looking at the Check form.

THE CHECK FORM

Click on the Check button to see the Check form (Figure 4.7). You can use this form to enter any transaction that *reduces* your bank balance: a check, a cash withdrawal, a charge to the account, and so on. You will use this in much the same way that you enter information into the Account Book window.

Keyboard shortcuts also work in the Checks & Forms window. For example, press + to increase a check number or date by one, or press " to insert information from the same field in the last-entered transaction.

These are the fields, in the order in which the cursor moves:

#	The check number; type **Print** if you plan to print this check
Date	The date
Pay To	The payee name
$	The transaction amount
Memo	A note explaining the purpose of the check
(blank box)	You can type a name and address in this box to be printed on the check for use with a window envelope

Category and subcategory boxes	The category and subcategory of the transaction; select one from the list.
Classification and subclassification boxes	The classification and subclassification of the transaction; if you haven't created classifications, these fields won't appear
Ending Balance	The balance as tallied by Money

Here's how you would write a check using the Check form. First, select the account or accounts you want to use from the Account drop-down list box. Click on the Check button, (or press Alt-C). The fields appear in the form, with the highlight in the # field (the same as the Num field in the Account Book window). If the check number that Money entered is correct, just press Tab—if it isn't, type the check number. The highlight moves to the Account name field if you selected multiple accounts from the Account drop-down list box. Type the account name or select it from the list box, and press Tab. In the Date field, press Tab if the date is correct, or type the correct date and then press Tab.

The cursor will then move to the Pay To field. This field is the same as the Account Book window's Payee field; type the payee name or select one from the list, and press Tab. In the Amount field, type the transaction amount. Since this is a check, there is only one Amount field, and it is the same as the Account Book's Payment field. Press Tab, enter the Memo, and press Tab again. You can enter an address if you want to print the address on the check or add the address to the Payee List. Press Tab again to move to the category field. Type or select a category name, press Tab, and type or select a subcategory name. If you have created classifications the cursor will move to the Item field when you press Tab. Select an item and press Tab. If your classification has subitems, the cursor then moves to the subitem field. Otherwise the transaction is entered into the account, the fields are cleared, the next check number is entered into the # field, and the highlight moves to that field.

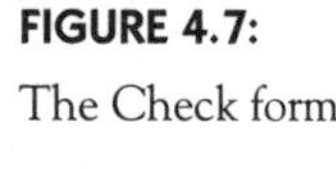

FIGURE 4.7:
The Check form

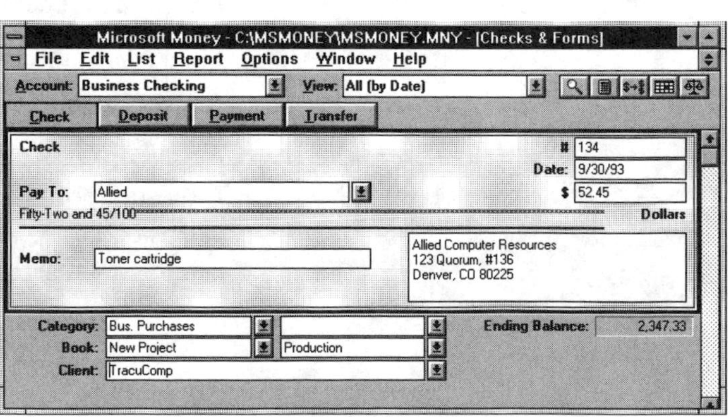

THE DEPOSIT FORM

Click on the Deposit button if you want to enter a deposit transaction. Figure 4.8 shows what the form will look like.

This form is much the same as the check, except that there is no address space, and a Pay To field replaces the Received From field.

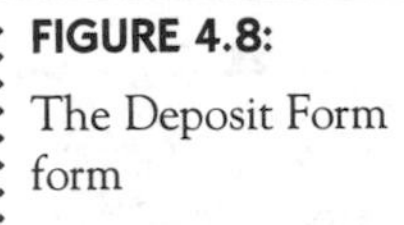

FIGURE 4.8:

The Deposit Form form

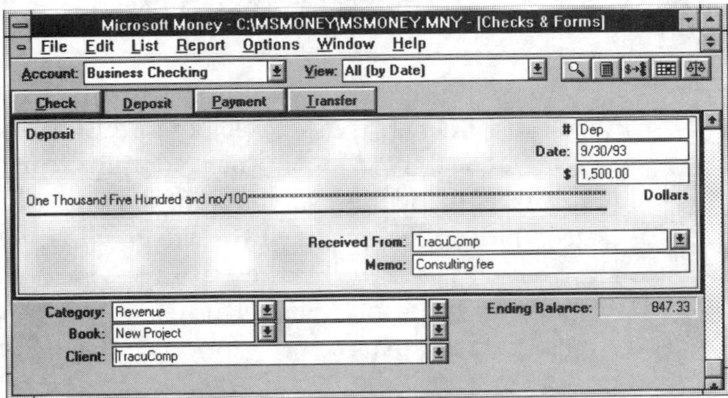

THE PAYMENT FORM

The Payment form is used in almost the exact same way as the Check form. In fact, the only significant difference is its lack of an address box. The Payment Form is functionally redundant; everything that you can do with the Payment Form can be done with the Check Form. The Payment Form simply lets you enter a non-check payment—an automatic withdrawal or account fee, for example—on a form that doesn't look like a check. Figure 4.9 shows the Payment form.

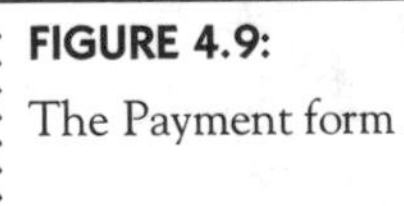

FIGURE 4.9:

The Payment form

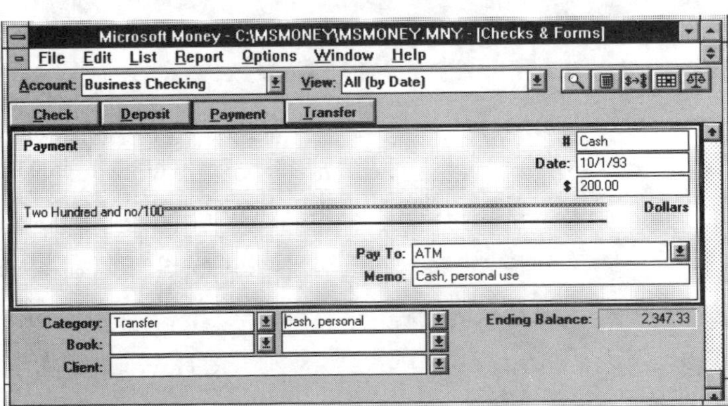

THE TRANSFER FORM

If you are transferring money from one account to another, click on the Transfer button. Figure 4.10 shows what the form looks like.

This form does not have a Category field; the From and To fields are, in effect, the category fields, because the category is Transfer.

You can still enter a check number in this form if you need to—this might be to record a check used to pay your monthly credit card bill, for example—but you can't enter an address. (If you want to enter an address, use the Check form and select the Transfer category.) You will need to enter the name of the account receiving the transfer, as well as the Pay To information. For example, if you are sending a check to the bank issuing your credit card (Pay To: First National Bank), the transaction is also a transfer (To: Credit Card Account).

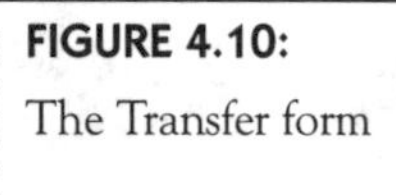

FIGURE 4.10:
The Transfer form

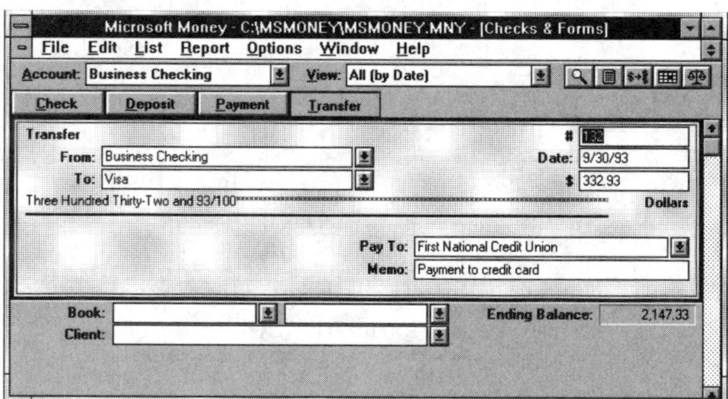

THE DIFFERENT FORMS

You have just seen what the Checks & Forms views look like when you are working with a checking account. If you are working with other accounts, they look slightly different. Each type of account has its own set of forms:

Bank Account	Check, Deposit, Payment, Transfer
Credit Card	Charge, Credit Transfer
Cash	Receive, Spend, Transfer

Asset	Increase, Decrease, Transfer
Liability	Increase, Decrease, Transfer
Multiple Types	Check, Receive, Spend, Transfer

Of course, these forms all work in much the same manner. If you understand the Account Book transaction entry procedure, you will understand the use of the Checks & Forms windows.

Something may have occurred to you while reading through these lessons so far. Although you have learned how to view exactly the transactions you want, how to enter transactions, and how to categorize them, what do you do if the transaction is especially complicated? What if a single transaction is actually several different transactions? What if a deposit is made up of several checks from different people, or if a check is used to pay one person for several different goods or services? You should be able to assign a transaction to several different categories at once, and that is what you will learn about in the next lesson.

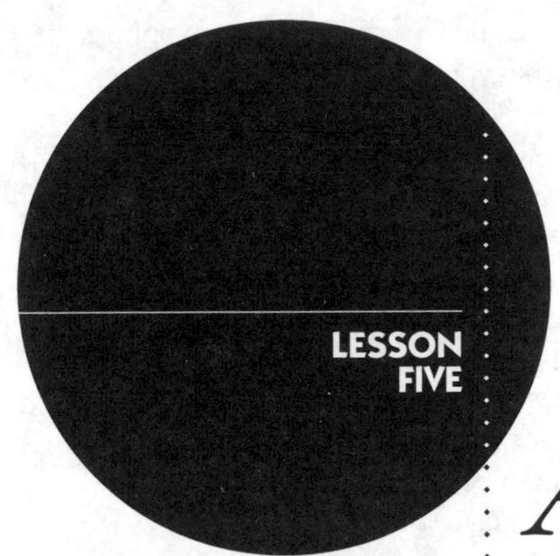

ASSIGNING TRANSACTIONS TO SEVERAL CATEGORIES

INTRODUCING

Splitting Transactions Before Entering a Total

Splitting Transactions After Entering a Total

Using Negatives in Split Transactions

Using the Calculator

You will sometimes have transactions that don't fit into any one category. If you go to a store and use a single check or credit card charge to buy clothing, sports equipment, and furnishings, to which category do you assign the transaction? If you want to deduct a portion of your monthly rent from your taxes for the office you maintain in your home, how do you categorize your rent check? If you receive a check from one client for several different projects, how do you assign each portion to the correct classification?

Fortunately, there's a simple way to categorize such transactions: the Split Transactions command. When you reach an entry that you want to split among two or more categories or classifications, do one of the following:

- Select Edit ➤ Split Transaction
- Press Ctrl-S
- Click on the Split Transaction icon button in the Toolbar

The Split Transaction dialog box will appear, into which you can add as many categories and classifications to the transaction as you wish. There are two ways to enter a split transaction. You can either split the transaction *before* entering a number in the Payment or Deposit column, so that Money enters the transaction total for you, or you can enter a transaction total first and *then* split the transaction, so Money knows how much the total should be.

Let's try both ways. We are going to work with the Account Book window, but you can also split a transaction in the Checks & Forms window.

SPLITTING A TRANSACTION BEFORE ENTERING A TOTAL

Let's try splitting a transaction *before* we enter a transaction total. Press End to move the highlight to the first blank entry. Press Ctrl-S and the Split Transaction dialog box appears, with the category list box dropped down from the first field (see Figure 5.1). Highlight an Expense category (preferably one with subcategories) and press Tab; Money enters the category into the first field and moves the cursor to the next field. The subcategory list box then appears. Highlight a subcategory and press Tab. Money enters the subcategory into the second field, and moves the cursor to the Description field.

Type a description and then tab to the Amount field. Type the portion of the transaction to be assigned to the first category and press the Tab key again. If you haven't created any classifications, the cursor moves directly to the next entry. If you have created a new classification, the cursor moves to the next line and opens the Classification drop-down list box. Select the classification and subclassification and press the Tab key to move to the next entry. Notice that Money copies the number in the Amount field into the Total box at the bottom of the dialog box.

To remove a portion of a split transaction, highlight the line and press Del. You can also press Ctrl-Del to delete the portion without displaying a confirmation dialog box.

FIGURE 5.1:

The Split Transaction dialog box

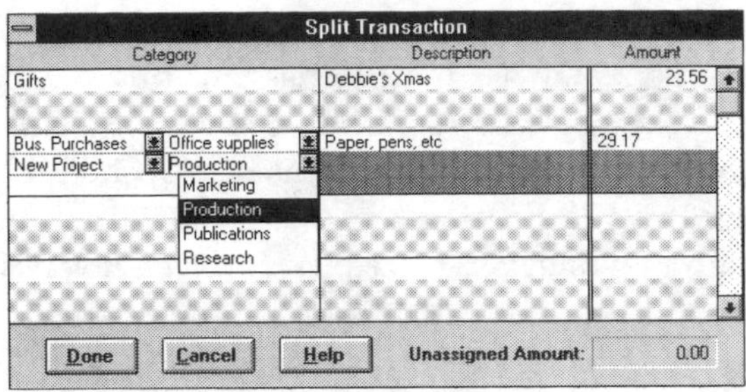

Enter the next portion of the split transaction in the same way. Each time you finish an entry, Money adds the number in the Amount box to the Total box. Continue in this manner until each of the portions has been entered. Make sure that the number in the Total box at the bottom of the Amount column equals the total transaction amount; if it doesn't, you entered one or more of the splits incorrectly.

When you have entered all of the portions of the transaction, click on Done. You will be asked if the transaction was money you spent or received (Figure 5.2). Click on Spend if the transaction is an expense, or Receive if the transaction is a deposit. Then click on OK and the Split Transaction dialog box closes. Money enters the number from the Total box into the appropriate amount box.

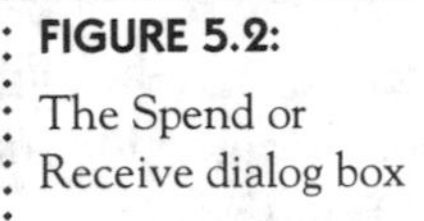

FIGURE 5.2:

The Spend or Receive dialog box

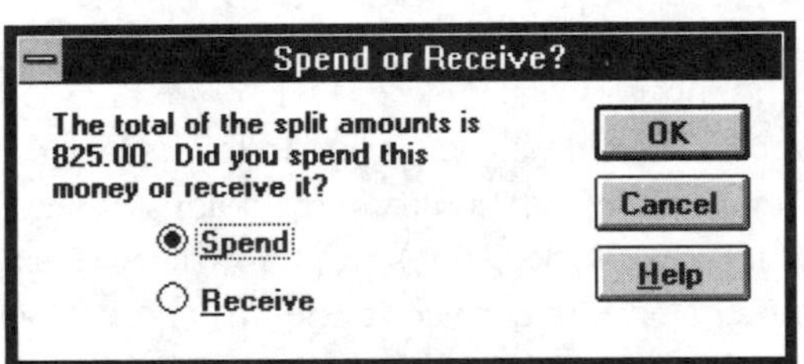

SPLITTING A TRANSACTION AFTER ENTERING A TOTAL

Instead of displaying the dialog box as soon as you select the entry, you can enter the transaction number, date, payee, and amount first, and *then* select Split Transaction. Money knows the final transaction total and keeps track of the unassigned (rather than assigned) transaction amount.

As you enter categories and amounts, Money calculates the amount of the transaction that has not been assigned to a category. When you close the Split Transaction dialog box, Money won't enter anything into the Payment or Deposit column, nor will it ask you if this is a "Spend" or "Receive" transaction; it already knows this information because it knows the total transaction and it knows the column in which you placed it. However, if you try to close the dialog box with a portion of the transaction total still unassigned, Money displays the Adjust Split Amount dialog box (Figure 5.3).

You now have three options:

Edit Splits: Returns you to the Split Transaction box in order to modify the split amounts.

Adjust Total: Changes the transaction total to match the sum of all the entries in the Split Transaction dialog box. You should do this only if you made a mistake when you entered the number into the Payment or Deposit column, and are sure that the new number is correct.

Continue With Unassigned Amount: Ignores the problem and continues. The unassigned amount may cause inaccuracies in some of your reports, of course.

The same Adjust Split dialog box will also appear if you enter too much money into the Split Transaction dialog box. For example, if the transaction total is $200, but the sum of the category assignments you entered is $250, Money will tell you that some of the money is still unassigned. You can tell whether the Split Transaction sum is greater or less than the transaction total by looking at the number at the bottom of the Split Transaction dialog box; if it's in parentheses, it's a negative number, which means you have assigned *too much* money to the various categories. So be careful—you might want to leave a portion of a transaction unassigned, but you will never want the split total to exceed the transaction total!

The Adjust Split dialog box will also appear if you ever modify the Payment or Deposit amount in the Account Book window.

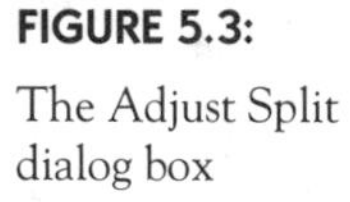

FIGURE 5.3:

The Adjust Split dialog box

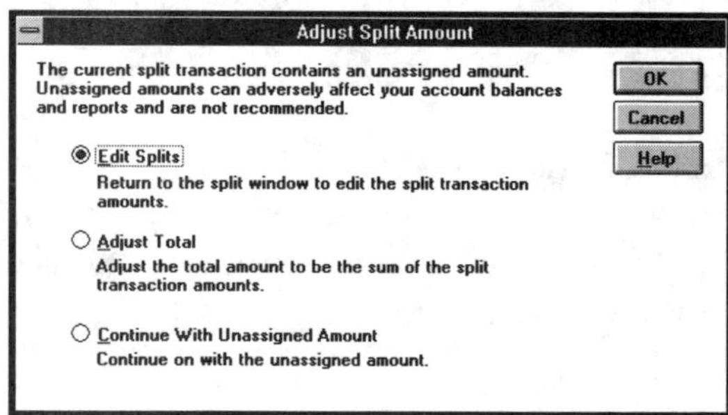

If you display transactions sorted by category, or exclude some categories, each part of a split transaction is displayed as a separate transaction. *A transaction split into three categories appears in three places in the Account Book window.*

Try entering a split transaction yourself. For example, imagine that you have been to an electronics store and purchased a calculator for $43.72 and a compact disk for $15.04. The calculator is a business expense and the compact disk is for personal use. In the Account Book or Checks & Forms window, press End to move to the first blank entry. Then press Ctrl-S to display the Split Transaction dialog box. The Category drop-down list box is already down. Select a business category, such as Office Expenses, and press Tab. In the subcategory box, select an appropriate subcategory, such as Equipment, and press Tab again. In the Description column, type **Calculator** and press Tab to move to the Amount column. Type **43.72** and press Tab. If you created a classification, the cursor moves to the classification field. Select the appropriate classification and subclassification and press Tab again. You will hear a confirmation beep to indicate that the first part of the split has been accepted.

In the category field of the next part, select a personal category, such as Leisure, and then select a subcategory, such as Tapes/CDs. Type **CD** in the Description field and type **15.04** in the Amount field. Enter the classification information and press Tab to complete the second part of the split.

Finally, click on Done or press Alt-D. The Spend or Receive dialog box appears. Make sure the Spend option button is selected and click on OK. Money enters the total—$58.76—into the Payment field automatically. Now all you have to do is enter the rest of the transaction information.

USING THE CALCULATOR

You may find that you must use the calculator to figure out the split amounts. To use the calculator, select Options ➤ Calculator (or press Ctrl-K, or click on the Calculator icon) *before* you open the Split Transaction dialog box. The Calculator command simply opens the Windows calculator, which is an independent application, so the calculator will disappear when you click on any Money window. When you need to use the calculator press Ctrl-Esc to see the Task List dialog box and double-click on Calculator in the list. Or you can press Alt-Tab until the calculator appears.

You can't open the calculator from the Money menus once you have opened the Split Transaction box. If you are halfway through a split transaction and find that you need the calculator, you can go to the Program Manager and load it from there.

Figure 5.4 shows the standard Windows calculator; if yours looks much more complicated than this, the calculator is probably in Scientific mode. You can use the calculator either by clicking on the calculator 'keys' with your mouse or by turning on your keyboard's Num Lock and using the numeric keypad. When you have the answer you need, select Edit ➤ Copy or press Ctrl-Ins, return to the Amount column in the Split Transaction box, and select Edit ➤ Paste (or press Shift-Ins or Ctrl-V) to paste the number into the field.

If you have problems with copying or pasting calculations, make sure that the Num Lock is turned off before using the numeric keypad's Ins key.

Of course, you can use the calculator at any time, not just in the Split Transaction dialog box. For a full list of the calculator's keys, their functions, and their keyboard equivalents, see Options ➤ Calculator in the Reference section.

Splitting transactions is a powerful tool for accurate record keeping. In the next chapter, you will learn about another powerful feature—the Future Transactions window, which reminds you about upcoming transactions and enters them into your accounts automatically.

FIGURE 5.4:
The Calculator

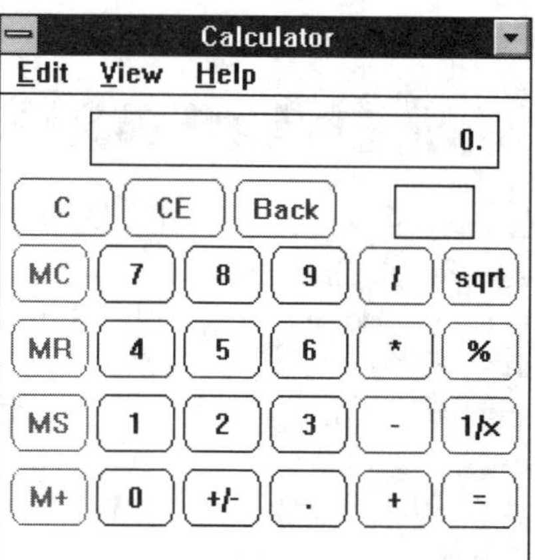

For More Information

See the following entries in the Reference section:

Appendix A: Setting Up Payroll

Edit ➤ Split Transaction

Options ➤ Calculator

Entering Future Transactions and Paying Bills

INTRODUCING

Scheduling Future Transactions
Using Existing Transactions
Using the Future Transactions Window
Setting Reminders
Using Scheduled Transactions

There are transactions that will occur at some time in the future of which you already know the total, payee or source, and category. These transactions fall into two groups—regular and irregular transactions.

Regular transactions are those that occur at regular intervals. In many cases, you will know all the necessary transaction information.

You know that you will pay your rent or mortgage once a month, that your employer will automatically deposit a check in your bank account every two weeks, or that you have to pay the kindergarten on the fifth of each month. In some cases, however, you don't know for sure how much the payment or deposit will be—you know you must pay your credit card bill at the beginning of each month, but you are not sure what the total will be on each bill.

Irregular transactions are those that will occur at some time in the future but will not be regularly repeated, or may not be repeated at all. Such transactions might include items such as the loan you must repay a friend in two months time, or the money that someone owes to *you* and will pay back "sometime."

Transactions can be scheduled as daily, weekly, biweekly, semimonthly, monthly, bimonthly, quarterly, semiannually, annually, biannually, or for a specific date in the future. For example, if you schedule a transaction for 9/15/93 and designate it as a Monthly transaction, Money will also schedule it for 10/15/93, 11/15/93, 12/15/93, 1/15/94, and so on. The transaction will appear only once in the Future Transactions window; when you actually make the transaction, Money will replace the date with the next scheduled date.

You can schedule either type of transaction. What is the advantage of this? Money will remind you of future transactions a few days before they occur. If you have ever had to pay a penalty because you were late with your rent, or lost insurance coverage because you were late with your premium, you will know that this can save you trouble. And scheduling transactions can save you time. Instead of entering a transaction each week or each month, you enter the information just once, and Money will enter it each time after that.

Here are a few suggestions for future transactions:

- Automatic payroll deposits
- Car loan payments
- Credit card bills
- Daycare payments
- Disability insurance premiums
- Gas and electric bill payments
- Health insurance premiums
- Individual Retirement Account deposits
- Internal Revenue Service quarterly estimated tax payments
- Life insurance premiums
- Mortgage payments

- Pension check deposits
- Phone bill payments
- Rent payments
- Social Security check deposits
- Water bill payments

There are two ways to enter future transactions. You can select an existing transaction in the Account Book or Checks & Forms window and schedule it to be paid in the future; Money will place the information in the Future Transactions window for you. Or you can go to the Future Transactions window and enter the transaction directly.

SCHEDULING AN EXISTING TRANSACTION AS A FUTURE PAYMENT

Using existing transactions is a convenient way to schedule future transactions. For example, you can display your checking account in the Account Book window and select and enter repeating transactions into the Future Transactions window. Or you can quickly schedule a transaction while you enter it in the Amount Book window. Here's how you do it.

Select a transaction, or, if you are currently entering a transaction, enter all the information as normal: the check number, date, payee, amount, memo, category, and classification. Then select Edit ➤ Schedule in Future (or press Ctrl-E, or click on the Schedule in Future icon button in the Toolbar). The Schedule Future Transaction dialog box appears (see Figure 6.1).

In the Frequency list box, indicate the interval with which the transaction recurs. The Next Date box will automatically show the next schedule date. Then click on OK and that's it. If you now go to the Future Transactions window (press Ctrl-Tab or select Window ➤ Future Transactions), you will see the transaction scheduled for the specified date.

What if the transaction total changes each time (as with a credit card payment)? Then schedule the transaction *before* you fill in the amount field. In other words, enter all the transaction information except the amount, schedule the payment, and *then* finish the current transaction. You don't have to finish entering a

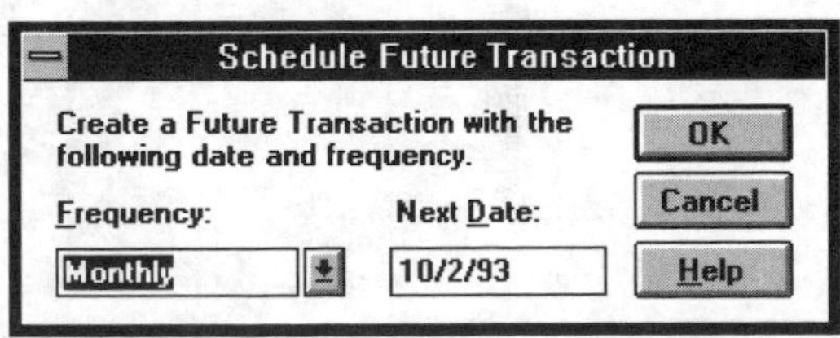

FIGURE 6.1: The Schedule Future Transaction dialog box

transaction before you schedule it. And what if you want to *print* a check? Just type the word **print** in the Num column, and "print" will be added to the future transaction. (See Lesson 7 for more information on printing checks.)

SCHEDULING A PAYMENT WITH THE FUTURE TRANSACTIONS WINDOW

The second way to schedule transactions is to enter them directly in the Future Transactions window (see Figure 6.2). To display this window, select Window ➤ Future Transactions, press Ctrl-Tab once or twice, or double-click on the Future Transactions icon at the bottom of the Money window (if it's visible).

This window is similar to the Account Book window, with a few important differences. You cannot select an account; the window displays *all* future transactions, regardless of the account. The only View options available adjust the order in which the transactions are displayed—chronologically or grouped by payee.

The entries themselves are slightly different as well. Of course, the Balance or C columns are not available. An additional column, the Freq/Acct column, displays the name of the account that the transaction relates to and how often the transaction occurs.

You enter transactions into this window in the same manner as you do in the Account Book window. Press End to move to the first blank entry and type the date of the first transaction. Press Tab to move the cursor to the Frequency field. Type a frequency or select one from the list. (The list will not automatically appear, so click on the arrow or press F4 to display it.) Then Tab to the Num field. If you are entering a check that you want to print, type **print**. Otherwise, leave this field

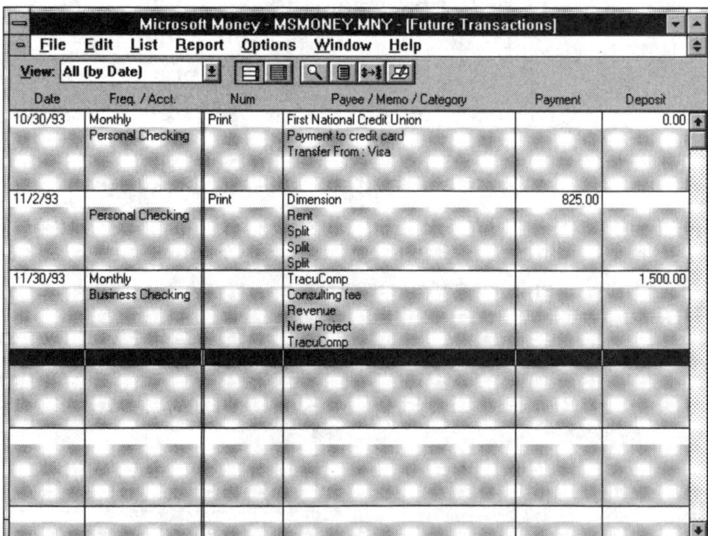

FIGURE 6.2:
The Future Transactions window

empty; you cannot enter a check number now, or any other kind of notation (such as dep or chrg). Enter the information in the Payee, Payment, Deposit, Account, Memo, Category, and Classification fields as normal. If you are not certain of some of this information, just leave those fields blank; you will be able to fill them in when the payment is made. And if you enter information that you later find is incorrect, you will be able to change the information.

If the transaction is a one-time transaction, select Only Once from the Frequency drop-down list box. If it will occur more than once, but irregularly, leave the Frequency field blank.

SETTING REMINDERS

Money will remind you a few days before a scheduled transaction is due. You can specify the exact number in the Settings dialog box (see Figure 6.3). Select Options ➤ Settings. When the dialog box appears, make sure that the Transactions Due Reminder check box has a check mark inside it; then enter a number in the Days In Advance to Remind text box, located on the right side of the dialog box. The default is 5 days, but you can enter any number from 0 (to remind you on the day the transaction is due) to 254 days.

FIGURE 6.3:

The Settings dialog box

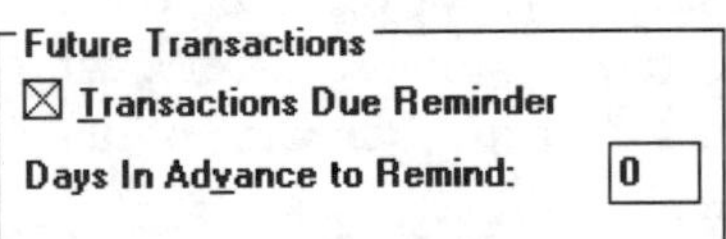

When you open Money the specified number of days before a transaction is due, the Reminder dialog box will appear (Figure 6.4). If you click on the Yes button, the Record Due Transactions dialog box will appear and you can immediately enter the transactions.

Money reminds you about transactions in the current file only. If another file has pending transactions, you won't see the Reminder dialog box until you open that file.

FIGURE 6.4:

The Reminder dialog box, showing that a transaction is due

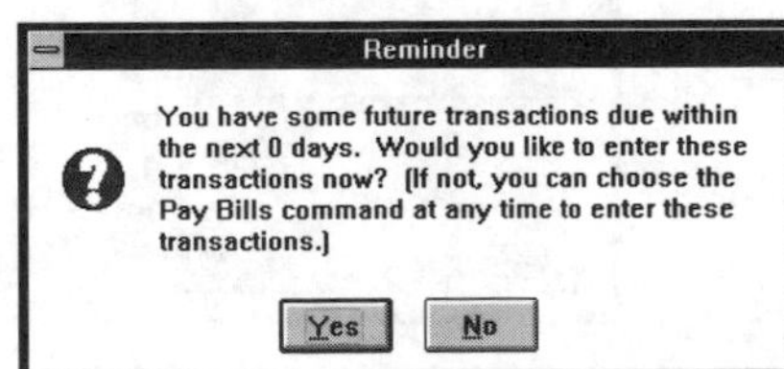

USING SCHEDULED TRANSACTIONS

When a transaction is due, you must tell Money to record it in the appropriate account. Of course, you have to do *your* part as well: write the check, make the deposit, and so on. If you have a number of bills that fall due at the same time, you could sit down with your checkbook and Money, and let Money tell you what to write and to whom. At the same time, Money will record the transactions into the various accounts.

There are two ways to handle scheduled transactions when they fall due. As you have just seen, you can click on the Yes button in the Reminder dialog box. Or you can select the Options ➤ Pay Bills command (Ctrl-P). In either case, Money will display the Future Transactions window along with the Record Due Transactions dialog box (see Figure 6.5).

You can also enter just one transaction. Display the Future Transactions window, select the transaction, and select Edit ➤ Enter from Schedule.

Enter the date up to which you want to perform the scheduled transactions and press ↵. The Enter Scheduled Transactions dialog box appears (see Figure 6.6).

The Enter Scheduled Transactions dialog box shows the information for the first due transaction. It shows the account in which the transaction should be recorded, the date, payee, amount, memo, category, and classification. If this is a check that you want to print, the word "print" will appear in the Num box. It also

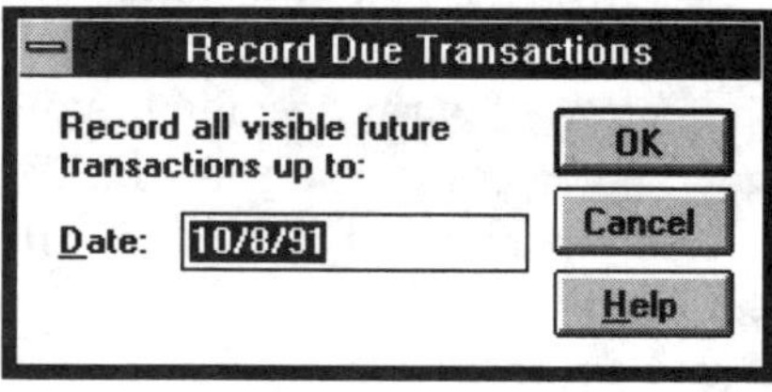

FIGURE 6.5: The Record Due Transactions dialog box

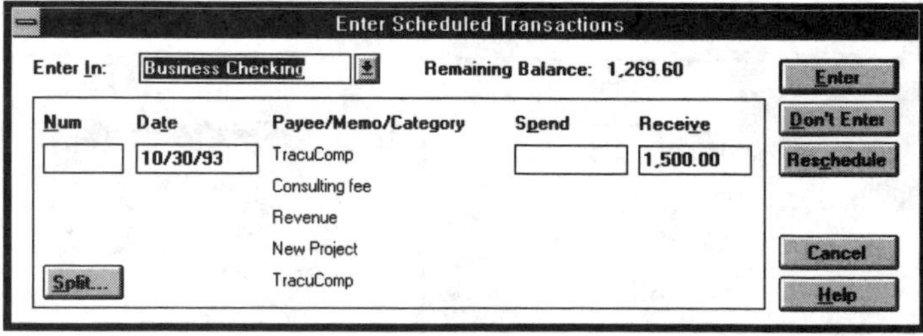

FIGURE 6.6: The Enter Scheduled Transactions dialog box

shows the current balance of the account—the balance *before* the displayed transaction—so you can tell if the account has enough money to cover the payments you are about to make.

If the transaction information is correct, there's no need to change anything, though you may need to enter a check number into the Num box, if you aren't printing checks. If some of the information *does* need to be modified, simply type the correct information into the appropriate box. Unfortunately, you can't directly change the payee, memo, category, or classification (unless it's a split transaction, in which case you can click on the Split button to see the Split Transaction dialog box). If you want to change these entries, close the dialog box and change them in the Future Transactions window, or simply proceed and change them in the Account Book window later.

After you have confirmed the transaction information, you have three options:

Enter: Enters the transaction into the appropriate Account and displays the next transaction.

Don't Enter: Displays the next transaction without entering the current one.

Reschedule: Reschedules the transaction for a later date (according to the Frequency information). If the Frequency field is blank, or if the Frequency is set to Only Once, the Reschedule Transaction dialog box will appear (see Figure 6.7), enabling you to specify a later date for the transaction.

So what exactly happens when you "enter" transactions? Well, Money records the information into the appropriate accounts saving you the need to do so yourself. You still need to write the checks when necessary, and make sure that scheduled deposits actually occurred. If you *print* checks—that is, if you typed "print" instead of a check number—the checks are now waiting to be printed. And that's what you will learn about in the next chapter.

FIGURE 6.7: The Reschedule Transaction dialog box

Reschedule Transaction

Change the next time this transaction is due to:

Date:

OK

Cancel

Help

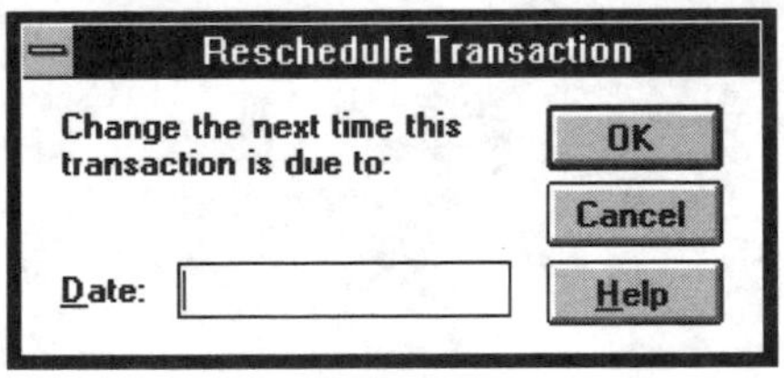

FOR MORE INFORMATION

See the following entries in the Reference section:

Edit ➤ Enter from Schedule

Edit ➤ Schedule in Future

Options ➤ Pay Bills

Window ➤ Future Transactions

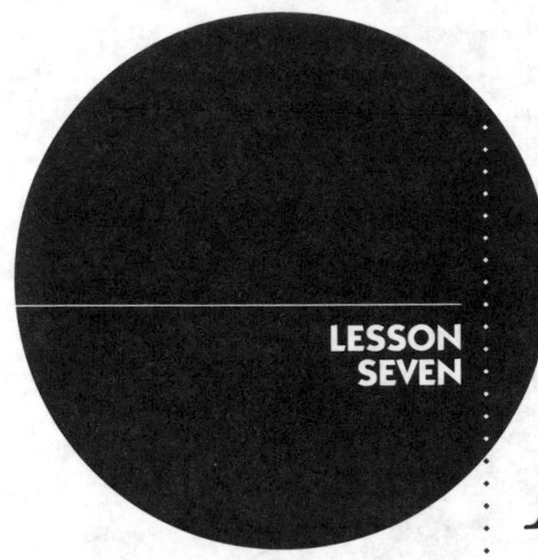

LESSON SEVEN

*P*RINTING CHECKS

INTRODUCING

Ordering and Preparing Checks
Entering Information
Preparing the Printer
Printing the Checks

If you are in the habit of sitting down once or twice a month and writing checks, or if you have a business that puts a lot of checks in the mail, you may want to have Money print your checks for you. You won't throw out your checkbook, of course. It's too much trouble to drag a computer and printer everywhere you go. Even when you write checks at home, pulling out your checkbook is easier than booting your computer. Also, computer checks are much more expensive than regular, pre-printed checks—often four or five times more.

Nonetheless, printing checks can be a real time-saver for some people. And you can instruct Money to print an address on the checks that can be seen through an envelope window. So if you mail lots of checks or if you employ other people, you might find it easier to print checks than to handwrite them.

PREPARING THE CHECKS

Naturally, the first step is to buy machine-printable checks. There are two laser and three continuous-feed printer formats you can use:

Laser Standard: Three checks per 8½″ x 11″ sheet

Laser Voucher: One check and two vouchers per 8½″ x 11″ sheet

Continuous-Feed, Wallet: Standard wallet-size checks, with a stub on the left side

Continuous-Feed, Standard: Full-size checks, with no stub; one-part or two-part (includes duplicate copy)

Continuous-Feed, Voucher: Full-size checks, with a stub; one-part or two-part

The vouchers are provided for record keeping; Money prints all the check information, except for the payee's address, on the voucher. It also prints the name of the account from which the check is drawn.

Your Microsoft Money package includes sample checks and order forms from Deluxe Business Systems. You can also call Deluxe at 1-800-328-0304 (in the U.S.) or 1-800-826-3714 (in Canada). Checks are also available from other sources, such as Nebs (1-800-225-6380). Always make sure that the checks are printed in the correct Money format; the supplier should know or may be able to send you samples. And shop around for the best price.

PREPARING THE INFORMATION

You have already learned how to prepare a check for printing; just type **print** in the Num column, and then fill in the rest of the information. If you want an address to appear on the check, enter the transaction in the Checks & Forms window, which includes an address box. Or, open the Payee List by selecting List ➤ Payee List, select the appropriate payee, and type the information into the Address box.

If you wish to enter transaction information that should not print on the check (such as a purchase order number or a contact name), just enter the information in braces { }. For example, typing **{per: Jean}** *prevents the words* **per: Jean** *from appearing on the check.*

PREPARING THE PRINTER

The first step is to install a driver for your printer by using the Windows Control Panel. If you haven't done that yet, check your Windows documentation for full instructions. If you have already installed the printer, select File ➤ Print Setup from Money's menu bar to enter the Print Setup dialog box (see Figure 7.1).

Click on the Check Printing option button at the top of the box to see the setup for check printing. When you first display this dialog box, the box shows the setup parameters for the Default Printer. (This is the Windows default printer, as defined in the Windows Control Panel.) If you want to use a different printer, click on the Specific Printer option button, and select a printer from the drop-down list box. This list displays all the device drivers that you have loaded in Windows—not only printers, but also slide makers, plotters, data communications drivers, and so on. Selecting a printer has no effect on other Windows applications; the Windows default printer remains unchanged (unlike some programs, which change the default printer when you select a different one). Next, select the check type. Money doesn't "ghost," or inactivate, the inappropriate ones, by the way, so make sure you pick the correct type. If you are printing on a laser printer, you can still select Wallet, but the results will be poor (unless you happen to have some custom checks that will match the same format).

Next load the paper. If you are using continuous paper, load the paper to the top-of-form position on your printer. If you are using a laser printer, make sure you load the checks with the proper side up and in the correct check-number order.

If you are using two-part checks, you may need to adjust the paper-thickness setting on your continous-form printer. Check your printer documentation.

FIGURE 7.1:

The Print Setup dialog box

PRINTING YOUR CHECKS

You are now ready to print checks. First, open either the Account Book window or the Checks & Forms window—Money will not let you print from the Future Transactions window. Then, use the Account drop-down list to select the bank account containing the checks you want to print. You can also select multiple accounts (*none* of which need be bank accounts).

It gets just a little odd here (but hold on, you'll get through). If you have selected a single, non-bank account or a bank account without any pending checks, Money will not let you print *any* checks. But if you have selected multiple accounts, you *can* print checks, even if none of the accounts are bank accounts or if the selected bank accounts don't contain any checks waiting to be printed.

When you want to print your checks, select File ➤ Print Checks. If you have multiple accounts displayed, the Select Account dialog box will appear. This box displays *all* the selected accounts, including bank accounts with no pending checks and even non-bank accounts—the ones you can't print checks from! Anyway, select the account you want to work with. You can select an account that isn't currently displayed in the Account Book or Checks & Forms window, but you can't select more than one account. Click on Continue and the Print Checks dialog box appears. Figure 7.2 shows the Print Checks dialog box used if you selected a laser-printer check format in the Print Setup dialog box. (If you selected a continuous-form check format, the information below line two will not be present.)

If you have a single bank account with pending checks displayed, the Select Account dialog box will not appear. Instead, the Print Checks dialog box appears as soon as you select File ➤ Print Checks.

If you want to print a sample check—to make sure you have set up your printer correctly—you can do so by clicking on the Print Test button. The test check will contain generic information: Xs in the date and number fields, "this is a void check" printed on it, and so on. You can use this check to make sure that continuous-form paper is lined up correctly, or to make sure that you have selected the correct type of laser check format.

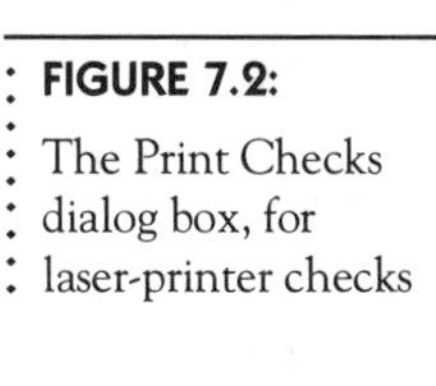

FIGURE 7.2:

The Print Checks dialog box, for laser-printer checks

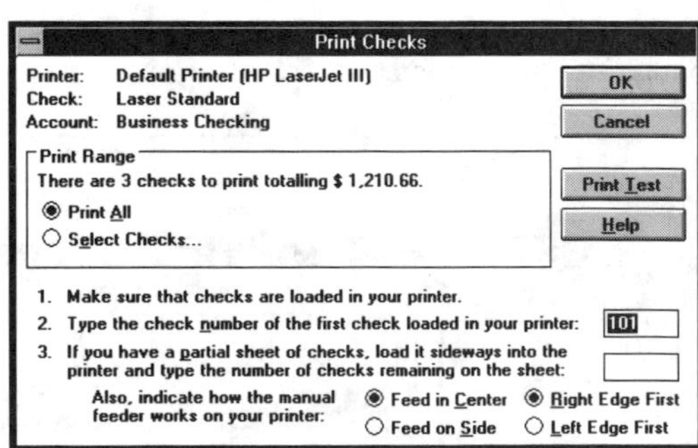

If you use a real check for a sample, remember to enter a transaction for that check, and mark it **VOID**.

Unfortunately, when Money prints the test check, it removes the Print Checks dialog box in order to give you a chance to go to the Print Setup dialog box and make any necessary adjustments. So, if the test check is fine, you must select File ➤ Print Checks again to return to the Print Checks dialog box.

Make sure the information at the top of the Print Checks dialog box (the printer, the type of check, and the account name) is correct; if it isn't, you'd better go back and fix it! Next, type the number of the first check into the box in the lower right corner. If you don't enter a number here, Money will assume that the first number is 101. (If you are using a laser printer, make sure you keep the checks in order when you load them in the printer.) If you have a partial sheet of laser checks, you will have to use your printer's manual feed. On line 3 near the bottom of the dialog box, enter the number of checks on the partial sheet and select the correct manual-feed option for your printer.

Now select the checks that you want to print. The Print All option is the default; if you want to print selected checks, click on Select Checks to enter the Select Checks dialog box (see Figure 7.3).

The Select Checks dialog box works in much the same way as the other selection boxes in Money. You can click on Select All and then click on the checks you *don't* want to print, or click on Select None and then click on the ones that you *do* want to print. Moving the cursor to a check and pressing the spacebar also selects the check. When you have the checks you want, click on OK to return to the Print Checks dialog box.

Finally, click on OK and Money prints your checks and displays the Confirm Printing dialog box. Before you close this box, make sure that your checks printed correctly. If there were any problems—the paper jammed, the paper wasn't lined up, the toner was too low—click on the Reprint button in the Confirm Printing box. Money then displays the Select Checks to Reprint dialog box, which looks

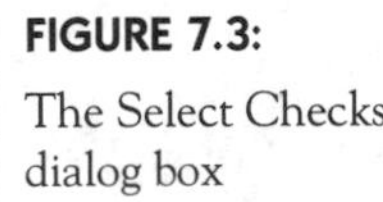

FIGURE 7.3:
The Select Checks dialog box

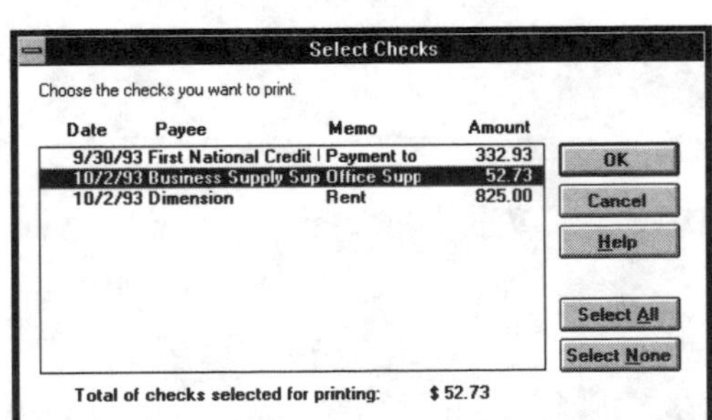

much the same as the Select Checks dialog box. You can then select the checks that need reprinting, and, if necessary, reset the first check number.

When you click on OK, Money will try to print the checks again. But if you click on Cancel, Money will cancel the operation entirely; the checks that were not printed will retain the word "print" in the Num column. If the check is printed, though, Money replaces "print" with the appropriate check number.

When you saw the Print Setup dialog box, you probably noticed the Report Printing option button at the top. This button lets you configure the printer for producing reports, which you will learn about in the next chapter.

FOR MORE INFORMATION

See the following entries in the Reference section:

File ➤ Print Checks

File ➤ Printer Setup

PRODUCING REPORTS

INTRODUCING

Displaying a Report
Customizing Reports
Selecting Rows
Selecting Columns
Selecting a Date Range
Selecting Accounts and Transactions
Adjusting the Report Width
Selecting a Font
Printing Reports
Exporting to ASCII Files

Now we've reached one of the most important functions of Money: taking all the information that Money holds and organizing it in a meaningful report. Money has seven basic finance reports, which you can customize to get the exact information you need. You might want to organize your tax records, for example, check on your business' profitability and projected income, list all checks to a particular person, or list your personal assets.

These are the report types that Money produces:

Register Report: This report lists transactions in the selected accounts, showing check numbers, dates, payees, reconciliation status, categories, classifications, and amounts (Figure 8.1). It is displayed from the Report menu.

Future Transactions Report: This report lists the transactions in the Future Transactions window. It is produced by selecting Register Report while in the Future Transactions window.

Summary Report: This report shows account totals grouped by account, payee, category or subcategory, classification or subclassification, week, or month. It is displayed from the Report menu.

Income and Expense Report: This report shows income and expenses grouped by category or subcategory (Figure 8.2). It is displayed from the Report menu.

Tax Report: This report shows taxable income and tax-deductible expenses, grouped by category. It is displayed from the Report menu.

Budget Report: This report compares budgeted amounts with actual expenditures. It is displayed from the Report menu.

Net Worth Report: This report lists your total assets (the balances in your bank, cash, and asset accounts) and your total liabilities (the balances in your credit card and liability accounts), and shows the difference between the two (your net worth). Figure 8.3 shows a sample Net Worth Report. The report is displayed from the Report menu.

Account List Report: This report lists the bank names, account numbers, shortcuts, and balances of all of your accounts. It is displayed from the Account List dialog box.

Payee List Report: This report lists all payees, along with their entry shortcuts, phone numbers, and the date of their last transaction. It is displayed from the Payee List dialog box.

Category List Report: This report lists all categories along with their entry shortcuts, indicates inclusion in Tax Reports, and provides budget information. This report is displayed from the Category List dialog box, shown in Figure 8.4.

Classification List Report: This report lists classification items and subitems, along with their shortcuts. It is displayed from the Classification List dialog box.

Each of these reports can be customized to show specific information. For example, you may want to know how much cash you could retrieve quickly. You could select

FIGURE 8.1:

A sample Register Report

Register Report

REGISTER REPORT
9/1/93 Through 10/22/93

Num	Date	Payee	C	Category	Amount
2035	9/26/93	Markhall		Gifts : For Famil	(6.00)
2036	9/28/93	Payless Drugs		Split	(20.26)
2037	9/29/93	Payless Drugs		Gifts : D to P	(12.14)
2038	9/29/93	Grocery Warehou		Groceries	(88.26)
1994	9/30/93	Dimension		Split	(825.00)
Total Month Ending 9/30/93					261.48
Month Ending 10/31/93					
1995	10/1/93	MasterCard		Transfer To : Ma:	(2,177.72)
1996	10/1/93	Water Co.		Split	(28.68)
	10/2/93	To Money Marke		Transfer From : E	3,000.00
	10/2/93	Account Adjustm	R		14.57
	10/2/93	Starting Balance	R		(14.57)
Dep	10/2/93	Met. Life		Split	97.17
2039	10/3/93	Montessori		Education : Tuitic	(190.00)
	10/7/93	To Money Marke		Transfer From : E	3,000.00
Dep	10/7/93	Met. Life		Healthcare : Insu	60.97
	10/14/93	To Money Marke		Transfer From : F	2,500.00
Total Month Ending 10/31/93					6,261.74
GRAND TOTAL					6,523.22

FIGURE 8.2:

A sample Income and Expense Report

Income and Expense Report

INCOME AND EXPENSE REPORT
1/1/93 Through 10/22/93

Category	Total
INCOME	
Book Advances	2,000.00
Book Royalties	6,210.30
Consulting Fees	38,966.00
Interest Income	980.94
Magazines	205.00
Income - Unassigned	7,336.83
TOTAL INCOME	55,699.07
EXPENSES	
Allowance	0.75
B: Advertising	289.57
B: Bank Charges	20.63
B: Car	403.04
B: Depreciation/Sec.179	1,707.18
B: Entertainment	15.50
B: Insurance	130.50
B: Legal & Professional	271.00
B: Meals & Entertainment	25.84

the Net Worth Report and then instruct Money not to include long-term investments, such as IRAs and pension plans. Or you may want to know how well your business is doing. You could select the Income and Expense Report and instruct Money to include only business-related transactions.

You can create all sorts of Summary reports. Perhaps you want to see your month-by-month expenditures for each category in the last year. Maybe you want to know how much each client has paid you in the last year: you can instruct Money to report only income categories.

FIGURE 8.3:

A sample Net Worth Report

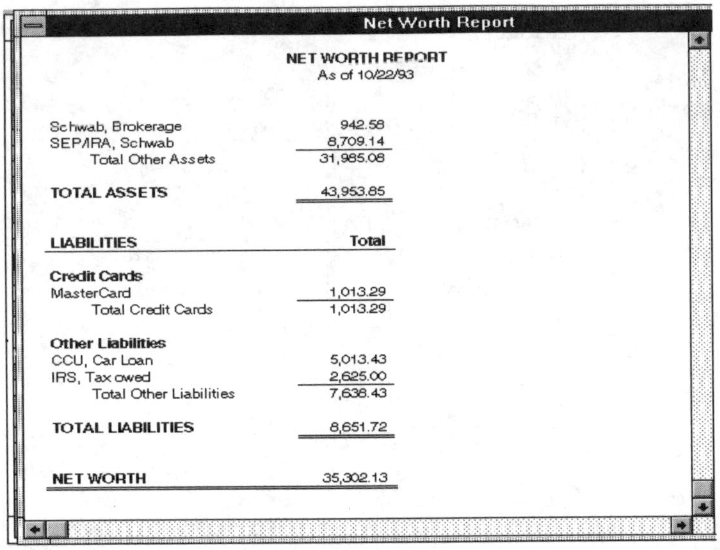

Net Worth Report

NET WORTH REPORT
As of 10/22/93

Schwab, Brokerage	942.58
SEP/IRA, Schwab	8,709.14
Total Other Assets	31,985.08
TOTAL ASSETS	43,953.65
LIABILITIES	**Total**
Credit Cards	
MasterCard	1,013.29
Total Credit Cards	1,013.29
Other Liabilities	
CCU, Car Loan	5,013.43
IRS, Tax owed	2,625.00
Total Other Liabilities	7,638.43
TOTAL LIABILITIES	8,651.72
NET WORTH	35,302.13

FIGURE 8.4:

A sample Category List Report

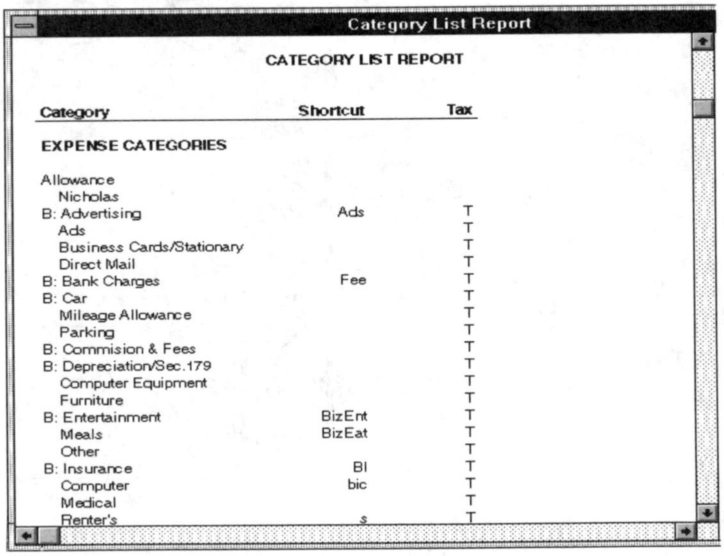

Category List Report

CATEGORY LIST REPORT

Category	Shortcut	Tax
EXPENSE CATEGORIES		
Allowance		
Nicholas		
B: Advertising	Ads	T
Ads		T
Business Cards/Stationary		T
Direct Mail		T
B: Bank Charges	Fee	T
B: Car		T
Mileage Allowance		T
Parking		T
B: Commision & Fees		T
B: Depreciation/Sec.179		T
Computer Equipment		T
Furniture		T
B: Entertainment	BizEnt	T
Meals	BizEat	T
Other		T
B: Insurance	BI	T
Computer	bic	T
Medical		T
Renter's	s	T

Money's report features are very flexible, enabling you to produce reports in numerous different formats. All the basic report types are described in the Reference section. In this chapter, we will examine just one report type, the Summary Report.

DISPLAYING THE SUMMARY REPORT

To see the Summary Report, select Report ➤ Summary Report. The Summary Report dialog box appears on your screen (see Figure 8.5). The report is composed of a column listing payees and a column indicating their transaction amounts. Amounts in parentheses indicate payments you have made. Amounts that are *not* in parentheses are the sums that you have received. The grand total is included at the bottom of the report. The Summary Report includes transactions from the beginning of the year to the current date.

In the Summary Report, a transfer from one account to another negates itself, equalling zero.

So, for example, imagine it's the middle of the year, and so far you have written six rent checks, each for $625. If you scan until you find your landlord's name in the Payee column, and then look across to the Amount column, you will see $3750—the sum you have paid your landlord this year.

This basic report may be all you need, but chances are that it's really *too* basic to be of much use. It only breaks down the account by payee, and it includes *all* payments since the beginning of the year. What if you only want information about the last three months? What if you want to break down the summary by category rather than payee? What if you want a month-by-month summary report? That's where the Customize feature comes in.

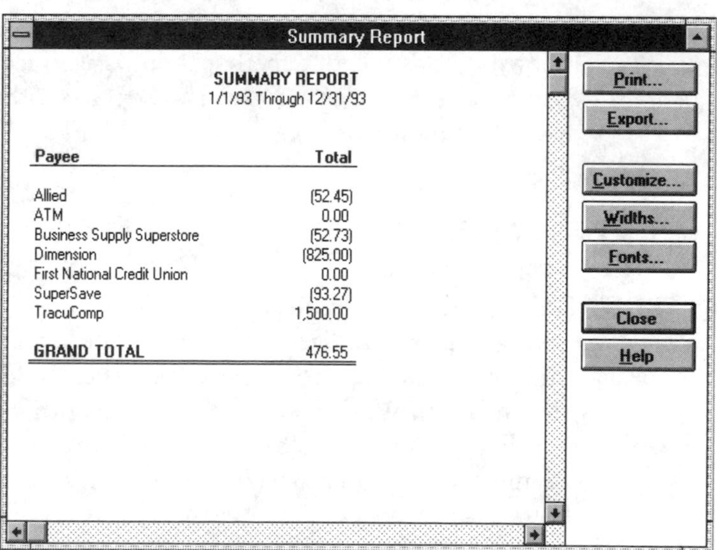

FIGURE 8.5: The Summary Report dialog box

CUSTOMIZING THE REPORT

Click on the Customize button and thc Customize Summary Report dialog box appears (Figure 8.6).

The Customize Summary Report dialog box lets you select exactly what you want to see in the report. You can change the report's title, of course, but let's look at the other elements in more depth.

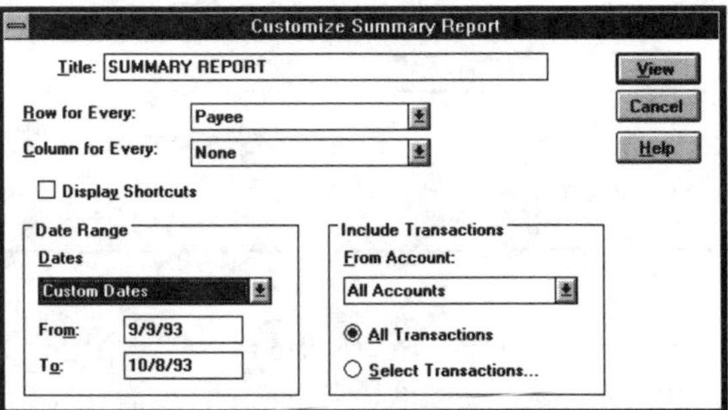

FIGURE 8.6:
The Customize Summary Report dialog box

SELECTING THE ROW

The Summary Report in Figure 8.5 has one row for every payee. You have a choice of these options, though: Account, Payee, Category, Subcategory, Classification, Subclassification, Week, or Month.

For example, you may wish to see a report showing how much money has been spent or received in each category or in each account. Or maybe you want to break it down by classification; perhaps you want to see the transaction totals related to each project or property. You can also opt to see the transaction totals broken down by week or month.

SELECTING THE COLUMN

The default Summary Report has two columns. The one on the left shows the selected group (payee, account, category, etc.), and the one on the right shows the total for each group. You can also add these columns: Account, Payee, Category, Classification, Week, Two Weeks, Half Month, Month, Quarter, and Year.

For example, let's say your rows are Payees, and you select the Category column. Money will produce a report with rows showing each payee and columns showing the exact portion of each payee's transactions that relate to each category.

The last column provides a total for all transactions for that payee. You may also want a monthly breakdown of transactions by payee. If you select Month, the report columns will display the transaction total for each payee in each month, with the total at the end.

SELECTING THE DATE RANGE

Money lets you select the dates from which the report's information will be taken. The available options are: All Dates, Current Month, Current Year, Month to Date, Year to Date, Previous Month, Previous Year, Last 30 Days, Last 12 Months, and Custom Dates.

The Year to Date option is automatically selected when you first select the report. If you select All Dates, all of the information in the file will be used, regardless of the date. If you select Custom Dates, you can enter the specific beginning and ending dates in the From and To text boxes. You could use this option, for instance, to track a specific project from the date it began.

SELECTING ACCOUNTS

You won't always want to include information from all your accounts in your report. You may have both business and personal accounts in a file, but want report totals for the business accounts only. Money lets you define exactly which accounts should be included in the report. Click on the down arrow in the From Account list box. This list box is almost identical to the Account drop-down list box that appears in the Toolbar, and is used in the same way. (The only difference is that there is no New Accounts option at the bottom of the list.) You can select a specific account directly from the list box, or use the Multiple Accounts option to pick exactly which accounts to use.

SELECTING TRANSACTIONS

There are two transaction options: All Transactions and Select Transactions. If All Transactions (the default) is selected, Money will use information for all transactions in the selected accounts. If you click on Select Transactions, the Select Transactions dialog box appears. You used this box in Lesson 4, when you learned how to select transactions using the Other option in the View drop-down list box. (The Select Transactions dialog box is virtually the same as the Other View dialog box.)

VIEWING THE REPORT

After you have created a customized report, click on View to see the new report in the Summary Report dialog box. Figure 8.7 shows an example of a report using categories for the rows and accounts for the columns.

To maximize the report, click on the arrow button in the top right corner of the dialog box, or press Alt-spacebar followed by X.

Let's try creating a Summary Report. First, select Report ➤ Summary Report. When the Summary Report dialog box appears, you will see two columns: Payee and Total. The left column lists all the payees with transactions that occurred since the beginning of the year. The right column lists the transaction totals for each payee. For example, if you have paid $500 rent eight times so far this year, you will see ($4000) in the Total column next to your landlord's name. Remember, the parentheses indicate that it is a negative number. The number is negative because the money left your account. Scan down the list and you should see a few numbers *not* in parentheses. These are transactions in which you *received* money, such as pay or investment income.

Now click on the Customize button. Select Category from the Row for Every box, and Quarter from the Column for Every box. Click on View, and look at the report. There are a couple of changes. First, category names have replaced payee

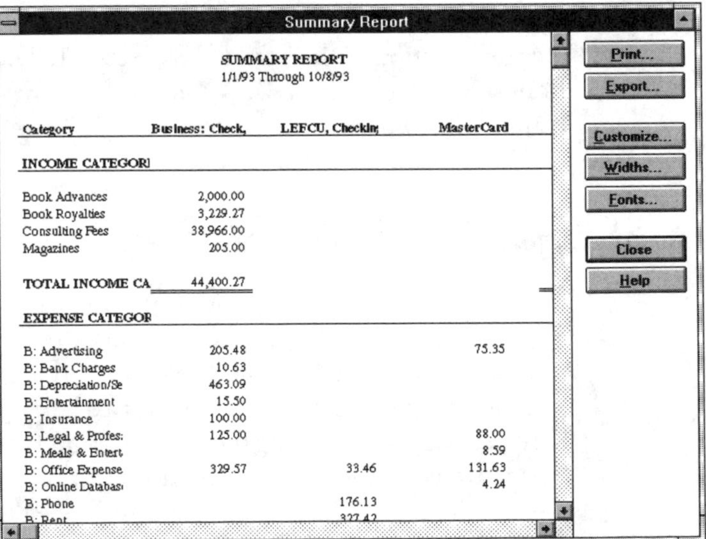

SUMMARY REPORT
1/1/93 Through 10/8/93

Category	Business: Check,	LEFCU, Checkin;	MasterCard
INCOME CATEGORI			
Book Advances	2,000.00		
Book Royalties	3,229.27		
Consulting Fees	38,966.00		
Magazines	205.00		
TOTAL INCOME CA	44,400.27		
EXPENSE CATEGOR			
B: Advertising	205.48		75.35
B: Bank Charges	10.63		
B: Depreciation/Se	463.09		
B: Entertainment	15.50		
B: Insurance	100.00		
B: Legal & Profes:	125.00		88.00
B: Meals & Entert			8.59
B: Office Expense	329.57	33.46	131.63
B: Online Databas			4.24
B: Phone		176.13	
B: Rent		327.42	

FIGURE 8.7:

A sample Summary Report

names in the left column. Also, there are now up to six columns instead of two: Category on the left, Total on the right, and a column for each quarter so far this year in between. This report allows you to find out how much you spent on each category for the year so far and how much you spent during each quarter.

Now click on Customize again. This time, click on the Select Transactions option button. When the Select Transactions dialog box appears, select Payments from the Types box and select a category from the Category box (make sure it's a category that you have used). Then click on OK and click on View. Now the report is much smaller. It only provides information for the category you selected, and the only transactions that will be included are payments.

As you can see, the reports are extremely flexible. You can create just about any type of report you want. You can also modify the report by changing its width and font.

ADJUSTING THE REPORT WIDTH

Your report may have too much blank space, or some text may be truncated. You can adjust the width of the report by clicking on the Widths button, which displays the Report Column Width dialog box (Figure 8.8).

Click on one of the widths—Narrow, Standard, Wide, Extra Wide—and click on OK to return to the Summary Report. Money increases the width by "padding" entries with extra spaces and decreases the width by truncating entries. If you make the columns too narrow, words or rows may "disappear." If you make them too wide, the report may not fit on the paper when you print it.

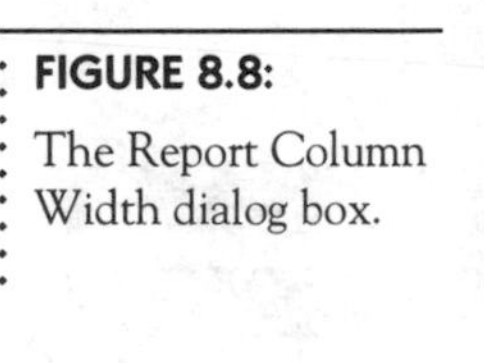

FIGURE 8.8:

The Report Column Width dialog box.

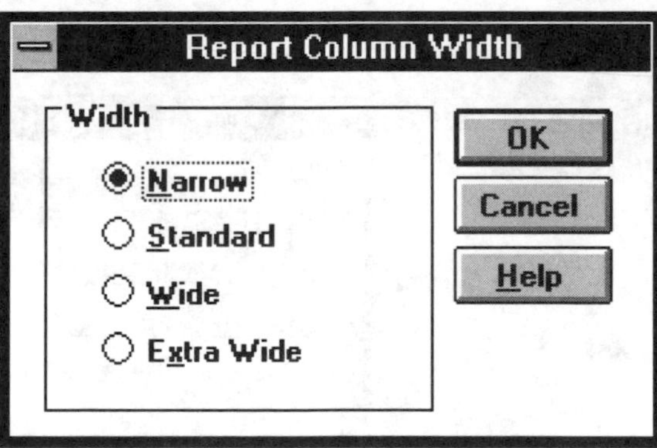

SELECTING THE FONT

Another way to adjust a report's appearance is to change the report's font. Click on the Fonts button to see the Select Fonts dialog box (Figure 8.9).

On the left side of the Select Fonts box is a list of the available fonts. These include Windows fonts (fonts installed when you loaded Windows), printer fonts (fonts supported by your printer, according to the printer driver that you selected earlier), and fonts loaded by programs such as Adobe Type Manager, Bitstream Facelift, or Atech's Publisher's PowerPak. A printer font is identified by a small picture of a printer in the column next to it.

You will usually want to use fonts between 8 and 14 points. Smaller fonts are hard to read, and larger fonts use too much space.

Select a font and then a font size in the list box to the right. Notice the Sample box at the bottom of the dialog box. When you have selected both a font and a size, the Sample box gives an example of what the font will look like (though this is not necessarily what it will look like when it is printed).

In some cases, Money will not work with the selected font very well. If a printer font does not have an associated *screen* font, the font displayed will not look like the font that will be printed. Also, although Money will display font sizes up to 72 points, it can't print a report using these very large fonts. (But of course, why would you want to?)

When you have selected the font you want to work with, click on OK to return to the Summary Report dialog box.

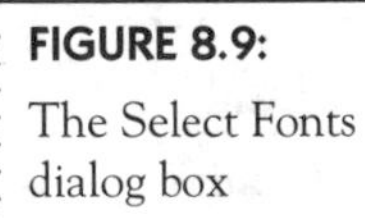

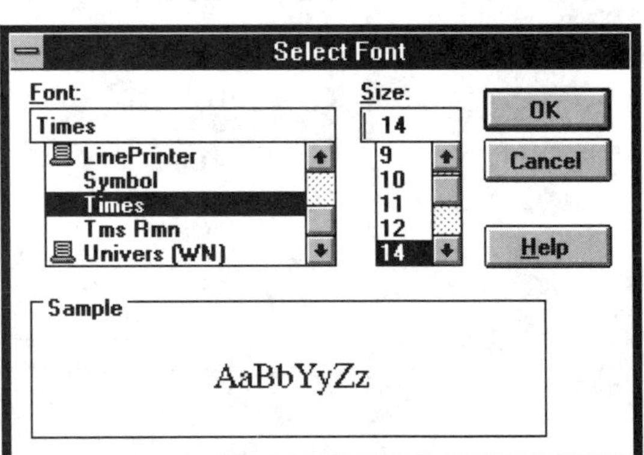

FIGURE 8.9:
The Select Fonts dialog box

PRINTING THE REPORT

If you want to print the report you have just created, click on the Print button at the top of the Summary Report dialog box. The Print Report dialog box appears (Figure 8.10).

First, make sure that the printer setup is correct; click on the Setup button to open the Print Setup dialog box (see Figure 8.11). You've seen this box before, of course, when you printed checks (in Lesson 7). There are no option buttons at the top of the dialog box this time though, because you can only change the report setup from this box.

Select the printer on which you want to print the reports from the drop-down list box or select Default Printer. You may also be able to select the print orientation, if your printer allows this. Portrait is the standard orientation—the "width" of the report will be across the shortest side (the 8½″ side). If you select Landscape, the report will be printed across the 11″ side. Some printers may also allow you to select the paper size and a paper source (such as Tray or Manual Feed). When you have set up the printer, click on OK to return to the Print Report dialog box.

Select the pages you want to print. Usually you will want to print the entire report (the default), but there may be cases when you only want a portion of it. Click on Pages and then enter the first page number in the From box and the last in the To

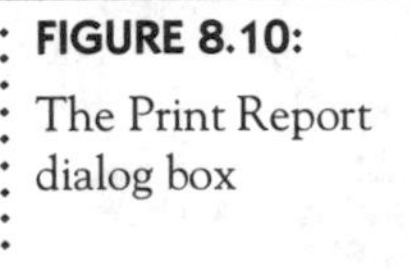

FIGURE 8.10:

The Print Report dialog box

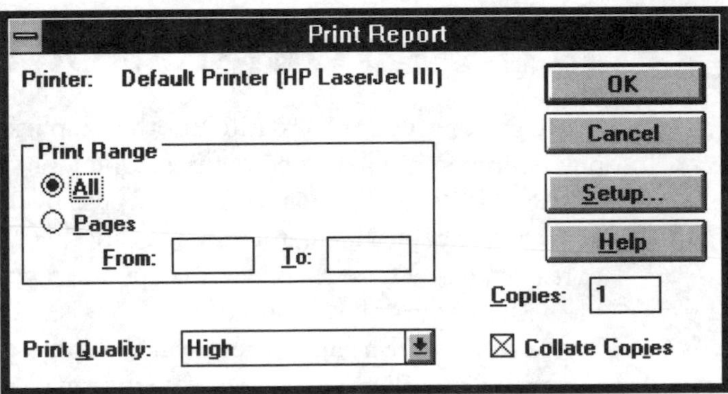

FIGURE 8.11:

The Print Setup dialog box

box. Unfortunately, there is no indication of page numbers in the display, so, unless you've printed the report before, you will have to guess at the page numbers.

To save time and paper, print the first page of the report to check the report layout before printing the entire report.

Next select the number of Copies you want. If you are printing multiple copies, you will probably want to leave the Collate check box selected. With Collate selected, Money prints the first copy, then prints the second, and then the third (pages 1, 2, 3, 1, 2, 3, 1, 2, 3). If you turn Collate off, Money will print all the copies of the first page, then all the copies of the second, and so on (pages 1, 1, 1, 2, 2, 2, 3, 3, 3). Now select the print quality: High, Medium, Low, and Draft. The effect of these options vary depending on your printer, so you will have to experiment. The lower-quality printouts are intended to be quicker, but won't look as nice. Some of the options may have no effect on your printer, or have unintended effects; for example, in some cases the Draft option will cause an almost blank page to print.

When you have made your selections, click on the OK button and Money will print the report.

EXPORTING YOUR REPORTS

You can copy your report into another application—a word processor, desktop-publishing program, database, tax program, or spreadsheet. Money lets you create an ASCII file, a common format accepted by most programs these days. (Even if you want to copy the information into another Windows application, you must export the data. There is no way to copy the report into Windows' clipboard.) The file will contain "tab-delimited" text; that is, tabs will be placed between columns. There will also be a carriage return at the end of each line. This allows database and spreadsheet applications to view the information as a group of fields or cells, with each field or cell being the text separated by tab characters. And if you are exporting to a word processor, you will use the tab marks to line up the columns.

ASCII files contain little format information. The width, font type, and font size are not exported with the report.

Click on the Export button in the Summary Report dialog box to see the Export dialog box (Figure 8.12). Choose a directory in which you want to place the file and enter a name in the File Name text box. You can change the extension if you don't want to use .TXT (perhaps you want to use .DOC, or another extension that is recognized by the program into which you are going to import the file.)

Click on OK and the new file is created.

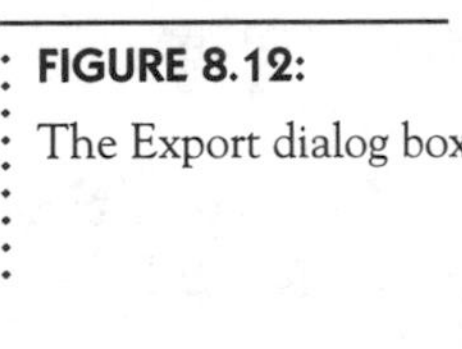

FIGURE 8.12:

The Export dialog box

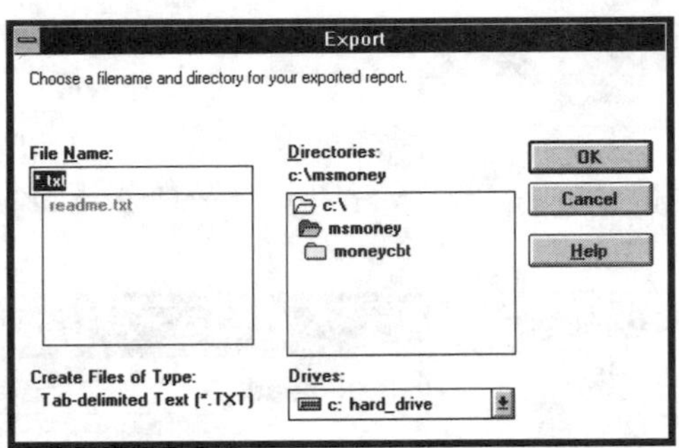

NOW THE BAD PART!

You've finished with your report. You created a custom report, selected a width and font, printed it, and maybe even exported it. Now you want to close the Summary Report dialog box. But wait! Where's the Save Report button?

Sorry, there isn't one. Money doesn't have any means to save customized reports. Microsoft knows that this is a problem and will fix it in a later version. In the meantime—fortunately—there *is* something you can do to get around the problem. You can use Windows Recorder to create a macro that will create your report for you.

OPENING THE WINDOWS RECORDER

Recorder is one of the applications that comes bundled with Windows (along with Calculator, Write, Notepad, and so on). It was loaded when you installed Windows, and an icon was placed in the Accessories program-group window. You can open it by double-clicking on the icon, or by selecting the icon and pressing ↵. If you don't want to search for the icon, select File ➤ Run from Program Manager's menu bar, type Recorder in the Run dialog box, and click on OK. The Recorder window opens (Figure 8.13).

FIGURE 8.13:

The Recorder window, showing two macros

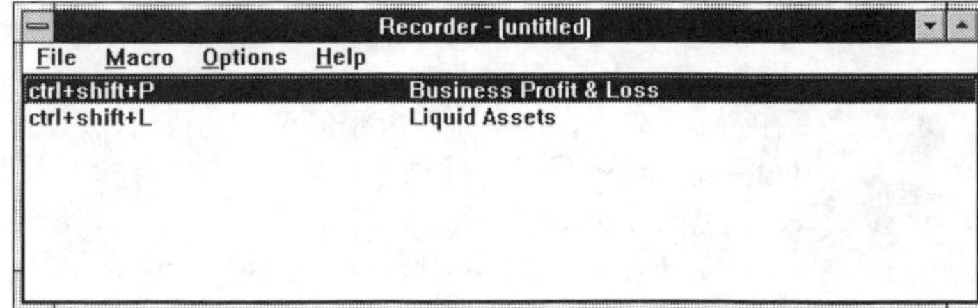

PREPARING RECORDER

Before we begin, let's set up Recorder to work the way we want. Select Options ➤ Preferences to see the Default Preferences dialog box (Figure 8.14).

FIGURE 8.14:

The Default Preferences dialog box

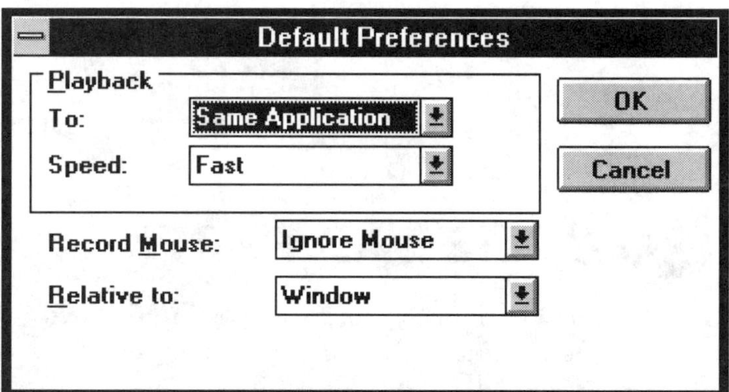

You want to select the following options in this box:

Playback To: Same Application: This setting instructs Windows to Use the macro only in the application in which it was created. Obviously, this macro is intended for use in Money only.

Playback Speed: Fast: This setting runs the macro without pausing. The other option, Recorded Speed, will build your report at the same speed as you created it.

Record Mouse: Ignore Mouse: This setting instructs the macro not to record mouse movements and clicks. For this macro, we don't want to use the mouse, because Recorder doesn't duplicate the original mouse movements very well, particularly when you set the Playback Speed to Fast. It's better to create a macro that uses only keyboard commands.

Relative To: Window: This setting is generally used for macros that use the mouse. It tells Recorder whether the mouse's position on the screen should be measured relative to the application's window or the entire screen. As ours is a keyboard-only macro, the setting won't make much difference.

Click on OK to set the default preferences.

RECORDING THE MACRO

When you are ready to begin recording the macro, go to the Money window. Then select Switch To from the Control menu (or press Ctrl-Esc). The Task List dialog box appears. Double-click on Recorder, or select Recorder and click on Switch To. When the Recorder window appears, select Macro ➤ Record. Recorder displays the Record Macro dialog box (Figure 8.15).

Type a name in the Record Macro Name text box. This can be any title (up to 40 characters) that will tell you exactly what the report is. You can also designate a shortcut key for the macro. Select a key from the Shortcut Key list, and then select Ctrl, Shift, or Alt (or any combination of the three). For example, you could run a macro by pressing Ctrl-Caps Lock or Shift-Ctrl-P. If you want to use a shortcut key to start the macro, you must make sure that the Enable Shortcut Keys check box is selected. Make sure you don't assign a shortcut already used by Money to the macro.

Finally, make sure that the Continuous Loop check box is *not* selected, and enter a macro description, if you want. The other dialog box options don't need to be changed—you set them earlier, in the Default Preferences dialog box.

Click on Start; the dialog box and Recorder window are removed, and you are back in the Money window. (The reason for going to the Money window and then coming straight back to Recorder is to make sure that when Recorder begins

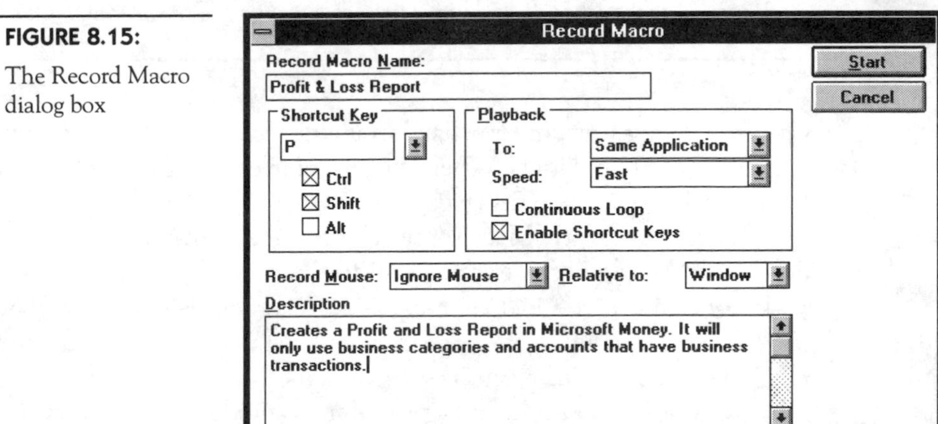

FIGURE 8.15: The Record Macro dialog box

recording the macro, it displays the Money window and not some other application.) Now you can create your macro, but *don't use the mouse*—Recorder will ignore all the mouse actions. (You may want to push your mouse away, so you don't unconsciously try to use it.)

If creating a Register or Future Transactions Report, select the window in the macro's first step (Alt-W plus A, C, or F). The window displayed when you select Report ➤ Register Report determines the report type.

Creating a report is really quite simple. First, press Alt-R to display the Report menu and type the underlined character in the name of the report you want to create (S for Summary Report, for example). When the Report dialog box appears, press Alt-C to customize the report. Continue in this manner. Remember that you can select options by holding down the Alt key while pressing the underlined character in the option's name. If the highlight is on a drop-down list box, you can open the list and move through it by pressing ↓, and then select the desired option by pressing Tab. You can also move the highlight through the dialog box by pressing Tab or Shift-Tab. When an option has two elements, pressing Tab moves you from one to the other.

If you need to select a payee name for a report, you should type the name into the Payee drop-down list box in the Select Transactions dialog box, rather than select it from the list. This is because the list changes each time a new payee is added. Also, you might find that if you press ↵ while the Select Accounts dialog box is displayed, both that dialog box and the Customize dialog box close at the same time, returning you to the Report dialog box. You can avoid the problem by pressing Tab to move the highlight to the OK button and then pressing the spacebar, or by simply leaving that part of the operation until last.

Continue in this way until you have set up the report exactly as you want it, including the report width and fonts. When you are completely finished, press Ctrl-Break. The Recorder dialog box appears (Figure 8.16).

Click on the Save Macro option button and then click on OK. The dialog box disappears. Now go back to the Recorder window by pressing Ctrl-Esc to view the Task List dialog box and double-click on Recorder. Select File ➤ Save, and when the File Save As dialog box appears, type a name (such as Money or MoneyMac). Click on OK and your macro is saved in a file.

Now you can use the same procedure to produce a macro for the next type of custom report. Each time you create a macro, return to the Recorder window and select File ➤ Save, and all the macros will be saved together in one file.

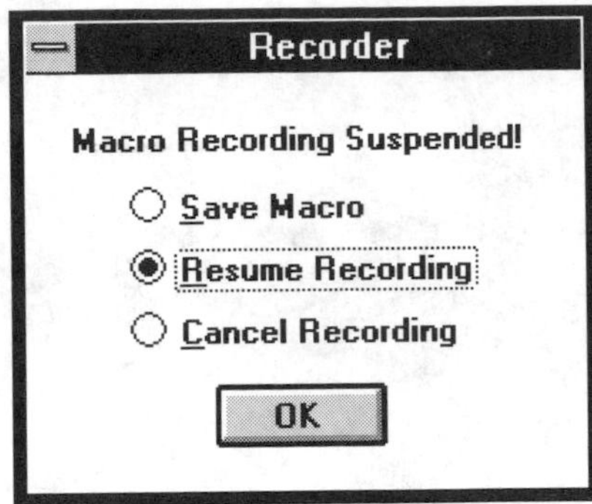

FIGURE 8.16:
The Recorder dialog box

DISPLAYING A REPORT USING RECORDER

When you want to view or print a report, you can instruct Recorder to do it for you. Open the Recorder window to see a list of macro names, and double-click on the name of the report you want to view (or select it and then select Macro ➤ Run). Recorder will then build it for you. Of course, if you assigned a keyboard shortcut, you can use it to run the macro.

If you use Money a lot you can make life a little easier for yourself by loading it automatically when you run Windows; you can also have Windows open Recorder and the Recorder macro file you created at the same time. For more information, see your Windows documentation.

FOR MORE INFORMATION

See the following entries in the Reference section:

Reports

Report ➤ Budget Report

Report ➤ Income and Expense Report

Report ➤ Net Worth Report

Report ➤ Register Report

Report ➤ Summary Report

Report ➤ Tax Report

File ➤ Print Setup

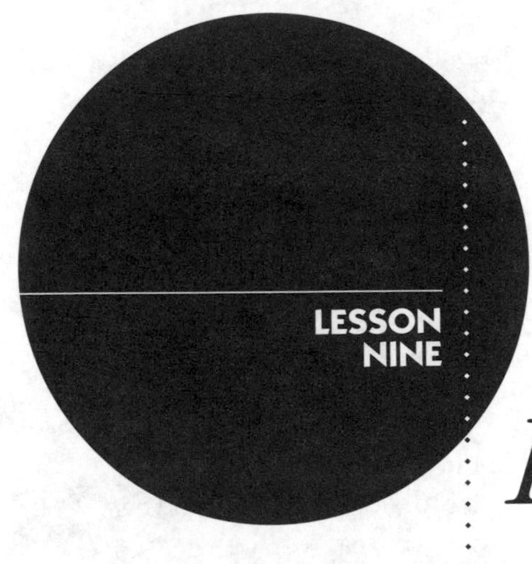

Balancing Your Checkbook

INTRODUCING

Preparing to Balance an Account

The Starting Balance Warning Dialog Box

Marking Transactions

SmartReconcile

Making Account Adjustments

Avoiding Balance Problems

Probably the most loathsome chore in personal money management is reconciling bank statements against check registers. Somehow, they just never seem to match. Well, Money can help you with the chore, and probably eliminate most—but not all—of the problems. For a start, Money keeps track of your balance for you, thereby eliminating the most common problem, mathematical errors. Money also has a system to help you reconcile your check register when your bank statement arrives, and even to check for some types of mistakes.

In this chapter we will assume that you are going to balance a checking account. For information about balancing other types of accounts, see Options ➤ Balance Accounts in the Reference section.

THE FIRST STEPS

Select the account you want to balance, and then select Options ➤ Balance Account (or press F9, or click on the Balance Account icon in the Toolbar). If there are multiple accounts displayed in the Account Book or Checks & Forms window, you will see the Select Account dialog box. Double-click on the name of the account you want to work with. The Account Balance dialog box appears (Figure 9.1).

If this is the first time you have balanced the account, the Starting Balance text box will contain the balance you entered when you first created the account. If this is not the first time, the box will contain the final balance from the last statement against which you reconciled the account.

Enter the final balance shown on your statement into the Ending Balance text box, and enter the date shown on the statement into the Statement Date text box. If you have balanced the account before, the Last Statement date will be shown below the Statement Date.

Look at your statement to see if there are any interest deposits or service charges. If there was just one of each, enter the information into the Service Charge and Interest Earned boxes, and select the appropriate category and subcategory. If you have more than one of either charge you can enter them as separate transactions later. After entering the transactions, mark them on the bank statement by crossing them out or putting a check mark next to them.

The next time you balance your account, Money will propose the same deposit and service charge categories.

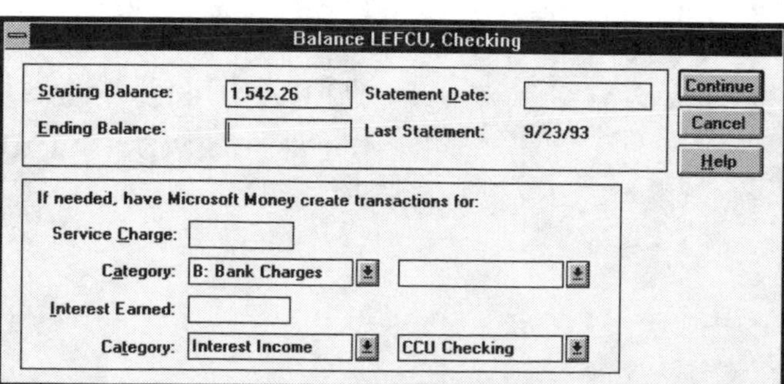

FIGURE 9.1:
The Balance Account dialog box

Click on Continue. Money will enter the service charge and interest transactions into the account for you.

CHECKING THE STARTING BALANCE

Money compares the starting balance shown in the box with a starting balance it has stored in its memory. Where does it find the starting balance? If you have never reconciled the account, the starting balance is the balance you entered when you first created the account. (You can see this value by selecting List ➤ Account List from the Money menu bar and clicking on the account name.) If you *have* reconciled the account before, this will be the Ending Balance from the last time the account was reconciled, and it should match the starting balance shown on the current statement.

See List ➤ Account List in the Reference section and Lesson 1 for more information about the starting balance.

The Starting Balance could be incorrect if you have done one of the following things:

- Entered an incorrect Starting Balance when you created the account
- Changed the original Starting Balance in the Account List
- Deleted a previously reconciled transaction
- Changed the reconciliation status of a previously reconciled transaction

It is quite possible that the Starting Balance will be wrong the first time you balance an account. If you were not conscientious in balancing your account in the past, the balance you show in your check register may not be correct. If, for whatever reason, the balance *is* incorrect, the Starting Balance Warning dialog box appears when you click on the Continue button in the Balance Account dialog box (Figure 9.2).

What now? Well, you can click on the Cancel button, and make sure that you are using the correct statement and haven't skipped any earlier statements. If you have just started using Money and this is the first time you have reconciled the account, you should check to see if you have entered any transactions that appeared on earlier statements; if so, mark them as reconciled by selecting the entry and pressing Shift-Ctrl-M.

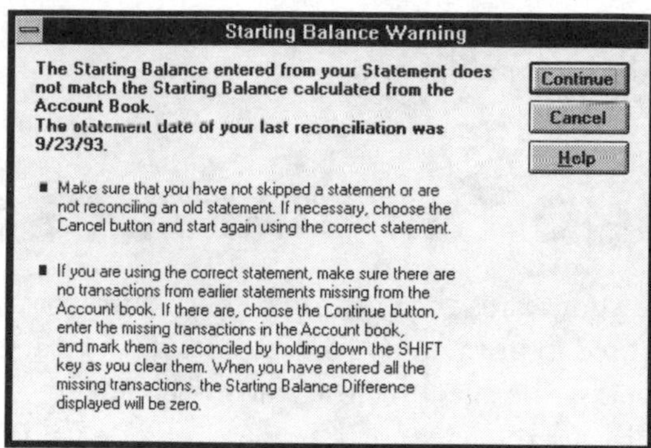

FIGURE 9.2:
The Starting Balance Warning dialog box

If, however, your past accounting is totally chaotic, you may want to forget about the problem for now, and use Money's "fudge factor" to fix the balance so that the account balancing procedure will work correctly next time. To follow this option, click on Continue.

MARKING THE TRANSACTIONS

Money now displays the Balance window (Figure 9.3).

The Balance window lists only those transactions that have not been reconciled. (Remember, reconciled transactions are marked with an R in the C column.) The window also does not show the service charge and interest payment that you just entered in the Balance Account dialog box, because Money automatically marks those as reconciled.

Look in the list on the screen for each of the transactions shown on your bank statement. When you find a transaction that appears on the statement, point to the

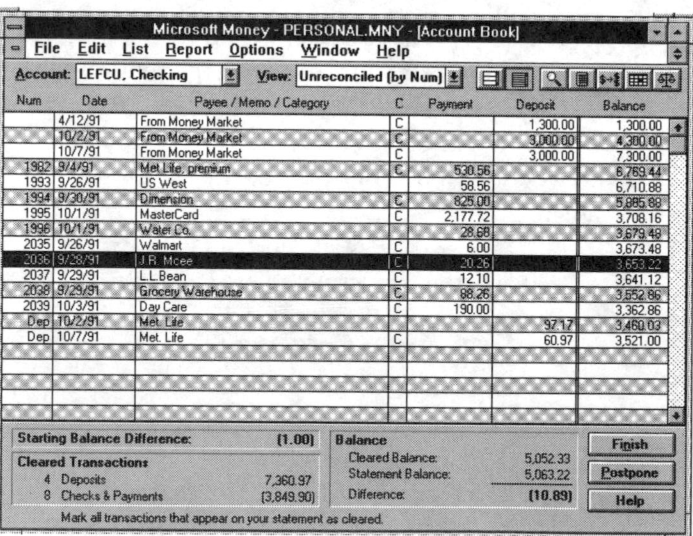

FIGURE 9.3:
The Balance window

C field and click the mouse (or select the transaction and press Ctrl-M) to place a C in that column. You can also press the spacebar to enter the C and move to the next transaction in the list. Each time you mark an item on the screen, mark it on the statement as well: cross it out or place a check mark next to it.

If you select the All (by Num) view from the View drop-down list box, Money places the transactions in order according to the number or notation in the Num column. The transactions without anything in the Num column will appear at the head of the list, then the checks in numerical order, and then the other transactions (Chrgs, Deps, and so on) in chronological order. This will help you search for missing items.

Listing checks in numerical order can also save you time. Many bank statements list cleared checks in numerical order. If this is the case with your statement, select the first check and press the spacebar to mark it; the highlight moves to the next line. When you reach a check that isn't included on the statement, press ↓ to skip it.

If you find items on the statement that are not in your list, add them to the list now. You can change to Entire Transaction View in order to categorize the new entries. At this time, you can also enter automatic withdrawals or bank charges other than those you entered into the Balance Account dialog box. Remember to mark each transaction as cleared (Ctrl-M) after entering it. You can also edit any transactions, if necessary.

Don't just look at check numbers. Make sure that the transaction amount on the statement matches the amount on the screen. If it doesn't, find out why and correct the problem.

As you mark transactions as cleared, they are added to the Cleared Transactions totals at the bottom of the window. When you have cleared all of the transactions on the statement, the Cleared Balance at the bottom of the window should match the Statement Balance.

The Cleared Balance is the Starting Balance you entered earlier, plus all cleared deposits and minus all the cleared payments. The Statement Balance is the Ending Balance you entered earlier, and if everything is correct, the Cleared Balance should match the Statement Balance. It may not.

If it doesn't, you have two options. You can click on the Postpone problem button to troubleshoot the problem later. Or you can click on the Finish button to complete the balancing operation.

FINISHING THE OPERATION

If all of the totals balance, you will see a dialog box when you click on the Finish button, congratulating you for balancing your account. But if the totals did not balance, you will see the Account Didn't Balance dialog box (Figure 9.4).

You now have three options:

Go back to reconciling the account: Money will return you to the Balance window, where you can look for the problem or click on the Postpone button to put off the problem for now.

Use SmartReconcile to help find the error: Money will try to find the error for you.

Automatically adjust the account balance: Money will add a transaction that will fix the problem for you. If the balance is too low it will add money, if it's too high it will withdraw some. You could call this the "fudge factor." The transaction will be called an "Account Adjustment."

SmartReconcile is a tempting option: let Money fix it for you! Of course, it probably won't be able to because it cannot read all your old bank statements and check registers. The problems it can help you with are very limited. Still, it's worth a click of the mouse to try it.

SmartReconcile can correct the following three types of errors:

- Entries that may have been typed incorrectly, such as 2535 entered for 25.35
- Uncleared entries that are exactly the same amount as the unresolved difference

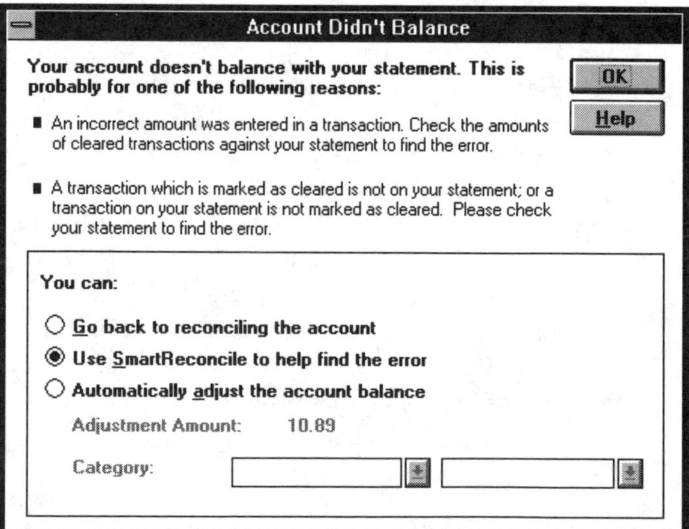

FIGURE 9.4: The Account Didn't Balance dialog box

- Cleared entries that are exactly the same amount as the unresolved difference

If SmartReconcile *can't* find the problem, within a second or two you will see a dialog box telling you so. But if it *can* find the problem, you will see the Possible Error dialog box (Figure 9.5). This box gives you a possible solution to the error and asks if you want to correct the error automatically.

The "fudge factor" is also an attractive option. However, if you have been using Money for a while and your account balanced last time you went through this process, *don't* use this option. Find the problem. But if this is the first time you have reconciled the account, you must decide if the hours or even days it will take to find the problem is really worth it. You survived this far without knowing the exact total in your account, so why not do so for one more day? Once you've made the adjustment, Money will be able to help you track the account accurately, but in the meantime, automatically adjusting the account balance might be the best thing to do.

To adjust the account balance, click on the last option in the Account Didn't Balance dialog box. You can then assign the adjustment to a category (Fudge?). Of course, don't assign this to a meaningful category that is used to track expenditures. In fact, you may want to leave the transaction uncategorized.

If you don't adjust the balance now, there will be a starting balance problem each time you reconcile the account.

Now, when you click on OK, Money will enter an Account Adjustment transaction and mark it as cleared. If you had a starting balance error when you began this process, you will then see the Starting Balance Adjustment dialog box (Figure 9.6).

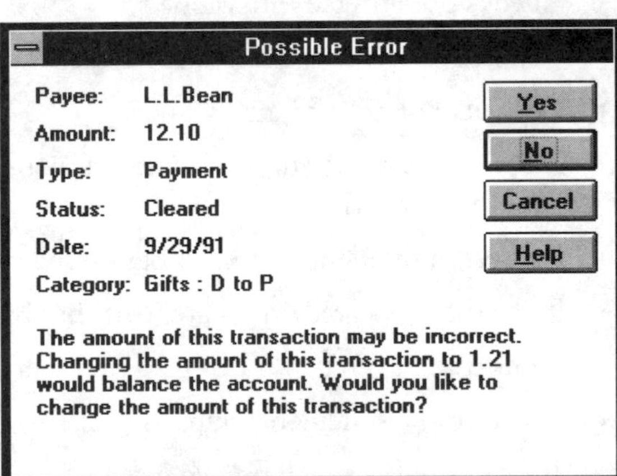

FIGURE 9.5: The Possible Error dialog box

FIGURE 9.6:
The Starting Balance Adjustment dialog box

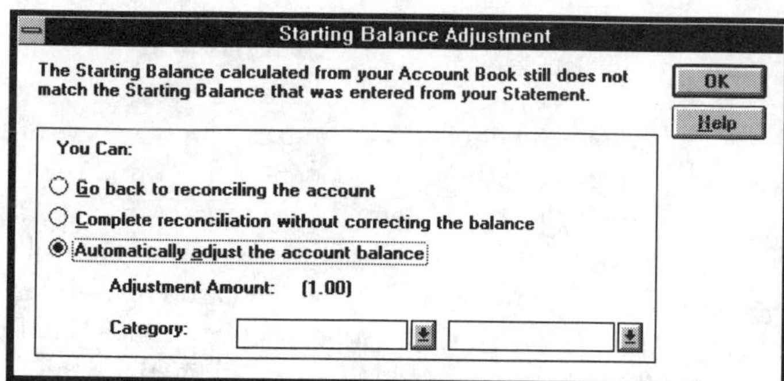

You can now return to reconciling the account, complete the reconciliation without correcting the balance, or automatically adjust the account balance by adding an Account Adjustment transaction. You might even find two adjustments that negate each other, one a credit and one a payment.

AVOIDING PROBLEMS

There are a number of problems that can cause an error when you balance your account:

- Automatic deposits not entered into Money
- Automatic withdrawals not entered into Money
- Bank charges not entered into Money
- Bounced checks that appeared as cleared on an earlier statement, but which you have not changed
- Checks not entered into Money
- Deposits incorrectly entered as payments and vice versa
- Deposits not entered into Money
- Incorrect amounts entered for transactions (such as $25.16 or $2561 instead of $25.61)
- Interest or dividend deposits not entered into Money
- Items that appeared on a statement that have not been marked as cleared
- Items that haven't appeared on a statement that are marked as cleared
- One or more statements skipped
- Transfers not entered into Money

Unless you were very diligent about reconciling it before, you will probably run into problems the first time you use Money to balance an existing checking account. The first attempt at balancing might take some work and adjustments. But once you've straightened out the account, it will be much easier to reconcile. Here's a few tips for keeping the account straight.

- Enter transactions carefully, being especially careful to enter the correct check number and amount.
- Make an entry in the Num column, even if the transaction is not a check. Coding each type of transaction will allow you to group them later using the All (by Num) view, enabling you to quickly scan for mistakes.
- When you receive a statement, first look for payments and deposits made by the bank, and add them to your account.
- If you have not reconciled this account before, make sure that the Starting Balance in the Balance Account dialog box matches the starting balance shown on your statement. If it doesn't, try to trace the problem.
- Be sure to enter the correct *ending* balance into the Balance Account dialog box.
- Check the Last Statement date in the Balance Account dialog box to make sure that you have not missed a statement.
- When you mark items in your account as cleared, make sure you verify that the amount is correct, not just the check number and date.
- As you mark items in your account as cleared, mark them on the statement as well by crossing them off or putting a check mark next to them. When you have finished, make sure that there are no items on the statement that have not been marked.

Using Money to reconcile your checking accounts can really save time and frustration. It's quick and (at least after the first time you do it) quite easy. The secret is simply to keep the transaction information up to date and accurate.

For information on balancing other account types, see Options ➤ Balance Account in the Reference section.

FOR MORE INFORMATION

See the following entry in the Reference section:

Options ➤ Balance Account

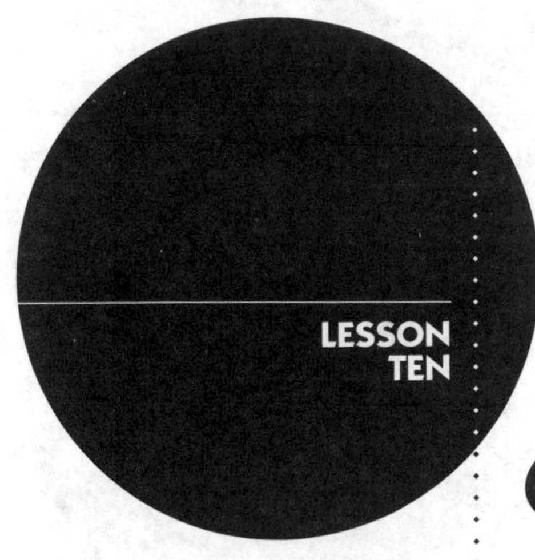

Creating a Budget

INTRODUCING

Assigning Budget Limits
Creating Budget Reports

Money lets you create a budget and compare your actual expenditure and income against the budgeted amounts. A budget shows how much you expect to spend or receive in specific categories. You might want to create a budget for your personal or business accounts as a way to track and control expenses.

Working with budgets is a two-step process. The first step is setting the budget amounts—the amount of money you expect (or hope!) to spend or receive in a particular category over a particular time period. The second step is viewing the budget report, which shows you the amount you budgeted and the amount you *actually* spent!

How do you decide how much to allow in each category? If you are budgeting a new business and have created a business plan, you could use the amounts from the plan. If you are budgeting accounts that have been in use for a while, you might want to create a Summary Report to find out how much you have been spending.

DEFINING BUDGET AMOUNTS

The budget amounts are linked to categories: you specify how much you want to limit expenses for each category that you wish to track. Begin by viewing the Category List—select List ➤ Category List. A box labeled Budget is at the bottom of the grey box inside the Category List dialog box (Figure 10.1).

Click on the first category or subcategory for which you want to budget. You may want to start by budgeting all of a category's subcategories first, so that when you get to the category itself, you can sum the subcategory amounts. Of course, there is no need to budget for subcategories if you don't want to—you can just budget for the category as a whole.

With the category or subcategory selected, click on one of the Budget option buttons.

Monthly Budget	To enter a monthly expense or income amount
Yearly Budget	To enter a yearly expense or income amount

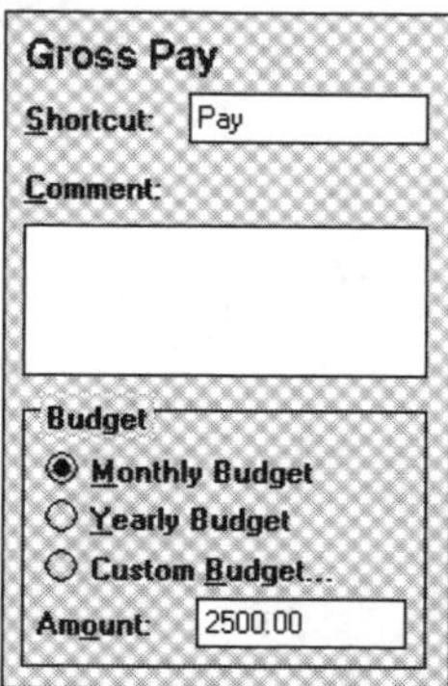

FIGURE 10.1: The Budget information in the Category List dialog box

Custom Budget	To enter a value that varies from month to month, or to budget a category and sum the values from the category's subcategories

If you selected the Monthly or Yearly option button, enter the budget value in the Amount box. If you selected Custom Budget, the Custom Budget dialog box appears (Figure 10.2).

This dialog box lets you enter a budget that varies month by month, such as utility bills or vacation expenses. Simply type a monthly amount in each of the boxes. If several consecutive months are the same, you can enter a value in the box for the first of the values and then click on the Fill Down button. Money will copy the value from the first box to all the subsequent boxes. For example, if you want to enter the same value in months March to June, type a value in the March box, click on Fill Down to fill all subsequent boxes, highlight the entry in the July box, type the new value, press Tab to move to the August box, and so on.

If you are budgeting a category and have already entered budget amounts for its subcategories, you can click on the Total Subcategories button. Money will add the monthly values from all of the subcategories and enter the monthly totals in the boxes. If you entered a yearly or custom budget amount for the subcategories, Money calculates the monthly amounts and totals them. You can then increase these values to allow for miscellaneous expenses that will be assigned to that category, but which do not have their own subcategory. When you have set the budget amounts to your satisfaction, click on OK to close the dialog box, select the next category or subcategory that you wish to budget, and repeat the procedure.

If you later delete a subcategory, Money will not *automatically recalculate the category-total budget amount.*

FIGURE 10.2:
The Custom Budget dialog box

Incidentally, Money will allow the total of the subcategory budgets to be *greater* than the parent category budget. For example, a category with a budget of $500 can have three subcategories with a budget of $300 each. In some instances, you may want the category budget to *exceed* the sum of the subcategory budgets to allow excess for miscellaneous expenses, but it's unlikely that you will want the category budgets to be *less* than the sum of the subcategory budgets. If you want to make sure that the category budget equals the total of the subcategory budgets, select Custom Budget and click on the Total Subcategories button.

You don't have to enter budget information before you start entering transactions. You could enter the information at the end of the year—it makes no difference to Money. As soon as you enter your budget information and enter enough transactions to make valid comparisons, you can create the Budget Report.

DISPLAYING A BUDGET REPORT

To create the Budget Report, first select Report ➤ Budget to see the Budget Report dialog box (Figure 10.3).

The Budget Report shows the budget for all subcategories, including those for which you have not entered a budget amount. The report has three columns for each month since the beginning of the year: an Actual expenditure and income column, a Budget expenditure and income column, and a Difference column. At the right edge of the report are the Actual, Budget and Difference totals for the entire year to date. Figure 10.3 shows the Total columns.

Let's take a look at Figure 10.3. The first entry in the Income Categories is Other Income. The report shows that you have assigned $125.00 to Other Income so far this year. You haven't entered a budget amount for this category, though, so

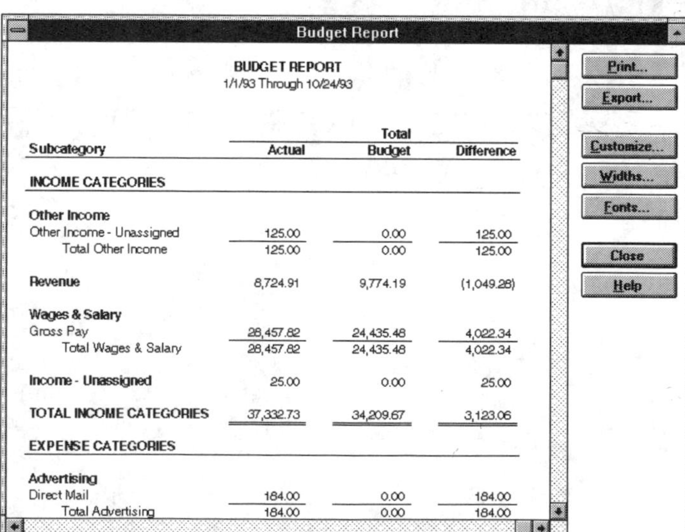

BUDGET REPORT
1/1/93 Through 10/24/93

Subcategory	Total Actual	Total Budget	Total Difference
INCOME CATEGORIES			
Other Income			
Other Income - Unassigned	125.00	0.00	125.00
Total Other Income	125.00	0.00	125.00
Revenue	8,724.91	9,774.19	(1,049.28)
Wages & Salary			
Gross Pay	28,457.82	24,435.48	4,022.34
Total Wages & Salary	28,457.82	24,435.48	4,022.34
Income - Unassigned	25.00	0.00	25.00
TOTAL INCOME CATEGORIES	37,332.73	34,209.67	3,123.06
EXPENSE CATEGORIES			
Advertising			
Direct Mail	184.00	0.00	184.00
Total Advertising	184.00	0.00	184.00

FIGURE 10.3:
A sample Budget Report

the Difference column shows $125.00—the actual sum exceeds the budget value ($0) by $125.00. You may want to reassign the transactions assigned to Other Income, or enter a budget value for Other Income.

The word "Unassigned" next to Other Income means that the transactions were not assigned to available subcategories.

The next entry is for Revenue, which might include such items as income from a small business. It shows that so far this year you have assigned $8724.91 to this category. It also shows that you expected to make $9774.19 by this time, so the value in the Difference column is (1049.28), meaning you are $1049.28 below the budget.

The next entry is Wages and Salary, and so far this year you have earned $28,457.82. When you set up your budget you expected to make $24,435.48 by this time, so you are actually ahead of the budget—by $4,022.34 according to the Difference column.

The final Income category is Income-Unassigned. This actually indicates money that has not been assigned to any category. You had $25 of income that was not assigned to any kind of category. You can't enter a budget amount for a "non-category," so the Difference column indicates that you exceeded the "budget" by $25. You should probably reassign this transaction to one of the other income categories.

At the bottom of the income categories are the totals. So far this year, you have earned $37,332.73. When you created your budget you only expected to earn $34,209.67, so you are $3,123.06 ahead of your budget.

The expense categories work in the same way, with an important, if obvious, difference. A positive value in the Difference column indicates that you spent more than you expected, while a positive value for an *income* category means you *earned* more than you expected. The Advertising-Direct Mail category shows that you have spent $184 so far this year, although you haven't budgeted for this type of expense. You should enter a budget value for this category so that you can track this expense the next time you create a budget or enter a value.

MODIFYING THE BUDGET REPORT

You can modify the Budget Report to select different dates, show categories instead of subcategories, remove non-budgeted categories, change the time-period (week, quarter, year, and so on), omit data from certain accounts, and remove certain types of transactions.

Before you customize a Budget Report, read Lesson 8 and decide if you want to create a macro that will let you save the new format.

Click on the Customize button in the Budget Report dialog box. The Customize Budget Report dialog box appears (Figure 10.4).

You can change the report title—you could put the business name at the top of the report, or something like "Household Budget '92." You can also select Category from the Row for Every drop-down list box to show only the category totals instead of the totals for every single category.

The default Budget report includes budget summaries for every month and three columns showing the year-to-date information. You can change this format by changing the selection in the Column for Every drop-down list box. You can include budget summaries—the Actual, Budget, and Difference columns—for every Week, Two Weeks, Half Month, Month, Quarter, and Year. You can also select None, meaning that only the total columns will be included.

What's the difference between None and Year settings? Don't they both simply show the information totaled for the year? Well, although the default report shows the year-to-date totals at the right side of the report, you can select a different time period using the Date Range options at the bottom of the Customize dialog box (we'll explain those in a moment). If you selected a multi-year time period, such as the last three years, the total columns at the right side of the report would be the totals for the last three years, not the year-to-date totals. If you select the Year option in the Column for Every drop-down list box, the report will include three columns, one for each year, plus three total columns that include all the data for the last three years.

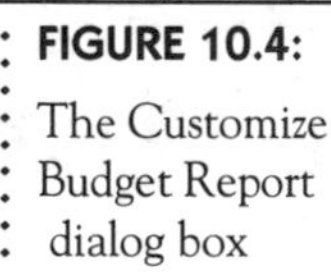

FIGURE 10.4:
The Customize Budget Report dialog box

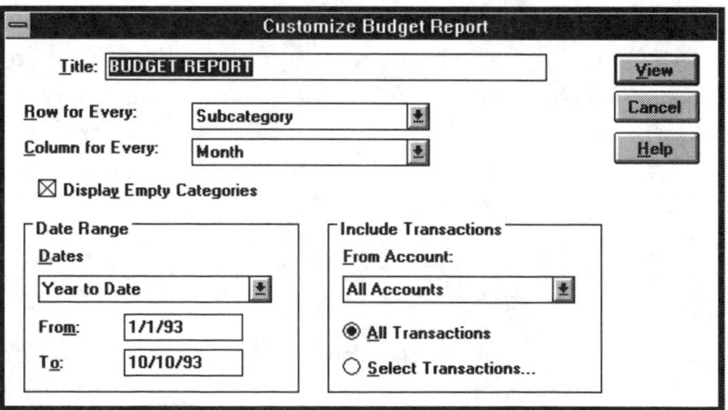

The next option in the Customize dialog box is the Display Empty Categories check box. If this box is marked (the default) *all* budgeted categories are shown on the report, even if there have not been any transactions assigned to a category. Turn this option off and only categories that have transactions assigned to them are included.

By default, if a category has a transaction assigned to it, it is *always* included in the report, even if you haven't budgeted for some of the categories. So how do you remove categories to which you have not assigned budget values? Unfortunately, Money does not have a Display Budget Categories Only option—you have to indicate the categories you don't want in the report one by one. Click on the Select Transactions option button at the bottom of the Customize dialog box. The Select Transactions dialog box will appear. (You have used this box before, in Lesson 8.) In the Category drop-down list box, select the Select Multiple Categories option to display the Select Category dialog box, select the categories that you want to include in the Budget Report, and click on OK.

You may also want to select the accounts (business or personal) that should be included in the report. This is done using the From Account drop-down list box, as you learned in Lesson 8. Finally, you can indicate the time span for the report using the Date Range options. Select a specific date range from the drop-down list box (Previous Month, Previous Year, and so on) or type the date range in the From and To text boxes.

When you've created the custom report you want, click on View and the new report is displayed. If you wish, you can now adjust the column width and font. You can also print the report or export it to an ASCII file. See Lesson 8 for more information.

FOR MORE INFORMATION

See the following lesson and Reference section entries:

Lesson 8: Producing Reports

List ➤ Category List

Report ➤ Budget Report

Reports

You have now finished the "tutorial" section of this book. You have learned enough to use Money in most situations. But there's more! The reference section explains Money's features in more detail, and describes those features that you haven't yet learned about, such as exporting to .QIF files, creating passwords, and archiving your files. Flip through the reference section to get an idea of the information available, and the features you might want to use. Then check the appendices, in particular Appendix B, which answers specific questions you may have about using Microsoft Money.

PART TWO

REFERENCE

ACCOUNT TYPES

There are five types of Money accounts:

- Bank account
- Credit card account
- Cash or Other account
- Asset account
- Liability account

BANK ACCOUNT

A bank account is an account such as the following, in which you keep cash:

- Checking account
- Money market account
- Savings account
- Share account (in a credit union)

Bank accounts may earn interest, but their funds are liquid, unlike asset accounts. Transactions are assigned as either a Payment or Deposit, and the balance shows the total funds remaining in the account.

You can print checks only from bank accounts—none of the other account types will allow you to print checks.

CREDIT CARD ACCOUNT

Credit card accounts "lend" you money each time you make a purchase or cash withdrawal, and are listed below:

- "Coin Loan" or line-of-credit account
- Charge account
- Credit card account

When you withdraw cash or make a purchase, the transaction is assigned as a Charge, and the balance increases. When you pay off part of the balance, the transaction is assigned as a Credit, and the balance drops. So the balance shows how much you owe. If the number is negative, the issuing bank actually owes you money (perhaps because of overpayment or some other credit to your account).

When you make a payment to this account, show it as a transfer from the other account to the credit card account. If your credit card account provides checks (some provide a limited number of checks), enter checks written in the same way you would enter a charge.

CASH OR OTHER ACCOUNT

Cash accounts are, quite simply, accounts from which you spend cash:

- Personal money spent
- Petty cash account

A cash account can be used to track your personal cash expenses or business petty cash. Each time you spend money, the transaction is entered in the Spend column, and the balance decreases. Each time you receive cash, the transaction is entered in the Receive column, and the balance increases. When you receive cash by cashing a check or by using an Automatic Teller Machine, enter the transaction as a transfer from the other account to the cash account. If you really want to track cash expenses, make sure you carry a small notebook wherever you go, to record each purchase.

ASSET ACCOUNT

An asset account can be any kind of investment or capital:

- Baseball card collection
- Certificate of deposit (CD)
- Gold coins
- Investments in stocks, bonds, and commodities
- Money owed to you (loans to others, accounts receivable, employee expense reports)
- Mutual fund
- Pension plan—IRA, SEP-IRA, Keogh plan, 401(k), company pension
- Real estate
- Stamp collection

When you purchase an asset, or when its value increases, the transaction is entered as an Increase, and the balance increases. When you sell an asset, or when its value drops, the transaction is entered as a Decrease, and the balance drops.

When you buy an asset, enter the transaction as a transfer from the account that paid for the item. When you sell an asset, enter the transaction as a transfer from the asset account to the account into which you deposit the money received from the sale.

Special care must be taken in tracking the value of the assets with asset accounts. An asset purchase is simply a transfer from one account to another—from, say, your checking account to your brokerage account—but if the asset changes in value, how do you account for the change? For example, suppose you purchase stock by sending a check to your broker. You enter this transaction as a transfer from checking to an asset account. The next week, you check the stock's value and notice a change. You cannot now go to the asset account and change the value of the purchased stock, because changing the amount of a transfer transaction changes the balance in *both* accounts.

Instead, you could enter a total equal to the *change* in the stock's value and name it something like Change In Value. Then, each time you check the stock's price, you can modify this transaction to show the current difference between the original and present prices. In this way, you will have two transactions for each stock purchase—the original transfer from your bank account and a second one used to show the total change in value since you purchased the stock. The advantage of this method is that you will always be able to see both the original value and the change in value, figures that you need for tax calculations. The disadvantage is that you have to calculate the difference between the present and original values each time you want to record the stock's value.

You could also assign the original stock purchase to a category such as Stock Purchase—or even create a category called Transfer-Stock Account—instead of transferring the funds to the asset account. You could then create an asset account with one entry for each stock; each time you check the stock's performance, modify the entries to show the new values.

If the asset is an investment such as a loan or certificate of deposit, you could show each increase or periodic interest payment as an individual transaction. And you can use the Future Transactions window to remind you when a payment is due.

LIABILITY ACCOUNT

A liability account is any kind of money that you owe:

- Accounts payable

- Business loans
- Car loans
- Money owed to physicians and hospitals
- Mortgages
- Personal loans
- Taxes owed by you
- Taxes withheld from employee payroll
- Tenant deposits

When you increase the amount you owe—when someone lends you money or you buy a product on credit—the transaction is entered as an Increase, and the balance goes up. When you decrease the amount you owe—when you make a monthly payment or pay off a loan—the transaction is entered as a Decrease, and the balance goes down. So, like the credit card account (which is a form of liability account), the balance shows how much you still owe.

Remember that when you make a payment to a liability account you are often paying both interest and principal, so you should make a split transaction, assigning part of the payment as a transfer from the paying account to the liability account, and part as an interest expense. You may not know exactly how much of the balance is interest and how much principal, but you can enter estimated figures and then enter the correct numbers when you receive a statement from the lender.

See Also

Appendix B: Questions and Answers

CUSTOMIZING MONEY

There are a number of ways in which you can modify the way Money works, so that you're more "comfortable" with the program. Money calls these options *settings*; you may have seen such options referred to in other programs as *preferences*. Here are the items that you can modify on the Settings dialog box:

Alternate Register Navigation: Makes the ↵ key work like the Tab key in transaction entries; pressing ↵ will move the cursor to the next field.

Automatically Drop Lists: Makes Money automatically display the list box when the cursor lands on a category or subcategory field.

Beep on Transaction Entry: Controls whether Money beeps when a transaction is entered.

Calculator Entry: Changes the manner in which numbers are entered into amount fields.

Colors: Changes the colors used for the entry lines and the Checks & Forms background. (You can also change the windows component colors using the Windows Control Panel.)

Confirm Transaction Changes: Controls whether Money displays a dialog box asking you if you want a new or edited transaction entered into the account book.

Reminder to Backup: Instructs Money to remind you to backup your file each time you close Money or open another file.

Show Message Bar: Removes the bar from the bottom of the Money window.

SmartFill On: Turn SmartFill and SuperSmartFill on and off.

Transactions Due Reminder: Instructs Money to remind you that you have future transactions due; you can set how many days in advance the reminder will be shown.

Type Size: Sets the font used in Money's entries: either Standard or Large.

The following Control Panel options also affect Money's operation:

International: Enables you to modify the way dates are displayed by changing the separator character, changing the month/day/year sequence, changing the number of digits in the year, and adding leading zeros to days and months. You can reduce the number of decimal places, change the decimal point character and thousands separator, and remove leading zeros from numbers.

Mouse: Enables you to change the mouse tracking speed, double-click speed, and mouse button positions.

Color: Enables you to change the colors of various Windows components.

Because of space limitations, we will only discuss the International option. For more information on the Mouse and Color options, see your Windows documentation.

THE SETTINGS DIALOG BOX

Select Options ➤ Settings to see the Settings dialog box.

Alternate Register Navigation With Alternate Register Navigation selected, pressing ↵ while entering a transaction moves the cursor to the next field, in the same way that pressing Tab works. With this option turned *off*, pressing ↵ ends the transaction entry and moves the cursor to the next entry. The option is *on* when the check box has a check mark in it.

Automatically Drop Lists By default, the category, subcategory, classification, and subclassification drop-down list boxes automatically open when the cursor lands on the field. You can place the cursor on the field by pointing and clicking with the mouse, or by pressing Tab.

You can turn this feature off, so that the drop-down list boxes do *not* open automatically. The option is *on* when the check box has a check mark in it.

This feature has no effect on the Account and Payee drop-down list boxes. These boxes never drop automatically; they can only be opened by clicking on ↓ or pressing F4, Alt-↑, or Alt-↓.

If you are editing a category, subcategory, classification, or subclassification field that already contains an entry, the drop-down list box will *not* automatically drop down, regardless of the Settings dialog box selection.

Calculator Entry Selecting the Calculator Entry mode in the Settings dialog box changes the way that numbers are entered into the amount fields. With Calculator Entry turned *on*, Money will assume that the last two digits you type are decimal places. Thus typing 298 and pressing Tab enters 2.98, not 298. With Calculator Entry turned *off*, you must type the decimal point.

By default, the Calculator Entry mode is turned *off* when you first install Money. The option is *on* when the check box has a check mark in it.

Color This section enables you to change the colors used for the "accent" lines (the lines that hold the memo, category, and classification fields) in the Account Book window and the background color of the Checks & Forms window. Click on the down arrow next to the box and select a color from the list.

You can also modify other screen colors using the Windows Control Panel.

Confirmation There are two types of transaction confirmation. You can instruct Money to display a dialog box asking you to confirm that you want to save the changes you have just made (Confirm Transaction Changes), and to beep each time a transaction is saved (Beep on Transaction Entry).

By default, when you first install Money the confirmation dialog boxes are *not* used, but the confirmation beep *is* used.

Display-Type Size Money lets you modify the size of the text used in the various windows to enable you to read the entries more easily. Entry text, message bar text, column headings, and text in the Checks & Forms window are all affected by modifying the type size. Text in dialog boxes, the menu bar, and the title bar is not affected. You can select Standard (the size used when you first install Money) or Larger. The option is *on* when the circle has a black mark inside it.

Reminder To Backup Each time you close a file (either when you close Money itself or when you use the File – Open command to open another file), Money will display a Backup dialog box that lets you copy the file onto another disk or directory. You can turn this reminder on and off by clicking on the Reminder to Backup check box in the bottom-left corner of the dialog box. A check mark in the check box turns the option on.

Show Message Bar The Money window has a bar at the bottom that provides messages describing dialog boxes and tells you what to do next. If you find that you don't use the message bar much, you may want to remove it to make the work area slightly larger. Click on the Show Message Bar check box near the top left of the dialog box.

SmartFill On SmartFill and SuperSmartFill are features that Money uses to help you enter transactions. Money keeps a list of previously entered payees; when you type a name into the payee field, Money searches its list looking for a match. When you have typed three or more characters that Money recognizes as the beginning of a name, it inserts the full payee name into the payee field. That's what Microsoft calls SmartFill. If you don't want to accept the new name that SmartFill gave you, you can simply continue typing and SmartFill will remove its guess.

If you now press Tab or click on another field, Money enters the amount, memo, and category that you used for the last transaction related to that payee. Microsoft calls this second stage SuperSmartFill.

SmartFill and SuperSmartFill can be turned on or off by clicking on the SmartFill On check box near the bottom right of the dialog box. A check mark in the check box indicates that the option is *on*.

Transactions Due Reminder If you have transactions scheduled for the future, you can instruct Money to remind you on the day they are due, or a few days before, by clicking on the Transactions Due Reminder check box below the buttons. In the Days In Advance to Remind text box, enter the number of days notice you want.

Now, Money will warn you the specified number of days in advance of a transaction due date. When you open a file—whether Money automatically opens the file when you open the program, or you use the File ➤ Open command—Money will display a dialog box informing you that a transaction is due. You will then have the option of going straight to the Record Due Transactions dialog box to enter a date and begin the bill-paying process. For more information, see Lesson 6, "Entering Future Transactions and Paying Bills," Edit ➤ Schedule in Future, and Options ➤ Pay Bills.

DATE AND NUMBER FORMATS

You display the Windows Control Panel by double-clicking on the icon in the Program Manager, or by selecting File ➤ Run, typing **Control**, and clicking on OK. Double-click on the International icon. The International dialog box appears.

Making changes to the Control Panel affects all your Windows applications, not just Money.

Date Formats Click on the Change button in the Date Format box to see the Date Format dialog box.

Order: The order in which the day, month, and year appear. You may select MDY (the standard US order), DMY (the standard British and Canadian order), or YMD.

Separator: The symbol you would like to use between dates. For example, you can use a slash, hyphen, or period, as in 1/7/93, 1-7-93, or 1.7.93.

Day Leading Zero: Adds a leading zero to the day part of the date; for example, 1/07/93.

Month Leading Zero: Adds a leading zero to the month part of the date; for example, 01/7/93.

Century: Enters the complete year; for example, 1/7/1993.

Long Date Format: These options have no effect on Money.

Number Formats Click on the Change button in the Number Format box to see the Number Format dialog box.

1000 Separator: The character you want used to separate thousands. For example, you can use a comma or a period, as in 1,000 or 1.000.

Decimal Separator: The character you want used as the decimal point, such as a comma or period, as in 5,1 or 5.1.

Decimal Digits: This option has no effect on Money. (Use the Currency Format dialog box for changing the number of decimal places.)

Leading Zero: Whether Money should use a leading 0 or not; for example, 0.98 or .98.

Currency Formats Click on the Change button in the Currency Format box to see the Currency Format dialog box.

Symbol Placement: This option has no effect on Money.

Negative: Defines how negative numbers are shown, either in parentheses or preceded by a negative sign. For example, (132.67) or –132.67. Whichever method you select, Money will recognize both. For example, if you select the parentheses method (the default), you can enter –132.67 and Money will change it to (132.67).

Symbol: This option has no effect on Money.

Decimal Digits: The number of decimal places in the number. You could, for example, enter 0, so all transactions would be rounded to the nearest dollar. If, however, you enter a number *larger* than 2, the last 2 digits in the number will be ignored by Money. If you select six digits, Money will still round the number to two decimal digits.

If you round values to the nearest dollar, the Find box may not be able to locate some entries since Money stores the original number. For example, if a transaction total of 29.65 is rounded to 30, Money will not be able to find the transaction when you search for 30. The transaction is still stored internally as 29.65.

NOTES You can also change the system date using the Control Panel; see your Windows Documentation.

EDIT ➤ COPY

Copies the highlighted text from an entry into the clipboard. See the entry Editing Transactions.

Keyboard Ctrl-Ins or Ctrl-C

EDIT ➤ CUT

Removes the highlighted text from an entry and copies it into the clipboard. See Editing Transactions.

Keyboard Shift-Del or Ctrl-X

EDIT ➤ DELETE TRANSACTION

Deletes the highlighted transaction. See Editing Transactions.

Keyboard Del or Ctrl-Del (to delete without confirmation)

NOTE Deleting a transfer transaction deletes *both* sides of the transfer. In other words, the transaction will be removed from both the account in which you deleted it and the account that includes the other part of the transfer.

EDIT ➤ ENTER FROM SCHEDULE

The Edit ➤ Enter from Schedule command appears only in the Future Transactions window, and is available only when a transaction is highlighted. It lets you enter the highlighted transaction into an account without needing to enter the date, as with the Options ➤ Pay Bills command. The Enter from Schedule command, however, only operates on the selected transaction; use this command when you want to enter one specific transaction, rather than several.

Keyboard Ctrl-E

See Also

Edit ➤ Schedule in Future

Options ➤ Pay Bills

EDIT ➤ FIND

The Edit ➤ Find command searches for a particular transaction in an account. It will only find transactions that are selected by the Account and View drop-down list boxes.

Keyboard Ctrl-F, F7 to repeat the last search

SEARCHING FOR A TRANSACTION

1. If you want to search for a scheduled transaction, double-click on the Future Transaction icon to open the Future Transactions window.
2. If you want to search for an existing account entry, open the Account Book or Checks & Forms window.
3. Select the account or accounts in which you want to search from the Accounts drop-down list box.
4. Select the type of transactions you want to search from the View drop-down list box.
5. Select Edit ➤ Find, or press Ctrl-F, or click on the Find icon button in the Toolbar. The Find dialog box appears.
6. Type the number or text which you want to search into the Find What text box.
7. In the Look In drop-down list box select the field in which you want to search. You can search these fields: All Fields (the default), Number, Payee, Amount, Memo, Category, Subcategory, Classification, and Subclassification.
8. Click on the Up or Down option button in the direction box. The search is normally performed from the current highlight position toward the *top* (first entry) of the account.

9. Click on Find Next. The highlight moves to the first entry that matches the search criteria. You can move the Find box out of the way, if you wish, by pointing at the title bar and dragging it.
10. Click on Find Next to go to the next entry, or click on Cancel to end the search.

Money will display a message box if it is unable to find the text or number you specified, or when it reaches the end or beginning of the list.

EDIT ➤ MARK AS CLEARED

Places a C in the C column of the Account Book window, to indicate that the transaction has appeared on a statement. There are three possible indicators in the C column:

Blank	The transaction has not yet appeared on a statement.
C	The transaction has appeared on a statement.
R	The transaction has appeared on a statement and has been reconciled by Money.

If the highlighted transaction has already been cleared, this option appears as Edit ➤ Mark as Uncleared. If the transaction has already been reconciled, the option appears as Edit ➤ Mark as Unreconciled.

Keyboard Ctrl-M, or Shift-Ctrl-M to mark as reconciled

Mouse Shift-Click in the C field to mark as reconciled; Click in the C field while balancing to mark as cleared

MARKING A TRANSACTION

Highlight the entry, and then select Edit ➤ Mark As Cleared/Uncleared/Unreconciled or press Ctrl-M. If the C field is blank, Money places a C in the field; if it contains a C or an R, Money removes the letter.

To mark a transaction as reconciled, highlight the entry and press Shift-Ctrl-M, or point to the C field, press the Shift key, and click the mouse button. This procedure also removes the R from the C field on a transaction already marked as reconciled.

MARKING WHILE BALANCING YOUR ACCOUNT

When you use the Options ➤ Balance Account command, Money displays all uncleared and unreconciled transactions from the account. You can then clear each transaction listed on your statement. To mark a transaction as cleared, point at the C field and click; Money will place a C in the field. You can also point at the C field, press and hold the Shift key, and click the mouse button to mark the transaction as reconciled, and remove it from the list.

See Also

Options ➤ Balance Account

EDIT ➤ MARK AS UNCLEARED

The Edit ➤ Mark As Uncleared command removes the C from the C field in the Account Book window, leaving the field blank. See Edit ➤ Mark as Cleared.

Keyboard Ctrl-M

EDIT ➤ MARK AS UNRECONCILED

The Edit ➤ Mark as Unreconciled command removes the R from the C field in the Account Book window, leaving the field blank. See Edit ➤ Mark as Cleared.

Keyboard Ctrl-M or Shift-Ctrl-M

Mouse Shift-Click on C field

EDIT ➤ PASTE

The Edit ➤ Paste command copies the text in the clipboard into the field in which the cursor is placed. See Editing Transactions.

Keyboard Shift-Ins or Ctrl-V

EDIT ➤ SCHEDULE IN FUTURE

The Edit ➤ Schedule in Future command copies an entry from the Account Book or Checks & Forms window into the Future Transactions window to instruct Money to remind you when the transaction is due again.

Keyboard Ctrl-E

NOTES If you have a number of similar transactions to enter into the Future Transactions window, you can highlight one entry in the Account Book window, issue the Edit ➤ Schedule in Future command several times, go to the Future Transactions window, and modify the specifics of each transaction.

See Also

Lesson 6: Entering Future Transactions and Paying Bills

Edit ➤ Enter from Schedule

Options ➤ Pay Bills

Window ➤ Future Transactions

EDIT ➤ SPLIT TRANSACTION

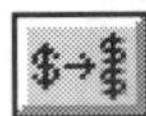

The Edit ➤ Split Transaction command lets you assign one transaction to two or more categories. See Lesson 5.

USING NEGATIVE AMOUNTS IN SPLIT TRANSACTIONS

In some cases, you will need to enter negative numbers in split transactions. For example, if your total monthly pay is $2500, but a portion of it is withheld for taxes, insurance, and automatic savings, you would enter $2500 in the Split Transaction dialog box and then enter a negative number for each of the withholdings. The $2500 amount could be assigned to a category such as Gross Pay, the savings amount could be shown as a transfer to a savings account and the taxes could be shown as an expense, assigned to a tax category. Money will enter the result in the transactions deposit field—$2500 less the sum of the withholdings.

Similarly, if you want to record a deposit less cash, you could enter the total deposit in the Split Transaction dialog box and then enter a negative number for the cash that you withdrew (you could assign the cash as a transfer to a cash account if you wish).

You enter negative numbers by typing a minus sign before the number, or by typing the number in parentheses.

NOTES If you change the amount of an existing split transaction, the Adjust Split Amount dialog box appears.

If you display transactions sorted by category, each part of a split transaction is displayed *as a separate transaction.* In other words, a transaction split into three categories will appear in three different places in the list.

See Also

Lesson 5: Assigning Transactions to Several Categories.

EDIT ➤ UNDO

This command reverses the last Edit ➤ Cut or Edit ➤ Paste command issued, or the last piece of text you typed. When you move on to another field, however, the Edit ➤ Undo command is no longer available. See Editing Transactions.

Keyboard Ctrl-Z or Alt-Backspace

EDIT ➤ UNVOID TRANSACTION

This command removes the **VOID** from the Balance column of the voided transactions in Account Book window, enabling Money to include the transaction in all the appropriate calculations.

See Also

Edit ➤ Void Transaction

EDIT ➤ VOID TRANSACTION

This command places ****VOID**** in the Balance column of the selected transaction in the Account Book window. The transaction is removed from all calculations, although the information remains displayed in the entry. The amount of the transaction is neither included in the balance calculations, nor added into the category to which the transaction was assigned.

If you void a transfer transaction, both sides of the transfer are voided.

See Also

Edit ➤ Unvoid Transaction

E

EDITING TRANSACTIONS

You can modify transaction information after it has been entered into Money.

Keyboard

Edit ➤ Undo: Ctrl-Z or Alt-Backspace

Edit ➤ Cut: Ctrl-X or Shift-Del

Edit ➤ Copy: Ctrl-C or Ctrl-Ins

Edit ➤ Paste: Ctrl-V or Shift-Ins

REPLACING INFORMATION IN AN ENTRY

You can edit entry information in the same manner as you entered it. Simply select the entry and press Tab to select the first field. Each time you move to a new field, all the characters in that field are selected. You can type a new entry or press Tab again to move to the next field.

MOVING INFORMATION AND UNDOING EDITS

Money lets you cut, copy, and paste information in the same way as most Windows applications. Highlight a portion of text. Select Edit ➤ Cut to remove the text and place it in the Windows Clipboard or Edit ➤ Copy to place a copy of the text into the Clipboard, leaving the original text unchanged. Placing the cursor in a field and selecting Edit ➤ Paste copies text from the Clipboard into the field.

You can also "undo" a cut or paste operation, or text that has just been typed. Just select Edit ➤ Undo and the text that has just been removed is replaced, or the text that has just been pasted or typed is removed. If you move to another field, though, the Edit ➤ Undo command will no longer work on the previous field.

DELETING TRANSACTIONS

Highlight the transaction and select Edit ➤ Delete or press the Del key to remove it. In either case, a dialog box will appear, asking you to confirm the deletion. You may also press Ctrl-Del to delete the transaction without having to confirm it.

If the transaction is a transfer, both sides of the transfer are deleted.

See Also

Entering Transactions

ENTERING TRANSACTIONS

Money provides a number of tools to help you enter information into a transaction.

THE TRANSACTION FIELDS

Each transaction entry contains these fields:

Num: A check number or a code to denote what the transaction is: dep, chrg, nsf, and so on. Choose your own codes. Using a code will help you sort the transactions using the All (By Num) option in the View drop-down list box; the transactions will be placed in order according to the number or code in the Num field.

Date: The transaction date.

Payee: The person to whom the money is paid, or from whom the money is received.

Debit: The debit column. The label used in this column depends on account type.

Checking—Payment

Credit—Charge

Cash—Spend

Asset—Decrease

Liability—Increase

Credit: The credit column. The label of the column depends on the type of account:

Checking—Deposit

Credit—Credit

Cash—Receive

Asset—Increase

Liability—Decrease

Account name: The name of the account. This field appears only if you used the Account drop-down list box to display two or more accounts.

Memo: A note explaining what the transaction is.

Category: The category to which the transaction has been assigned.

Subcategory: The subcategory to which the transaction has been assigned.

Classification 1: The first classification to which the transaction has been assigned. This and the remaining fields appear only if you have created new classifications.

Subclassification 1: The first subclassification to which the transaction has been assigned.

Classification 2: The second classification to which the transaction has been assigned.

Subclassification 2: The second subclassification to which the transaction has been assigned.

SELECTING A BLANK ENTRY

Press the End key to move to the first blank entry, or use the scroll bar to display the first blank entry and then click on it. If you are in the Checks & Forms window, click on one of the buttons.

BEGINNING THE ENTRY

Begin typing and the text is entered into the first field. Or, press Tab or ↵ and the cursor is placed in the first field.

MOVING THE CURSOR WITHIN AN ENTRY

You can move within an entry by pointing to the position and clicking with the mouse. Or you can use the following keyboard actions.

Moving between Fields Press Tab to move from one field to another. If Alternate Register Navigation has been selected in the Settings dialog box, you may also press ↵ to move from one field to another. Press Shift-Tab or Shift-↵ to move to the previous field.

Moving to the Beginning or End of a Field Press Home to move to the beginning of a field, or End to move to the end.

Moving to the First or Last Field With the cursor positioned at the first or last position in a field, press Home to move to the first field in the entry, or End to move to the last. You may have to press the key twice; the first press will move the cursor to the beginning or end of the current field, and the next press will move it to the first or last field.

Moving within a Field Use the arrow keys to move within a field. If you reach the end of the text in a field, the cursor jumps to the next field with the next press of the arrow key. Press Backspace to delete the preceding character, or Del to delete the following character.

SELECTING TEXT

You can select text so that you can cut, copy, or delete it. Double-click on the text, or press Shift while you press the arrow keys. You can also place the cursor, press and hold the mouse button, and drag the mouse across the text.

ENTERING NUMBERS AND DATES

If a number in the amount or balance field is too large to be shown, Money will replace it with ########. Increase the window size and the number will be displayed.

Money helps you with the check numbers and dates. It will automatically enter the next check in sequence, as well as the current date or the last date entered during the current Money session. Money then highlights the text it has entered. If you wish to change the information that Money entered for you, just type over it.

You can also type just part of the date, and let Money fill in the rest. Type one number and press Tab, and Money assumes the number is the day and fills in the current month and year for you. Or type two numbers (8/1, for example) and press Tab. Money then adds the year for you.

Be careful when entering transactions that are more than four months old. Money changes the year in such transactions. Say, for example, the current date is 10/1/92, and you enter a transaction as 5/31 and press Tab—Money will enter the date as 5/31/93, not 5/31/92.

You can enter an amount without the decimal point if it is a whole number (i.e., type **25** to enter 25.00), but you must include the decimal point if it is a decimal number (i.e., type **25.32**, not 2532). Money has an optional Calculator Entry feature which allows you to enter numbers without decimal points (i.e., type **2532** to enter 25.32).

You can also use the following keystrokes to enter numbers:

+	Increases the entered number by one or the date by one day
–	Decreases the entered number by one or the date by one day

Ctrl-D	Enters the current date
Shift-"	Enters the text you placed in the same field in the transaction you entered immediately before the current one.

ENTERING THE PAYEE AND MEMO

You can type a payee name, or select it from the drop-down list box. If you print your checks, the information you enter in the Payee and Memo fields (and the Address field in the Checks & Forms window) will be printed on the checks. You can prevent information in these fields from being printed by enclosing them in braces { }.

If Money has more than one payee with the same name, entering the name in the Payee field displays a dialog box with a list of names. You can then select the correct name from the list. You may want to add something to identical names to make them unique, such as a code enclosed in braces, so that typing the name and code would select the correct name but the code would not print on checks.

OPENING DROP-DOWN LIST BOXES

Several of the fields have drop-down list boxes. You can type the entry into the field or select it from the list box.

Account Name

Payee

Category

Subcategory

Classification

Subclassification

When the cursor lands on a blank Category, Subcategory, Classification, or Subclassification field, the drop-down list box automatically opens (*unless* you turned off the Automatically Drop Lists option in the Settings dialog box). You can also open list boxes by clicking on the down arrow or by pressing F4, Alt-↑, or Alt-↓.

You can then select from the list by using the scroll bar and clicking on the name with the mouse, or by pressing the arrow keys to highlight the item and pressing Tab to select it and move to the next field. Or type the first character of the name and the list jumps to that position.

Unlike with most drop-down list boxes, pressing Home and End will *not* move the highlight to the beginning or end of the list, because these keys are used to move the cursor in and between fields. Also, pressing ↵ will not usually select the item either—you must press Tab instead—*unless* you have turned on Alternate Register Navigation (in which case ↵ operates like the Tab key).

There's a shortcut when using categories and subcategories. If you skip the category field and go straight to the subcategory field, the list will show both category and subcategory names. You can select from the list, type a subcategory name, or type a subcategory shortcut, and then move to the next field. Money will fill in both the subcategory and category names. This method also works for classification items and subitems.

E

COPYING INFORMATION FROM THE PREVIOUS TRANSACTION

Pressing Shift-" (quotation mark) copies the information from the same field in the last transaction you entered. This is a great time saver for entering a group of similar transactions—instead of typing the same entries in each transaction you can just press Shift-" and Money will enter the information for you. (Shift-" has no effect in the Num field, so you can't use it to enter **Print** into transactions.)

SMARTFILL AND SUPERSMARTFILL

Money uses two systems called SmartFill and SuperSmartFill to help you enter information. It keeps a list of payees from your previous entries (see List ➤ Payee List). Then, each time you enter a transaction, Money searches the list for matching payee names. If you type three characters, and the list includes one payee name with the same first three characters, SmartFill enters the full payee name.

Money highlights the characters of the payee name that it entered for you, so if Money's guess is incorrect, you can continue typing to delete the name. But if Money's guess is correct, you can just press Tab to move to the next field or ↵ to end the entry. SuperSmartFill then enters the rest of the information associated with that payee—it will fill in the same amount, memo, and category that was used in the last transaction related to that payee.

SmartFill also assists you in entering text in any field with a drop-down list box. For example, if you type the first three characters of a category name, SmartFill will enter the rest of the name. If the information SmartFill enters is correct, you can just Tab to the next field. If SmartFill is wrong, you can continue typing over the characters that it entered. One advantage to this system is that you don't need to worry about the correct capitalization of a name: SmartFill will enter correct capitalization when you move to the next field.

SmartFill can even recognize shortcuts. If you type a shortcut that SmartFill recognizes, it will complete the shortcut for you. When you press Tab, Money will then enter the name associated with that shortcut.

You can turn off SmartFill and SuperSmartFill if you wish (see Customizing Money).

USING SHORTCUTS

You can use the Account, Payee, Category, and Classification Lists to add shortcuts to each account name, payee name, category subcategory, classification, and subclassification. Then, when you enter a transaction, you can type the shortcut and press Tab to insert the full entry. For example, you might assign the shortcut "V" to the category named Vacations. When you want to assign a transaction to Vacations, you can just type **v** and press Tab.

If you assign shortcuts to subcategories, you can tab past the category field without entering anything, type the subcategory shortcut, press Tab again, and Money will enter both the subcategory and *category*. This works only if the subcategory shortcut is unique, of course.

If you use a lot of category shortcuts, you may want to turn off the Automatically Drop Lists option in the Settings dialog box, so that the drop-down lists don't open each time the cursor lands on the field.

CREATING NEW ACCOUNTS, CATEGORIES, AND CLASSIFICATIONS

As a quick method for creating new accounts, categories, subcategories, classification items, and subitems while you are entering a transaction, simply type the new name—a name that Money doesn't recognize—in the field and then press Tab. Money will ask if you want to create a new object. Click Cancel to return to the transaction and replace the name you typed, or continue through the normal procedure for creating that object. After you have finished, Money returns you to the transaction.

CANCELLING AN ENTRY

Press Esc to cancel the entry, removing all the information you have entered so far. If a drop-down list box is open, the first time you press Esc will close the list box—press Esc again to cancel the entry.

You can also use Edit ➤ Undo (Alt-Backspace or Ctrl-Z) to undo the last text you typed, so long as you have not left that field.

FINISHING AN ENTRY

Point and click on another entry, or press ↵ anywhere in the entry. (If you have selected Alternate Register Navigation in the Settings dialog box, pressing ↵ only finishes the entry if the cursor is in the *last* field.) Move the cursor to the last field and press Tab. Selecting another window and most dialog boxes will also end the entry, entering the information into the account.

If you are in the Account Book window, when Money saves the transaction it moves it to its correct position in the list. If, for example, you enter a date earlier than the last transaction, and you are displaying the account in chronological order, Money moves the transaction to the correct chronological position.

CONFIRMATIONS

When you finish an entry, Money will beep to indicate that it has saved the information. You can turn this beep off by unchecking the Beep On Transaction Entry check box in the Settings dialog box. Selecting Confirm Transaction Changes from that dialog box displays a confirmation box each time you finish an entry. The confirmation box has two buttons, allowing you to save the information you entered or return to the transaction.

See Also

Lesson 2: Entering Transactions

Customizing Money

Editing Transactions

Keyboard Shortcuts

List ➤ Payee List

List ➤ Other Classification

Moving the Cursor and Highlight

FILE ➤ ARCHIVE

The File ➤ Archive command is used to create an archive copy of the current file, and if you wish, remove all the data from the current file. You may want to archive old information at the end of a year, removing the previous year's information from the file. You can always reopen the archive file if you need the information later.

ARCHIVING INFORMATION

1. Select File ➤ Archive. The Archive dialog box appears.
2. Indicate whether you want to create an archive file or remove old trans actions from the current file by marking the appropriate check boxes.
3. If you opt to remove old transactions, enter a date in the text box at the bottom of the dialog box. Money will remove all transactions with dates *before* the entered date.
4. Click on OK. The large Backup dialog box appears.
5. If necessary, select the drive name from the Drives drop-down list box.
6. If necessary, select the directory name from the Directories list box.
7. Enter a name for the archive file in the File Name text box.
8. Place a formatted disk in the selected drive, if necessary.
9. Click on OK. Money copies the current file to the new file.
10. If you selected remove transactions, Money removes all transactions dated earlier than the date you entered into the Archive dialog box.

Of course, you can also create an archive file without removing any transactions or remove transactions without creating an archive file, by making the appropriate check box selections in the Archive dialog box.

If you mark the first check box in the Archive dialog box and leave the second marker, Money removes the transactions without first creating a backup file. You will not be given a warning or a chance to abort the operation.

RESTORING AN ARCHIVE FILE

Archive files have the same format as Money files, so you can open them in the same way you would any other kind of .MNY file. See File ➤ Open for more information.

NOTES If you choose to remove old transactions, only those that have been reconciled against a bank statement (that is, transactions with "R" in the C column) will be removed from the file. However, *all* transactions in the file are copied into the archive file, including unreconciled transactions and those after the specified date. In fact, the archive file is simply a copy of the original.

If a transfer transaction has been reconciled in one account but not in the other, the transaction will *not* be removed from the file. Only transfers that are reconciled in both accounts are removed from the files.

If you get a message telling you that you are using an invalid file name, it may be because you actually *are* using an invalid file name *or* because the disk is write protected.

Archiving a file is much like making a backup (File ➤ Backup). There are slight differences, though. Money will not let you open a .BAK file without first giving it a new file name. This prevents you from opening a backup file and making changes to the original information.

SEE ALSO File ➤ Open; File ➤ Backup

F

FILE ➤ BACKUP

The File ➤ Backup command creates a backup file of the currently displayed file.

BACKING UP A FILE

1. Select File ➤ Backup. The Backup dialog box appears.
2. Enter the drive, path name, and file name of the backup file you want to create.
3. Place a formatted disk in the selected drive.
4. Click on OK. Money then saves all the information from the current file in the backup file.

SETTING AUTOMATIC BACKUPS

You can instruct Money to remind you to backup your file each time you close Money or open another file. Select the Reminder to Backup option in the Settings dialog box. Each time you try to close Money or select File ➤ Open to open another file, Money will display the Backup dialog box.

OPENING BACKUP FILES

You can open backup files at any time.

1. Select File ➤ Open. The Open dialog box appears.
2. If necessary, select the drive name from the Drives drop-down list box.
3. If necessary, select the directory name from the Directories list box.
4. Select Backups (*.BAK) from the List Files of Type drop-down list box.
5. Double-click on the name of the backup file you want to open in the File Name list box, or click on the file name and click on OK. The Restore Backup dialog box appears.

Do not leave Money at this point. If you use the Windows commands to move to another application at this point—perhaps to use File Manager to search for a file—Windows may crash when you return to Money.

6. If you want to save the new file in a different drive and directory, select them from the Drives drop-down list box and the Directories list box.
7. Notice that the File Name list box in the Restore Backup dialog box contains a list of existing .MNY files in the selected directory. Enter a new name in the File Name text box at the top of the list, and click on OK.
8. Money creates a new file, loading the information from the backup file to the new file. The backup file itself remains unchanged.

NOTES If you get a message telling you that you are using an invalid file name, it may be because you *are* using an invalid file name or because the disk is write protected.

While it's important to make sure you have a backup of your Money files, you may not want to bother using the Money backup feature if you back up your hard disk regularly.

SEE ALSO Customizing Money; File ➤ Archive; File ➤ Open

FILE ➤ EXIT

File ➤ Exit command closes Money.

Keyboard Alt-F4

CLOSING MONEY

There are several ways to close Money.

- Select File ➤ Exit
- Press Alt-F4
- Select Close from the Control menu
- Double-click on the Control menu

NOTES When you close Money, it saves information concerning the session in a file called MSMONEY.INI, which is stored in the MSMONEY directory. The next time you open Money, it looks in this file to find the following information:

- The size and position of the Money window
- The size and position of the Account Book, Checks & Forms, and Future Transactions windows
- The options selected in the Settings dialog box
- The current file's directory and name

Money uses this information to reopen with the same file, window positions, and Settings options as when you closed it.

You can instruct Money to automatically remind you to make a backup file when you close Money. Select Options ➤ Settings and select the Reminder to Backup check box in the bottom left corner of the Settings dialog box.

SEE ALSO Customizing Money; File ➤ Backup

FILE ➤ EXPORT

Money lets you export an account into Quicken format. Quicken is a popular finance program published by Intuit. When you export an account, Money creates a .QIF file that can be used by Quicken; the original file is left unchanged. You can export only one Money account at a time.

The File ➤ Export command can also be used to split Money files, and, in conjunction with File ➤ Import, to merge Money files.

TO EXPORT AN ACCOUNT TO QUICKEN FORMAT

1. Select File ➤ Export. The Export dialog box appears.
2. Mark the Strict QIF Compatibility check box if you are going to use the file in Quicken. Money will shorten the category names to 15 characters, and if you have created two classifications, will export only the first.

   If you plan to import the .QIF file into another Money file (using File ➤ Export and File ➤ Import to move accounts between files), make sure that the Strict QIF Compatibility check box is not marked, so that all the information is retained.
3. If you want to create the new file in a different drive and directory, select them from the Drives drop-down list box and the Directories list box.
4. The File Name list box in the Export dialog box contains a list of existing .QIF files in the selected directory. Enter a new name in the File Name text box at the top of the list and click on OK.
5. If more than one account is displayed in the Money window, the Select Export Account dialog box appears.

   Select the account you want to export and click on OK. If only one account is displayed in the Money window, that account will be exported.
6. Money creates the new .QIF file.

THE .QIF FILES The .QIF files are ASCII files that list account and transaction information line-by-line. Each line begins with a letter that indicates the type of information on that line. Lines of the same type are grouped together. The first group shows the account's opening balance and account information. Subsequent entries show the individual transactions. The following list describes each code:

!Type:	The first line in the file shows the account type, such as "!Type:Bank" for a Bank account, or "!Type:CCard" for a Credit Card account.
D	The transaction date.
T	The amount of the transaction. For example, "T123.45" indicates a $123.45 credit to the account while "T-123.45" shows a similar debit. In the first group, this amount is the opening balance.
CC	Indicates that the transaction has been cleared (a "C" appears in Money's C column).
CX	Indicates that the transaction has been reconciled (an "R" appears in Money's C column).
N	The check number or notation in Money's Num column. If the notation is "Print," the .QIF file will show "*****."
P	The payee. In the first group, this will say "POpening Balance."
M	The memo.
A	The address. this is a field that is used by Quicken, but not by Money; it is not the same as the address field in the Checks & Forms window or the Payee list. The Address is neither imported nor exported.
L	In the first group, this is the account name ("L[Checking]," for example). In subsequent groups, this is the category, subcategory, classification and subclassification, such as "LHealthcare:Premiums." If the transaction is a transfer, it will appear in brackets, like "L[Mastercard]." If the transaction includes classifications, they will be preceded by /, such as "LOther Income:Consulting/Acme Corp:Doc Project/First Phase:Installation Guide." If there are classifications but no categories, a / will immediately follow the L, as in "L/Acme Corp:Doc Project."

F

S	If the transaction is split, each individual category is shown on a line beginning with "S."
E	For each category in a split transaction, the information from the Description column is placed on a line beginning with "E."
$	For each category in a split transaction, the amount is placed on a line beginning with "$."
^	This symbol follows each group in the file.

Note also that some symbols may be modified. Periods and slashes are replaced by dashes, for example.

NOTES You can use .QIF files to merge two Money files, or even to merge two accounts in the same file. Export the accounts you want to move, and then import them into the other file. You will lose some information, such as payee addresses and bank names and account numbers, but the important transaction information will remain.

You can also export information to other applications by creating a tab-delimited ASCII file from the Report dialog boxes. See Reports.

SEE ALSO File ➤ Import; Reports

FILE ➤ IMPORT

The File ➤ Import command lets you access .QIF files created by the Quicken personal finance program. If you have been using Quicken and now want to use Money, you can import the Quicken files directly into Money.

You can only import one Quicken account at a time, so when you export from Quicken, you must export each account into a separate file. Each time you import an account, Money will ask you in which Money account you want to enter the information. So before you import your Quicken accounts, create a Money account for each one.

IMPORTING A QUICKEN FILE

1. Create a Money account without categories, or delete the categories you don't want to use from a existing Money file. When you import the Quicken files, Money will create categories to match the ones used in the files.
2. If your Quicken files include classes, create these classifications in the Money account *before* importing the Quicken file. When you import the accounts, the names will be entered from the Quicken file, but the classification and subclassification must already exist in the Money file.
3. Select File ➤ Import. The Import dialog box appears.
4. Double-click on the name of the file you want to import. (If the name of the file you want doesn't appear in the Import dialog box, type *.* in the File Name text box and click on OK to see all the file names.) The Select Import Account dialog box appears.

   Indicate whether to import both sides of a transfer transaction by marking the check box at the bottom of the dialog box (see Notes).
5. Click on the account to which you want to import the Quicken account information, and click on Continue.
6. If Money needs to import a transfer transaction, and the transfer names an account that does not exist in your Money file, the Assign Import Account dialog box will appear.

   You can then do one of the following options:

   - Click on an account and then click on Assign to select that account as the transfer partner.
   - Click on Create to create a new account to be used as the transfer partner.
   - Click on Stop Import to abort the .QIF import operation.
7. Make your selection and Money imports the file.

NOTES The first time you import an account into a file, the "Import only one side of transfers" check box has no effect—Money will import both sides of any transfer transactions in the .QIF file. That is, it will enter the transaction into both the account to which you choose to import the Quicken account and to the account named as the transfer partner. However, what happens the *next* time you import an account *does* depend on what you select in this check box. If you selected "Import only one side of transfers," Money will check to see if the transfer transactions already exist.

For example, when you import Account A, which has a transfer to Account B, Money imports both sides of the transfer, entering the transaction in both Accounts A and B regardless of the check box setting. Then, when you import Account B, and leave the "Import only one side of transfers" check box marked, Money sees that the transfer between A and B is already in B, so it doesn't import the information again. If you had left the listed check box unmarked, Money would have imported the transfer again, so it would appear in both Account B and Account A *twice*.

You can use File ➤ Import in conjunction with File ➤ Export to merge two Money files together, to merge two accounts in the same file together, or to break files down into smaller files. See File ➤ Export.

SEE ALSO File ➤ Export; List ➤ Other Classification; Reports

FILE ➤ NEW

Money lets you create your own files, although it is not always necessary to do so. When Money is first opened, it creates a file named MSMONEY.MNY, which is automatically opened each time you open Money. You may, however, want to create your own files to keep different accounts separate.

NOTES You can split files apart or merge them together using File ➤ Export and File ➤ Import. See File ➤ Export.

SEE ALSO Lesson 1: Getting Ready; Customize Money; File ➤ Backup; File ➤ Open

FILE ➤ OPEN

If you have more than one Money file, you can use the File ➤ Open command to close one file and open another.

OPENING A FILE

1. Select File ➤ Open. The Open dialog box appears.
2. Select the drive and directory in which the file is stored.

3. Double-click on the name of the file you want in the File Name list box. The Backup dialog box appears, unless you have turned off the Reminder to Backup option in the Settings dialog box.
4. Backup the current file if you wish (place a formatted disk in the drive and click Yes), or click on No. The selected file is opened.

The Open dialog box has a list box at the bottom labeled List Files of Type. You can click on the down arrow and select Backups (*.BAK) or All Files (*.*). This allows you to display only backup files in the list box, or to display Money files that have been given a different extension.

NOTES If a file has become corrupted after a system crash, Money may not let you open it. Try going to your MONEY.INI file and removing the CurrentFile-line. MONEY.INI is in the MSMONEY directory and can be opened with the Windows Notepad.

SEE ALSO Lesson 1: Getting Ready; Customizing Money; File ➤ Backup; File ➤ New

FILE ➤ PRINT CHECKS

Money prints checks for you. You must have special checks in the correct format for your printer.

NOTES You can only print checks from checking accounts. You cannot print checks from credit card, liability, or asset accounts that provide checks.

SEE ALSO Lesson 7: Printing Checks; File ➤ Print Setup; List ➤ Payee List; Window ➤ Checks & Forms

FILE ➤ PRINT SETUP

The File ➤ Print Setup command lets you select the printer configuration that Money will use for printing checks and reports.

NOTES Before you can select a printer, a Windows printer driver must be installed. For information on this procedure, see your Windows documentation.

Money lets you configure the printer differently for checks and reports. This allows you to use one printer for checks and one for reports. If you want to use both printers on the same port, connect one of the printers to LPT*n*.OS2 in the Windows Control Panel. For example, one printer could be attached to LPT1, and one to LPT1.OS2. Both printers will print to the LPT1 port, but the one connected to the LPT1.OS2 port will bypass the Windows print-management software. Connecting a printer in this way lets you swap printers without going to the Control Panel and activating the one you want to use.

Changing the printer setup in Money has no effect on the printer when it is used by other Windows applications.

SEE ALSO Lesson 7: Printing Checks; Lesson 8: Producing Reports; File ➤ Print Checks; Reports

HELP MENU OPTIONS

Money's online help system provides information and examples of Money operations. It can be accessed directly from the Money menu bar.

Keyboard: F1

HELP OPTIONS

Index	Displays an index of help topics
Keyboard Shortcuts	Displays a list containing most of Money's keyboard shortcuts
How to Use Help	Displays a window that explains the use of the help system
Windows Basics	Starts a lesson that teaches you the basics of working with Microsoft Windows
Previews	Runs the Money previews, the same previews that you had the opportunity to view when you first installed Money
About Microsoft Money	Displays the About message box that shows you the Money version number and the serial number

CONTEXT-SENSITIVE HELP

Press F1 at any time to see help about the action you are performing. If a dialog box is displayed you will see information about that dialog box. Otherwise, you will see the Help index.

NOTES Many dialog boxes contain Help buttons. Clicking on Help will display a Help window with information about that dialog box.

LIST ➤ ACCOUNT LIST

The List ➤ Account List option lets you view a list of all the accounts in the current file. From the Account List dialog box, you can create new accounts, rename or delete existing accounts, and edit account information. You can also print or view an Account Report.

Account List	A list of the existing accounts and their account types (Bank, Credit Card, Cash, Asset, or Liability). Click on an account name to see its information in the grey box next to the list, or to delete or rename it.
Shortcut	Up to six characters that can be used instead of the full account name when entering a transaction. You cannot use these characters in shortcuts: \ [ ] ? * ".
Opening Balance	The beginning balance, the starting point for tracking account transactions.
Bank Name	The name of the bank holding the account. This field is for information only; Money does not use it.
Account Number	The account number. This field is for information only.
Comment	Information about the account, such as phone numbers, contact names, date established, and so on. Start new lines by pressing ↵. This field is for information only.
New button	Click on this button to create a new account.
Delete button	Select an account and click on this button to delete the account.
Rename button	Select an account and click on this button to rename the account.
Close button	Closes the dialog box.

Report button	Lets you view and print a list of the accounts containing information about each one.
Help button	Displays information about the Account List box.

DISPLAYING THE ACCOUNT LIST

Select List ➤ Account List to display the Account List

CREATING A NEW ACCOUNT

1. Click on the New Button or press Alt-N. The Create New Account dialog box appears.
2. Enter an account name. The name can be up to 32 characters long, and can include any character except \ [ ] ? * or ″.
3. Click on one of the option buttons to select an account type.
4. Click on OK. The Opening Balance dialog box appears.
5. Type the beginning balance and click on OK. The new account is added to the list.
6. Enter the Shortcut, Bank Name, Account Number, and Comment.

You can also create a new account by using one of several other methods:

- Select New Account from the Account drop-down list box.
- If multiple accounts are displayed, you can type a new account name in the transaction's Account Name field.
- Select the Transfer category and then enter a new account name in the transfer-to field.

In each case Money will lead you through the account-creation procedure.

Which Account Balance You have a number of options for the account balance, depending on how accurate you want your records to be.

If you want to show all activity in the account since you opened it, enter 0. Later, you will need to enter all the transactions, including the opening deposit.

If you want to start recording transactions from the end of the last statement, enter the ending balance from the last statement. Later, you will need to enter all the transactions that have not yet appeared on your statement.

If you want to start recording transactions from the present time, enter your current register balance. Then you will record transactions as they occur.

If you want to start recording transactions from the present time, but you have no idea of the account's present balance, enter 0. Then record transactions as they occur. When you balance your account, you will need to let Money enter an account adjustment to bring the balance into line with the statement balance.

If you open a new account by making an initial deposit, *don't* enter that sum as the beginning balance. Enter 0 as the beginning balance, and then enter the initial deposit as the first transaction. This enables you to assign the deposit to a category and have it appear on reports. Otherwise, the opening deposit becomes a "missing transaction."

If your check register balance is not correct, you will need to let Money enter an account adjustment. Once the balance has been adjusted and there are no more outstanding transactions, you will be able to balance the account without making adjustments each time.

DELETING AN ACCOUNT

1. Select the account name.
2. Click on the Delete button, or press Alt-D.
3. If the account does not have any transactions, Money deletes it. If it does contain transactions, Money displays a dialog box asking you to confirm that you want to delete the account. If you are sure, click on Yes.

If you delete an account that includes transfers to another account, Money creates a new category called Xfer From Deleted Account and assigns the transfer transactions to it. If you delete an account that has transfers from another account, Money creates a new category called Xfer To Deleted Account.

RENAMING AN ACCOUNT

1. Select the account name.

2. Click on the Rename button, or press Alt-R. The Rename Account dialog box appears.
3. Type a new name and click on OK.

VIEWING AN ACCOUNT LIST REPORT

1. Click on the Report button. The Account List Report dialog box appears.
2. Click on the Customize button. The Customize Account List Report dialog box appears.
3. Enter a new report title if you wish.
4. Select the options for the information you want to include:

   Shortcuts: Includes the account shortcuts in the report.

   Bank Information: Includes the Bank Names and Account Numbers in the report.

   Account Balances: Includes the Opening Balances and Current Balances in the report.
5. Click on the View button.

EDITING ACCOUNT INFORMATION

1. Move the cursor to the appropriate text box by clicking on it with the mouse, pressing Tab, or pressing Alt and the letter underlined in the item name.
2. Type the new information.
3. You can cancel any changes you make by pressing Esc before you move to another name or close the dialog box.

NOTES The Create New Account dialog box is also displayed when you install Money or when you create a new file.

SEE ALSO Lesson 1: Getting Ready; Account Drop-Down List Box; Account Types; Options ➤ Balance Account; Reports

LIST ➤ CATEGORY LIST

The List ➤ Category List option lets you view a list of all available categories (with the exception of the Transfer category, which cannot be deleted or modified). From the category list dialog box, you can create new categories, rename or delete existing categories, and edit category information. You can also print or view a Category Report.

Category List	A list of the existing categories. Select a category name to see its information or to delete or rename it.
Subcategory List	A list of the existing subcategories in the highlighted category. Select a subcategory name to see its information, or to delete or rename it.
Shortcut	Up to six characters that can be used instead of the full category name when entering a transaction. You cannot use these characters: \ [ ] ? * ″.
Comment	Information about the category or subcategory, possibly including explanations of the category's accounting purpose or the types of transactions assigned to the category or subcategory. End a line by pressing ↵. This field is for information only.
Budget box	Contains information about the budgeted amount for the selected category or subcategory. See Lesson 10: Creating a Budget for more information.
New button	Click on the New button below the Category List to create a new category, or the one below the Subcategory List to create a new subcategory.
Delete button	Select a category or subcategory and click on the button below the list to delete it.

Rename button	Select a category or subcategory and click on the button below the list to rename it.
Close button	Closes the dialog box.
Report button	Lets you view a print a list of the categories, with information about each one.
Help button	Displays a Help screen with information about the Category List.

DISPLAYING THE CATEGORY LIST

Select List ➤ Category List to display the Category List.

CREATING A NEW CATEGORY

1. Click on the New Button below the Category List, or press Alt-N. The Create New Category dialog box appears.
2. Enter a category name. The name may be up to 32 characters long, and can include any character except \ [ ] ? * or ″.
3. Click on one of the option buttons to select an account type.
4. Click on one of the option buttons to indicate whether this category will be an income or expense category.
5. Turn on the Include on Tax Reports check box if you want to include this category in tax reports.
6. Click on the OK button. The name of the new category is entered into the Category List.
7. Enter the Shortcut, Comment, and Budget information.

You can also create a new category or subcategory while entering a transaction by typing a new name in the Category or Subcategory field. When you move to the next field, Money will lead you through the creation of the category.

DELETING A CATEGORY AND REASSIGNING TRANSACTIONS

1. Select the category name.
2. Click on the Delete button, or press Alt-D.
3. If the category contains subcategories, a dialog box is displayed warning you that the subcategories will be deleted. Click on OK.
4. If there are transactions that have been assigned to the category, the Delete Category dialog box appears.
5. If you want to change the category to which those transactions were assigned, select the category and subcategory if you wish and click on OK. If that category has a budgeted amount, the amount will be added to the category to which you are transferring the transactions.

RENAMING A CATEGORY

1. Select the category name.
2. Click on the Rename button, or press Alt-R. The Rename Category dialog box appears.
3. Type a new name and click on OK.

DELETING AND RENAMING SUBCATEGORIES

The procedures used for deleting and renaming subcategories are the same as those for deleting and renaming categories.

CREATING A NEW SUBCATEGORY

1. If you wish, select the category to which you want to add the subcategory.
2. Click on the New Button below the Subcategory List, or press Alt-W. The Create New Subcategory dialog box appears.
3. Enter the name of the new subcategory.
4. Mark the Include on Tax Reports check box to include the subcategory in tax reports. Note, however, that doing so will also include the parent category and other subcategories.

5. If you selected the category to which you want to add the subcategory in Step 1, click on OK. If you didn't select the category in Step 1, use the Subcategory For drop-down list box to select the category to which you want to assign the subcategory. Then click OK.

VIEWING A CATEGORY LIST REPORT

1. Click on the Report button. The Category List Report dialog box appears.
2. Click on the Customize button. The Customize Category List Report dialog box appears.
3. Enter a new report title if you wish.
4. Select the information you want to include in the report.

    Shortcut: Includes the category and subcategory shortcuts in the report.

    Tax Flag: Displays a T next to the categories that will be included on tax reports.

    Basic Budgets: Includes a column with the amount budgeted for each category and subcategory, and a column showing the time period (per week, per month, etc.).

    Detailed Budgets: Includes a column for each month of the year, showing the amount budgeted for the categories and subcategories for that month.

5. Click on the View button.

EDITING CATEGORY INFORMATION

1. Move to the appropriate text box by clicking with the mouse, pressing Tab, or pressing Alt and the letter underlined in the item name.
2. Type the new information.
3. You can cancel any changes you make by pressing Esc before you move to another name or close the dialog box.

NOTES If you delete an account that includes transfers to another account, Money will create a Xfer From Deleted Account category and assign the transactions to it. You can use the new category in the same way as you use any other.

SEE ALSO Lesson 3: Creating Categories and Editing Payee Lists; Reports; Reports ➤ Tax Reports

LIST ➤ OTHER CLASSIFICATION

Money lets you create your own classifications to which you can assign transactions. You can think of categories as a form of classification; assigning transactions to a category groups the transactions according to type. You can create your own classifications to group transactions according to different criteria, such as project, client, or property. You may create up to two new classifications.

CREATING A NEW CLASSIFICATION

This is described in detail in Lesson 8.

DELETING A CLASSIFICATION ITEM

1. From the List menu, select the name of the classification containing the item you want to delete. The Classification List dialog box appears.
2. Select the item you want to delete.
3. If the item contains sub-items, a dialog box is displayed warning you that they will be deleted. Click on OK.
4. If transactions have been assigned to the item, the Delete Classification dialog box appears.
5. If you want to change the item to which those transactions were assigned, select the item—and sub-item if you wish—and click on OK.

DELETING AN ENTIRE CLASSIFICATION

1. Select List ➤ Other Classification.
2. Click on the Delete button under the classification name.

CHANGING A CLASSIFICATION NAME AND ADDING SUBITEMS

1. Select List ➤ Other Classification.

2. When the Other Classification dialog box appears, click on the Modify button under the classification name. The Modify Classification Scheme dialog box appears.
3. Enter the new name and click on the Allow Sub-Items check box. If you turn this box *off*, the sub-items will be removed, but you will *not* be warned if transactions are using the sub-items.

EDITING CLASSIFICATION INFORMATION

1. Move to the appropriate text box by clicking on the text box with the mouse or pressing Tab, or pressing Alt and the letter underlined in the item name).
2. Type the new information.
3. You can cancel any changes you make by pressing Esc before you move to another name or close the dialog box.

PRODUCING A CLASSIFICATION LIST REPORT

1. Click on the Report button. The Classification List Report dialog box appears.
2. Click on the Customize button. The Customize Classification List Report dialog box appears.
3. Enter a new report title, if you wish.
4. Click on the Include Shortcut check box if you want the shortcuts assigned to the classifications to appear in the report.
5. Click on the View button.

SEE ALSO Lesson 3: Working with Categories, Classifications, and Payee Lists

LIST ➤ PAYEE LIST

Money keeps a list of payees. This list is used by SmartFill and SuperSmartFill to enter information into transactions automatically, and to provide the addresses that are printed on the checks.

USING THE PAYEE LIST

To see the Payee List, select List ➤ Payee List.

New	Click on New to add a new payee name. Payee names can be up to 32 characters long, but may not include these characters: \ [ ] ? * ". If you enter an existing name, you will be given the option of combining the transactions for both payees or keeping them separate.
Delete	Select a payee and click on Delete to remove the name from the list. If you delete the name, you will not be able to select this payee from the View drop-down list box, but the transactions in your accounts remain unchanged—the payee name is not removed.
Rename	Select a payee and click on Rename to change the payee's name.
Shortcut	Enter up to six characters that can be used instead of the full payee name when entering a transaction. You might use the payee's account number, for example, or the name of the product you buy from that company. You cannot use these characters in shortcuts: \ [ ] ? * ".
Phone	The payee's phone number. For your information only.
Address	The payee's address, up to four lines. Start new lines by pressing ↵. This address is printed on any check for that payee. Information typed in braces, such as {Attn: Janet}, will not be printed on the check. If you entered an address in the Checks & Forms window when entering a transaction, it will automatically be entered in the Payee List.

Comment	A comment about the payee, such as a contact name or a note about the preferred form of payment for this payee. Start new lines by pressing ↵.

PRODUCING A PAYEE LIST REPORT

1. Click on the Report button. The Payee List dialog box appears.
2. Click on the Customize button. The Customize Payee List dialog box appears.
3. Enter a new report title, if you wish.
4. Select the options for the information you want to include in the report:

   Shortcut: Includes the payee shortcuts in the report.

   Last Date Used: Includes the last transaction date for each payee in the report.

   Phone Number: Includes the payee's telephone number in the report.

5. Click on the View button.

EDITING PAYEE INFORMATION

1. Click on the payee name.
2. Move to the appropriate text box by clicking in the box with the mouse, pressing Tab, or pressing Alt and the letter underlined in the item name.
3. Type the new information.
4. You can cancel any changes you make by pressing Esc before you move to another name or close the dialog box.

NOTES There is no way to stop Money from adding payees to the Payee List. Each time you enter a transaction Money copies the information to the list, replacing the payee's previous information when necessary. This means you will end up with a lot of unnecessary payee data that you will never need again. You may want to periodically clear the list by deleting the names you don't want.

If you delete a payee name, you will not be able to select that payee from the View drop-down list, or display it in a report, even though the payee name remains in the payee field of the relevant transactions.

Once a payee name is in the list with the correct capitalization, you can enter the name in transactions without worrying about capitalization. Money will enter the correct capitalization when you move to the next field.

SEE ALSO Lesson 2: Entering Transactions; Lesson 3: Working with Categories, Classifications, and Payee Lists; Entering Transactions

OPTIONS ➤ BALANCE ACCOUNTS

Money helps you to reconcile an account balance against a bank statement. This ensures that you have entered all of the appropriate transactions correctly, and that your bank has not made any mistakes.

For detailed information about balancing an account, see Lesson 10.

Keyboard F9

BALANCING A CASH, ASSET, OR LIABILITY ACCOUNT

If you try to balance a Cash, Asset, or Liability Account, you will see the Adjust Account Balance dialog box.

This dialog box lets you enter an account adjustment and assign it to a category. Or you may click on the Balance button to use the account-balancing procedure outlined above.

NOTES Once you have reconciled transactions, you should not have to modify their amounts later. Modifying a reconciled amount will cause problems with the account balance calculations, and you will have to enter an account adjustment the next time you balance the account.

SEE ALSO Lesson 9: Balancing Your Checkbook

OPTIONS ➤ CALCULATOR

The Calculator command displays the Microsoft Windows calculator. You can use the calculator to make calculations and then copy the result to a transaction. If you removed the Windows calculator file (CALC.EXE), this menu option will not work.

Keyboard Ctrl-K

DISPLAYING THE CALCULATOR

There are three ways to display the calculator from Money:

- Select Options ➤ Calculator
- Press Ctrl-K
- Click on the Calculator icon in the Toolbar

CHANGING THE MODE

Select View ➤ Standard or View ➤ Scientific to display the standard or scientific calculator configuration.

USING THE CALCULATOR

To operate the calculator, click on the keys with the mouse or use your keyboard. The following table explains the function of each calculator key and its keyboard equivalent.

BUTTON	KEYBOARD EQIVALENT	FUNCTION
+	+	Addition
–	–	Subtraction
*	* (on Num keypad)	Multiplication
/	/ (on Num keypad)	Division
=	= or ↵	Equals
1/x	r	Calculates the reciprocal of the displayed number
%	%	Calculates the percentage; 200*25% means calculate 25% of 200
sqrt	@	Calculates the square root of the displayed number

BUTTON	KEYBOARD EQIVALENT	FUNCTION
+/–	F9	Changes the sign of the displayed number
.	. *or* ,	Enters a decimal point
Back	Backspace or ←	Deletes the last digit or decimal point in the displayed number
CE	Del	Clears the last displayed number; the previous steps in the calculation remain in memory
C	Esc	Clears the current calculation
MC	Ctrl-C	Clears the value in memory
MR	Ctrl-R	Copies the value stored in memory into the calculator display
MS	Ctrl-M	Removes the value stored in memory, and replaces it with the displayed value
M+	Ctrl-P	Adds the displayed value to the value stored in memory

COPYING NUMBERS BETWEEN THE CALCULATOR AND MONEY

You can copy numbers between the calculator and Money. To copy a number in the calculator, press Ctrl-Ins or select Edit ➤ Copy (you need not select the number first). To paste that number into the transaction, place the cursor in the amount field and press Shift-Ins (or Ctrl-V or select Edit ➤ Paste).

To copy from the transaction to the calculator, select the number in the amount field and then press Ctrl-Ins (or Ctrl-C or select Edit ➤ Copy). Then go to the calculator and press Shift-Ins or select Edit ➤ Paste.

FINDING THE CALCULATOR

If you click on the Money window (or any other window or dialog box), the Calculator will disappear. You can retrieve it by one of three procedures:

- Press Ctrl-Esc and double-click on Calculator in the Task List dialog box
- Select Switch To from the Control menu and double-click on Calculator in the Task List dialog box
- Hold down Alt and press Tab until the outline of the calculator appears

NOTES Calculator is an independent application. It runs independently of Money or any other Windows program. You can close Money and Calculator will remain open.

SEE ALSO Your Windows documentation

OPTIONS ➤ ENTIRE TRANSACTION VIEW

The Account Book and Future Transactions windows have two views—Top Line View and Entire Transaction View. The Top Line View shows only the first line of each transaction—the check number or notation, the date, the payee, and the amount. The Entire Transaction View shows *all* information related to each transaction, including its memo, category, and classification.

This command changes the view from the Top Line View to the Entire Transaction View. You can also click on the Entire Transaction View icon button in the Toolbar, or press Ctrl-T.

Keyboard Ctrl-T

SEE ALSO Options ➤ Top Line View; Window ➤ Account Book; Window ➤ Future Transactions

OPTIONS ➤ PASSWORD

You may add a password to your data file so that the file cannot be opened by an unauthorized person. You may want to do this if you use a computer that others have access to while you are not present.

ASSIGNING A PASSWORD TO YOUR FILE

1. Select Options ➤ Password. The New Password dialog box appears.
2. Type the password you want to use. Money will display an asterisk in the text box for each key you press. You can enter up to 16 characters. You may use any characters you wish.
3. Click on OK. The text box is cleared and Money asks you to re-enter the password. This is to confirm the password you entered.
4. Type the password again and click on OK.

If you enter the password incorrectly the second time, Money will display a dialog box telling you to try again. You can click on the Cancel button at any time to abort the operation and start again.

USING YOUR PASSWORD

1. When you try to open a password-protected file (either upon starting Money or using the File ➤ Open command), Money displays the Password dialog box.
2. Type the password and click on the OK button. Money will allow you to continue.

CHANGING THE PASSWORD

1. Select Options ➤ Password. Money displays the password dialog box.
2. Type the password and click on the OK button. Money will display the New Password dialog box.
3. Continue as if you were entering a new password.

REMOVING THE PASSWORD

To remove a password use the same procedure as for changing the password, but instead of typing a new one, leave the text box empty and click on OK twice.

WHAT HAPPENS IF YOU FORGET YOUR PASSWORD?

Call Microsoft Money technical support at 1-206-635-7131. They will talk you through a procedure that will find the password for you. I'm not going to include that procedure in this book; that would defeat the purpose of having a password! Only a few Microsoft support people know this procedure, so it may take several days for a technician to call you. So *don't* forget the password! If *absolutely* necessary, write it down somewhere safe, away from the computer that has your Money files.

NOTES If you have trouble remembering passwords, another way to protect the file is to rename it, use an extension other than .MNY, and put it in another directory. It won't stop anyone from *opening* the file if they do find it, but it makes it less likely that it will be found.

No password system is perfect. If you want to be absolutely sure that nobody can get into your files, keep them on a floppy disk and remove them from the computer when you leave.

OPTIONS ➤ PAY BILLS

The Options ➤ Pay Bills command helps you enter transactions from the Future Transactions window into an account. This is a quick way to process transactions that occur more than once, or that you know will be occurring some time in the future. See Lesson 6 for detailed information.

NOTES When you want to enter one specific transaction, rather than several, display the Future Transactions window, select the transaction, and select Edit ➤ Enter from Schedule.

You can instruct Money to remind you that you have bills ready to be paid. See Customizing Money.

Transactions with no date in the Future Transactions window Date field are ignored by the Options ➤ Pay Bills command. You must use Edit ➤ Enter from Schedule to process these transactions.

SEE ALSO Lesson 6; Customizing Money; Edit ➤ Enter from Schedule; Edit ➤ Schedule in Future

OPTIONS ➤ SETTINGS

The Settings dialog box lets you change the way that Money works in certain situations: the effect that the ↵ key has, the way numbers are entered into the amount fields, the type of confirmations you will receive, and so on. The settings you select are stored in the MONEY.INI file, which Money refers to each time you open the program.

The Settings dialog box is not the only way you can customize Money. For more information, see Customizing Money.

OPTIONS ➤ TOP LINE VIEW

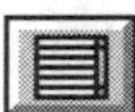

The Account Book and Future Transactions windows have two views—Top Line View and Entire Transaction View. The Top Line View shows only the first line of each transaction—the check number or notation, the date, the payee, and the amount. The Entire Transaction View shows *all* the information related to each transaction, including its memo, category, and classification.

This command changes the view from the Entire Transaction View to the Top Line View. You can also click on the Top Line View icon button in the Toolbar, or press Ctrl-T.

Keyboard: Ctrl-T

If you have two or more accounts selected (from the Account drop-down list box), you will probably want to use Entire Transaction View. If you use Top Line View the Account Name field is not displayed, so you can't tell to which account each transaction belongs.

SEE ALSO Options ➤ Entire Transaction View; Window ➤ Account Book; Window ➤ Future Transactions

REPORTS

Money has a number of different reports that let you display or print your account information in a useful form. Each report may be customized so that you can get just the information you need.

WHERE ARE THE REPORTS?

Money has several reports that can be found in different places. Reports are displayed by selecting an option from the Report menu, or by clicking on the Report button in one of the List dialog boxes:

Budget Report (Report menu)

Income and Expense Report (Report menu)

Net Worth Report (Report menu)

Register Report (Report menu)

Future Transactions Report (Report menu; this report is a Register Report selected from the Future Transactions window)

Summary Report (Report menu)

Tax Report (Report menu)

Account List Report

Payee List Report

Category List Report

Classification List Report

The List reports are very simple reports, and are described elsewhere in this reference section (see List ➤ Account List, and so on). The Report dialog boxes have a number of common features. The following illustration shows the Summary Report dialog box.

Notice that the Report window can be sized; it has a control menu that can be used to enlarge or shrink the window, and it has a sizing button in the top right corner. You can also drag the box's borders to increase its size.

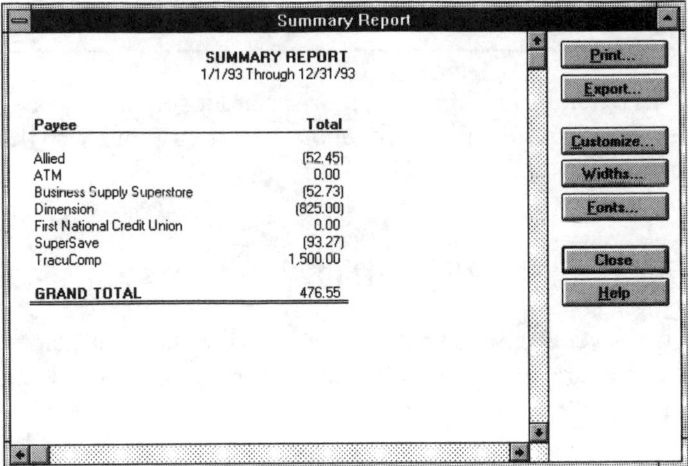

THE BUTTONS

Each of the report dialog boxes contain the following buttons:

BUTTON	FUNCTION
Print	Prints the report
Export	Creates an ASCII file containing the report information
Customize	Lets you select the information you want to include in the report
Widths	Lets you select the spacing between columns in the report
Fonts	Lets you choose the font for the report
Close	Closes the Report dialog box

CUSTOMIZING A REPORT

All of the reports can be customized in some way. Because the custom options vary so much between report types, customizing reports is explained in each individual report's reference section. Two important options are common to the reports on the Reports menu, though: the From Account drop-down list box and the Transactions option buttons. (The next figure shows the Include Transactions box that appears in most of the Report dialog boxes.)

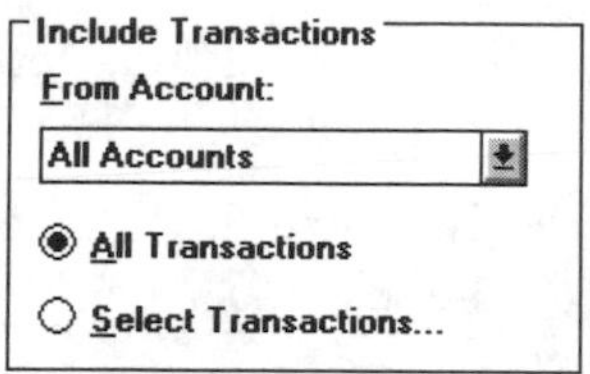

The From Account drop-down list box lets you select which accounts should be used to provide information for the report. You can select a single account by name, All Accounts, or Multiple Accounts. If you select Multiple Accounts, the Select Accounts dialog box appears.

Clicking on the All Transactions option button instructs Money to include all the transactions in the selected accounts and between the selected dates. Clicking on the Select Transactions option button, however, lets you select specific transactions to be included in the report. The Select Transactions dialog box appears.

Selecting Accounts If you selected Multiple Accounts in the From Account drop-down list box, the Select Accounts dialog box appears.

There are four ways to select accounts:

- Click on the account name
- Use the arrow keys to move the highlight to the account and press the spacebar
- Click on the Select All button to select all accounts, and then click on the ones you *don't* want
- Click on the Select None button, and then click on the ones that you *do* want

If you are using the keyboard instead of a mouse, sometimes pressing ↵ while the Select Accounts dialog box is open will close both that dialog box *and* the Customize dialog box, returning you to the Report dialog box. You can avoid the problem by pressing Tab to move the highlight to the OK button and then pressing the spacebar.

After you have selected the accounts you want, click on OK to return to the Customize Report dialog box.

Selecting Transactions If you clicked on Select Transactions, the Select Transactions dialog box appears.

The box contains the following options:

FIELD	OPTION	FUNCTION
Type	Payments	Displays only payments from the selected accounts
	Deposits	Displays only deposits to the selected accounts
	Unprinted Checks	Displays only transactions with the word 'print' in the Num column
	Transfers	Displays only transfers to or from the selected accounts
	All Types	Displays all transactions in the selected accounts
	No Amount	Displays only transactions that have 0.00 in both amount columns
Payee	Payee names	Displays only transactions related to the selected payee
	All Payees	Displays transactions for all payees
	Blank Payees	Displays only transactions that do not have a name in the Payee field
Cleared	Unreconciled Transactions	Displays only transactions *without* an "R" in the C field
	Reconciled Transactions	Displays only transactions *with* an "R" in the C field
	Reconciled & Unreconciled	Displays transactions regardless of the letter in the C field
Category	Category name	Displays only transactions related to the selected category

FIELD	OPTION	FUNCTION
	All Categories	Displays all transactions, including those not assigned to a category
	Income Categories	Displays only trans-actions assigned to Income categories
	Expense Categories	Displays only trans-actions assigned to Expense categories
	Tax Categories	Displays only transactions assigned to categories that have the "Include on Tax Report" option selected
	Blank Categories	Displays only transactions that have not been assigned to a category
	Select Multiple Categories	Displays only transactions related to the categories selected in the list box that appears
Classification	Classification name	Displays only transactions assigned to the selected classification
	All Classification	Displays transactions assigned to any classifications
	Blank Classification	Displays only transactions that have not been assigned to a classification
	Select Multiple Classification	Displays only trans-actions related to the classifications selected in the displayed list box
Date	From/To	Displays only transactions between the From and To dates

R

FIELD	OPTION	FUNCTION
Number	From/To	Displays only transactions with check numbers between the From and To numbers
Amount	From/To	Displays only transactions with a value between the From and To amounts

These settings are combined, of course. For example, if you select a Payee name, and then select the Food category, only transactions that are assigned to *both* the named Payee *and* the Food category will be displayed.

When you finish selecting the transactions, click on OK to return to the Report dialog box. Then click on View to see the customized report.

SELECTING A REPORT WIDTH

You can control the amount of space between columns in the report. If space is too narrow, the information in some columns may be truncated. If the space is too wide, some columns may not fit on the printed report (they will still be visible in the displayed report).

To change column width:

1. Click on the Width button. The Report Column Width dialog box appears.
2. Click on one of the Widths in the dialog box and then click on OK.

Remember that the width of the report is also dependent on the size of the font that you select.

SELECTING A REPORT FONT

You can use any Windows-compatible font for your report. All the text in the report uses the same font.

To change a report font:

1. Click on the Fonts button to see the Select Fonts dialog box.

   The list on the left side of the dialog box displays all the available fonts, including fonts installed when you loaded Windows, fonts supported by your printer, and fonts loaded by programs such as Adobe Type Manager. The printer fonts are identified by small printer icons next to the font name.

2. Click on a font name.
3. Select a font size in the list box to the right of the font list.

When you have selected both a font and a size, the Sample box shows an example of what the font will look like. However, if a printer font does not have an associated screen font, the font will appear different on-screen than when it is printed.

Unlike most custom-report information, the font size is saved with the Money file. Once you have selected a font size all the other reports in that file will use that font size.

PRINTING A REPORT

1. Click on the Print button. The Print Report dialog box appears.
2. Click on the Setup button to see the Print Setup dialog box. This is the same dialog box as that displayed when you select File ➤ Print Setup and click on the Report Printing option button.
3. Select the printer on which you want to print the reports: either the Default Printer or one from the drop-down list box.
4. Depending on your printer, you may also be able to select the print orientation. Portrait is the standard orientation; the "width" of the report will be across the shortest side. If you select Landscape, the report will be printed across the long side.
5. Depending on your printer, select the paper size and a paper source (such as Tray or Manual Feed).
6. Click on OK to return to the Print Report dialog box.
7. Select the pages you want to print. Select either All, or click on Pages and then enter the first page number in the From box and the last in the To box. The report display does not give an indication of page numbers, so you may have to guess.
8. Select the number of Copies you want.
9. You will normally want to leave the Collate check box selected. With Collate selected Money prints the first report entirely, then prints the second copy, then the third, and so on (pages 1, 2, 3, 1, 2, 3, 1, 2, 3). If you turn Collate *off* Money will print all the copies of the first page, then all copies of the second, and so on (pages 1, 1, 1, 2, 2, 2, 3, 3, 3).

10. Select the print quality: High, Medium, Low, or Draft. The effect of these options varies depending on your printer, so you may have to experiment. The lower quality printouts tend to be quicker, but don't look as nice. Some of the options may have no effect on your printer, or may even have unintended effects.
11. Click on the OK button and Money will print the report.

If a report is too wide for the paper, Money will print the information that didn't fit on another sheet. If it's too wide, though, try printing in Landscape, reducing the width, and reducing the font size.

EXPORTING A REPORT

You can export your Money report as a tab-delimited ASCII file for use in other programs—word processors, desktop publishing programs, databases, tax programs, or spreadsheets.

1. Click on the Export button in the Report dialog box. The Export dialog box appears.
2. Choose a directory in which you want to save the exported file.
3. Type a name in the File Name text box. You can change the extension if you don't want to use the default .TXT.
4. Click on OK and the new file is created.

NOTES Sometimes the word "Unassigned" will appear in a report. This simply means that the transaction was not assigned to a category, or was assigned to a category, but not a subcategory.

Money does not provide a command or procedure for saving customized report formats. However, you can use Windows Recorder to build report macros that will create the reports each time you need them. See Lesson 8 for more information.

You cannot copy a report to the Windows clipboard. The only way to move information into another application is using the Report Export feature.

SEE ALSO Lesson 8: Producing Reports; File ➤ Print Setup; List ➤ Account List; List ➤ Payee List; List ➤ Category List; List ➤ Classification List; Report ➤ Budget Report; Report ➤ Income and Expense Report; Report ➤ Net Worth Report; Report ➤ Register Report; Report ➤ Summary Report; Report ➤ Tax Report

REPORT ➤ BUDGET REPORT

The Budget Report compares the amount you have spent or earned in the specified time period with the amount that you budgeted. (For information on entering budget figures, see Budgets.) Select Report ➤ Budget to see the Budget Report dialog box.

CUSTOMIZING THE BUDGET REPORT

Click on the Customize button. The Customize Budget Report dialog box appears.

Title	You can enter a new title for the report in this box.
Row for Every	This selection enables you to display every subcategory or to group them by category.
Column for Every	All Budget reports have three Totals columns: Actual amount spent, Budgeted amount, and Difference. This setting enables you to add columns displaying the totals for every Week, Two Weeks, Half Month, Month, Quarter, or Year. If you select None, only the Totals columns are displayed.
Display Empty Categories	Mark this check box to include categories that have no transactions assigned to them in the report. Turn this option *off* if you only want to see those categories that have been used. (This applies only to categories, not subcategories.)
Dates	Indicate the dates of the transaction information to be included in the report by selecting All Dates (all the information in the account regardless of the date), Current Month, Current Year, Month to Date, Year to Date, Previous Month, Previous Year, Last 30 Days, or Last 12 Months. Or, enter a specific range of dates in the From and Two fields, in which case Money displays Custom Dates in the Dates text box.

From Account	Indicate the account or accounts that should be included in the report. You can select a single account by name, All Accounts, or Multiple Accounts. If you select Multiple Accounts, the Select Accounts dialog box appears (see Reports).
All Transactions	Click on this option button if you want to include in the report all transactions in the selected accounts that occur between the selected dates.
Select Transactions	Click on this option button to select specific transactions to be included in the report. The Select Transactions dialog box appears (see Reports).

NOTES Because transfers cannot be budgeted, they will not appear on the budget report.

SEE ALSO Lesson 8: Producing Reports; Lesson 11: Creating Budgets; Reports

REPORT ➤ INCOME AND EXPENSE REPORT

The Income and Expense Report compares income deposited in selected accounts with expenses paid from those accounts over a specified period. Transactions are subtotaled by category, without showing individual transactions. This report is a good way to gauge business cash flow, or to see if your income is keeping up with your expenses.

When you first display this report, all the transactions from all the accounts for the Year To Date are included. You can change these selections.

CUSTOMIZING THE INCOME AND EXPENSE REPORT

Click on the Customize button to see the Customize Income and Expense Report dialog box.

Title	You can enter a title for the report in this box.
Row for Every	This selection enables you to display every subcategory or to group them by category.
Column for Every	You can display a column for every Week, Two Weeks, Half Month, Month, Quarter, or Year. If you select None only the Total column is displayed, showing the total expense or income for each category or subcategory.
Dates	Indicate the dates of the transaction information included in the report by selecting All Dates (all the information in the account regardless of the date), Current Month, Current Year, Month to Date, Year to Date, Previous Month, Previous Year, Last 30 Days, or Last 12 Months. Or, enter a specific range of dates in the From and Two fields in which case Money displays Custom Dates in the Dates text box.
From Account	The account or accounts that should be included in the report. You can select a single account by name, All Accounts, or Multiple Accounts. If you select Multiple Accounts the Select Accounts dialog box appears (see Reports).
All Transactions	Click on this option button if you want to include all transactions in the selected accounts that occur between the selected dates.
Select Transactions	Click on this option button if you want to select specific transactions to be included in the report. The Select Transactions dialog box appears (see Reports).

R

Report Transfers By	Click on Income Statement if you want to ignore transfers. Click on Expenditures if you want the report to contain a separate section for transfers to and from *asset* and *liability* accounts. The amounts will be included in the Income Less Expenses total; transfers to other account types are not shown. Click on Cash Flow to show the flow of money in and out of the selected accounts. Transfers between accounts that are included in the report will not appear, but transfers to accounts not included in the report *will* be shown.

SEE ALSO Lesson 8: Producing Reports; Reports

REPORT ➤ NET WORTH REPORT

The Net Worth Report is based on the balance in the selected accounts, so customizing the report is fairly simple, as you don't need to select transactions.

CUSTOMIZING THE NET WORTH REPORT

Click on the Customize button to see the Customize Net Worth Report dialog box.

Title	You can enter a new title for the report in this box.
Date	In this box, enter the date you want the calculation to be based upon. The current date will be displayed here, but you can enter another date to see your past net worth.
All Accounts	Click on this option button to base the calculations on all of your accounts.
Multiple Accounts	Click on this option button to exclude some accounts from the calculations. The Select Accounts dialog box appears (see Reports).

SEE ALSO Lesson 8: Producing Reports; Reports

REPORT ➤ REGISTER REPORT

The Register Report displays a list of all the transactions in the selected account. The transactions displayed in the report depend on the window from which you selected the report. If you were in the Account Book or Checks & Forms window, the report will display information from the accounts selected in the Account drop-down list box. If you were in the Future Transactions window, the Register Report will actually be a Future Transactions Report, a listing of all the transactions pending in the Future Transactions window.

You can customize the report by adding or removing accounts and transactions.

CUSTOMIZING THE REGISTER REPORT

Click on the Customize button to see the Customize Register Report dialog box.

Title	You can enter a new title for the report in this box.
Memo	Mark this box if you want to include a column for the memo field.
Account	Mark this box if you want to include a column for the account name field.
Cleared Flag	Mark this box if you want to include a column for the C field.
Category	Mark this box if you want to include a column to show the transaction's category and subcategory.
Classifications	If you have created classifications, you can click on the classification names to include a column showing the transaction's classification.

Dates	Indicate the dates of the transaction information to be included in the report by selecting All Dates (all the information in the account regardless of the date), Current Month, Current Year, Month to Date, Year to Date, Previous Month, Previous Year, Last 30 Days, or Last 12 Months. Or, enter a specific range of dates in the From and Two fields in which case Money displays Custom Dates in the Date text box.
Subtotal by	**None:** Displays a chronological list of transactions in the selected accounts, one row per transaction. **Account:** Displays a list of transactions grouped by account name, chronologically ordered and subtotaled within each account. **Category:** Displays a list of transactions grouped by category name, chronologically ordered and subtotaled within each category. **Subcategory:** Displays a list of transactions grouped by subcategory name, chronologically ordered and subtotaled within each subcategory. **Classification:** Displays a list of transactions grouped by classification name, chronologically ordered and subtotaled within each classification. **Subclassification:** Displays a list of transactions grouped by subclassification name, chronologically ordered and subtotaled within each subclassification. **Week:** Displays a chronological list of transactions in the selected accounts, with a total line at the end of each week. **Month:** Displays a chronological list of transactions in the selected accounts, with a total line at the end of each month.
Display Splits	Select this check box to display split transactions with the transaction total on one line and each split on its own line.

From Account	Indicate the account or accounts that should be included in the report. You can select a single account by name, All Accounts, or Multiple Accounts. If you select Multiple Accounts, the Select Accounts dialog box appears (see Reports).
All Transactions	Click on this option button if you want to include all transactions in the selected accounts that occur between the selected dates.
Select Transactions	Click on this option button to select specific transactions to be included in the report. The Select Transactions dialog box appears (see Reports).

CREATING A FUTURE TRANSACTIONS REPORT

If you select Report ➤ Register Report from the Future Transactions window, Money will produce a Future Transactions Report. This report lists all the pending transactions. The Customize Future Transactions Report dialog box is similar to the Customize Register Report dialog box. The Subtotal by drop-down list box and the Cleared Flag check box are not included in this dialog box, but several options are added.

Number	The check number. Although the future transactions window doesn't show actual numbers, it will show the word "Print" if a check is going to be printed.
All	Click on this option button to see all pending transactions.
Payments	Click on this option button to see all pending payments.
Deposits	Click on this option button to see all pending deposits.

NOTES The transactions included in the Register Report are those currently displayed in the window—the ones selected from the View drop-down list box. In the Future Transactions Report, *all* pending transactions are included.

Unlike some of the other reports, the Register Report does not treat Transfers any differently from other categories.

SEE ALSO Lesson 8: Producing Reports; Reports

REPORT ➤ SUMMARY REPORT

The Summary Report shows the total of transactions for a specified group of transactions, such as all transactions with a certain payee, or all transactions in a specified category or classification. When you first display the report, it shows a list of payees, with the total of all the transactions for each payee, for the Year To Date.

CUSTOMIZING THE SUMMARY REPORT

Click on the Customize button. The Customize Summary Report dialog box appears.

Title	You can enter a new title for the report in this box.
Row for Every	Select what information you want on each row: Account, Payee, Category, Subcategory, Classification, Subclassification, Week, or Month.
Column for Every	Select the columns you want: None, Account, Payee, Category, Classification, Week, Two Weeks, Half Month, Month, Quarter, or Year. If you select None, the report will have a Total column only.
Display Shortcuts	Mark this check box to display shortcuts after the category and subcategory names. The payee, account, and classification shortcuts will *not* be displayed.

Dates	Indicate the dates of the transaction information to be included in the report by selecting All Dates (all the information in the account regardless of the date), Current Month, Current Year, Month to Date, Year to Date, Previous Month, Previous Year, Last 30 Days, or Last 12 Months. Or, enter a specific range of dates in the From and Two fields, in which case Money displays Custom Dates in the Dates text box.
From Account	Indicate the account or accounts that should be included in the report. You can select a single account by name, All Accounts, or Multiple Accounts. If you select Multiple Accounts the Select Accounts dialog box appears (see Reports).
All Transactions	Click on this option button if you want to include all transactions in the selected accounts that occur between the selected dates.
Select Transactions	Click on this option button to select specific transactions to be included in the report. The Select Transactions dialog box appears (see Reports).

Some of the Row choices are not compatible with some of the Column choices, of course. You could not select Account for the row and Account for the column, for instance, nor could you select two date options.

NOTES The Summary Report treats transfers as a payment or deposit. If you produce a Summary Report for just one account, transfers out of the account will appear as money spent, and transfers in will appear as deposits. If the Summary Report shows multiple accounts, of course, these transfers will cancel each other out as a transfer from one account shows up as a transfer *into* another.

SEE ALSO Lesson 8: Producing Reports; Reports

R

REPORT ➤ TAX REPORT

The Tax Report shows the total transactions for tax-related categories. You could produce a report that lists the tax-related categories and shows how much was spent or received in each category in each of your accounts.

CUSTOMIZING THE TAX REPORT

Click on the Customize button. The Customize Tax Report dialog box appears.

Title	You can enter a new title for the report in this box.
Tax Summary	Select this option to see the transactions totaled by category or subcategory.
Tax Transactions	Select this option to include individual tax-report transactions, grouped by category or subcategory.
Row for Every/ Subtotal By	If you selected the Tax Summary option, this drop-down list box is labeled Row for Every. You can opt to list all the subcategories or just categories. If you selected the Tax Transactions, the list box is labeled Subtotal By. You can opt to group and subtotal the transactions by category or subcategory.
Column for Every	If you selected the Tax Summary option this drop-down list box appears. Select what columns you want to display: None (meaning only a Total column), Account, Payee, or Category.
Display Shortcuts	If you select the Tax Summary option, the Display Shortcuts check box is displayed. If you mark this check box, the category and subcategory shortcuts will be included in parentheses. The payee, account, and classification shortcuts will *not* be displayed.

Dates	Indicate the dates of the transaction information to be included in the report by selecting All Dates (all the information in the account regardless of the date), Current Month, Current Year, Month to Date, Year to Date, Previous Month, Previous Year, Last 30 Days, or Last 12 Months. Or, enter a specific range of dates in the From and Two fields in which case Money displays Custom Dates in the Dates check box.
From Account	Indicate the account or accounts that should be included in the report. You can select a single account by name, All Accounts, or Multiple Accounts. If you select Multiple Accounts the Select Accounts dialog box appears (see Reports).
All Transactions	Click on this option button to include all transactions in the selected accounts that occur between the selected dates.
Select Transactions	Click on this option button to select specific transactions to be included in the report. The Select Transactions dialog box appears (see Reports).

CAUTION The Tax Report should be used with great care. It totals your taxable income and tax-deductible expenses, and then subtracts the expenses from the income, producing a figure that might at first glance appear to be the Adjusted Gross Income. It isn't, however, because different expenses are deductible to different degrees. For example, you may not have enough deductions to itemize them. Money does not calculate the actual *allowable* deductions from your income; it merely subtracts tax-deductible expenses from taxable income.

The Tax Report can give you useful information if you understand your taxes. The totals shown on the report should generally be ignored, and the individual category information used independently.

NOTES In order to be included in a Tax Report, a category must be defined as a Tax-Report-related category. This is done by selecting the "Include on Tax Reports" check box in the Category List dialog box. See List ➤ Category List for more information.

Categories that are taxable income (such as salary or investment income) or tax deductible expenses (such as mortgage interest or business expenses) should be set up as tax-report categories if you intend to produce Tax Reports.

You can export the Tax Report to any tax program that accepts ASCII files. You might want to use the tax program's category codes as shortcuts for each of the tax categories. Then, when you export the file, include the shortcuts by clicking on the Display Shortcuts check box. See your tax program documentation for more information.

SEE ALSO Lesson 8: Producing Reports; List ➤ Category List; Reports

STARTING MONEY

There are several ways to start Money. You can open Money and Windows at the same time, or open Money after you have opened Windows. You can also make Windows open Money automatically for you.

OPENING MONEY FROM DOS

To open Money from DOS:

- Type **C:\MSMONEY\MSMONEY** and press ↵.

Both Windows and Money will open. If you have entered any Run= or Load= commands in WIN.INI, those programs will also be opened.

To open Money along with a specific file:

- Type **C:\MSMONEY\MSMONEY C:*directory**filename*.MNY** and press ↵.

OPENING MONEY INSIDE WINDOWS

You can open Money in one of several ways:

- Double-click on the Microsoft Money icon.
- Select File ➤ Run from the Program Manager and type **C:\MSMONEY\MSMONEY**. You can also open Money with a specific file by adding the file name after the program name in the command line, such as **C:\MSMONEY\MSMONEY C:\TEMP\RENTALS.MNY**.
- Start the File Manager, display the MSMONEY directory, and double-click on MSMONEY.EXE or on any .MNY file. (See Notes.)
- Modify the Load= or Run= lines at the beginning of the WIN.INI file to instruct MSMONEY to open each time you start Windows. If you add **c:\msmoney\msmoney.exe** to the Load= line, Money will load as an icon when you open Windows. If you add **c:\msmoney\msmoney.exe** to the Run= line, Money will load as a window.

NOTES Money will only run in Windows' Standard or 386 Enhanced mode.

You could create batch files to open Money with various files. For example, if you create a batch file called Rent (in your root directory) with the line **C:\MSMONEY**

MSMONEY C:\MSMONEY\ RENTALS.MNY, you can just type RENT at the DOS prompt and press ↵ whenever you want to work on the file called RENTALS.

If you enter the line **MNY=c:\msmoney\msmoney.exe ^.MNY** in the WIN.INI file, you can click on a .MNY file *anywhere*, regardless of the directory it is in and open Money. To make this change, select File ➤ Run from the Program Manager. Type **WIN.INI** and press ↵. When Notepad opens, select Search ➤ Find and type MNY. Press ↵ and Notepad will move the cursor to the MNY line. Make the changes and press Alt-F4 to close Notepad.

SEE ALSO Lesson 2: Entering Transactions

TOOLBAR ICON BUTTONS

The Money window Toolbar, the gray strip immediately below the menu bar, contains several buttons with icons on them. You can click on these icon buttons to carry out commands. All the icon buttons have corresponding menu commands; clicking on the buttons is simply an alternative method for selecting the commands.

THE ICON BUTTONS

These are the icons and their associated commands:

Options ➤ Entire Transaction View

Options ➤ Top Line View

Edit ➤ Find

Options ➤ Calculator

Edit ➤ Split Transaction

Edit ➤ Schedule in Future

Options ➤ Balance Account

Options ➤ Enter from Schedule*

*Future transactions window only

SEE ALSO The individual commands that the icon buttons replace.

VIEW DROP-DOWN LIST BOX

The View drop-down list box is used to select which types of transactions will be displayed in the window. It is found in the middle of the Toolbar in the Account Book and Checks & Forms windows, and on the left side of the Toolbar in the Future Transactions window.

The Account drop-down list box is used to determine which accounts will provide information. The View drop-down list box is used to select the types of transactions that will be used from those accounts.

Keyboard Alt-V to open the list box; Ctrl-O to open the Other View dialog box

NOTES When you exclude some transactions from a view, the Ending Balance field at the bottom of the window is renamed Total.

When you view transactions sorted by category, each part of a split transaction is displayed *as a separate transaction*. In other words, a transaction split into three categories will appear in three different places in the list.

SEE ALSO Lesson 4: Viewing Different Accounts and Transactions

WINDOW ➤ ACCOUNT BOOK

The Account Book window lets you enter transactions into a window that looks like an account or checkbook register. You can select the type of transactions that you want to display, the order in which they are shown, and the accounts from which they came.

DISPLAYING THE ACCOUNT BOOK WINDOW

You can display the Account Book window by one of the following methods:

- Select Window ➤ Account Book
- Double-click on the Account Book icon, if it is visible
- Press and hold the Ctrl key while you press Esc once or twice

Account drop-down list box	Lets you select the accounts you want to display
View drop-down list box	Lets you select the type of transactions you want to display
Toolbar icon buttons	Shortcut buttons that duplicate several menu options
Num column	Enter a transaction's check number or some kind of notation in the Num column
Date column	Enter a transaction's date in the Date column
Payee/Memo/Category column	Contains each transaction's payee, memo, category, subcategory, classification item, and subitem fields
C	This column indicates whether the transaction has been cleared (C) or reconciled against a bank statement (R)

Payment	The amount of a payment transaction; the column title changes depending on the type of account displayed: Checking account—Payment; Credit account—Charge; Cash or multiple accounts—Spend; Asset account—Decrease; Liability account—Increase
Deposit	The amount of a deposit transaction; the column title actually changes depending on the type of account displayed: Checking account—Deposit; Credit account—Credit; Cash or multiple accounts—Receive; Asset account—Increase; Liability account—Decrease
Balance	The balance in the account at each transaction or the total balance of the multiple accounts at each transaction
Ending Balance	The current balance in the account; if you used the View drop-down list box to select specific transactions, the Ending Balance box is labeled Total

CHANGING THE WINDOW DISPLAY

You can display the Account Book window in Top Line View, which shows only the first line of each transaction, or Entire Transaction View, which displays all three, four, or five lines of each transaction. To change the view. Select Options ➤ Entire Transaction View or Options ➤ Top Line View, or press Ctrl-T to toggle between the views.

SEE ALSO Account Drop-Down List Box; Entering Transactions; Toolbar Icon Buttons; View Drop-Down List Box; Window ➤ Checks & Forms; Window ➤ Future Transactions

WINDOW ➤ CHECKS & FORMS

The Checks & Forms window provides a user interface that is similar to paper forms, such as checks and deposit slips.

DISPLAYING THE CHECKS & FORMS WINDOW

You can display the Checks & Forms window in one of the following ways:

- Select Window ➤ Checks & Forms
- Double-click on the Checks & Forms icon (if it is visible)
- Press and hold Ctrl while you press Esc once or twice

Account drop-down list box	Lets you select the accounts you want to display
View drop-down list box	Lets you select the type of transactions you want to display
Toolbar icon buttons	Shortcut buttons that duplicate several menu options
Form Buttons	Clicking on a button displays a form for that type of transaction. The available buttons depend on the account type selected from the Account drop-down list box. *Bank account:* Check, Deposit, Payment, Transfer *Credit card account:* Charge, Credit, Transfer *Cash account:* Receive, Spend, Transfer *Asset account:* Increase, Decrease, Transfer *Liability account:* Increase, Decrease, Transfer

The window's components depend upon which form is displayed. The fields in the forms are the same as the Account Book window fields, only rearranged to replicate a transaction form, such as a check or a deposit slip.

NOTES Entering transactions into a form in the Checks & Forms window is much the same as entering it into the Account Book. The keys work in the same way; the fields are just in different positions. SmartFill and SuperSmartFill work the same as well.

The Checks & Forms window does not indicate whether a transaction has been cleared or reconciled. Go to the Account Book window and look at the C column.

The Checks & Forms window is linked to the Account Book window. Selecting another option from the Account or View drop-down list boxes in one of the windows changes the setting in the other. Also, the Checks & Forms window always displays the transaction that is selected in the Account Book window. And clearing a form in the Checks & Forms window moves the highlight in the Account Book window to the first blank entry.

SEE ALSO Lesson 4: Viewing Different Files and Transactions; Account Drop-Down List Box; Account Types; Entering Transactions; Toolbar Icon Buttons; View Drop-Down List Box; Window ➤ Account Book; Window ➤ Future Transactions

WINDOW ➤ FUTURE TRANSACTIONS

The Future Transactions window contains a list of transactions that have been scheduled for a later date. Some entries are one-time transactions; others occur at regular intervals, such as once a month or once a week.

When you want to process the transactions, you can use the Options ➤ Pay Bills or Edit ➤ Enter from Schedule commands to automatically enter the transactions into the appropriate accounts.

DISPLAYING THE FUTURE TRANSACTIONS WINDOW

There are several ways to display the Future Transactions window:

- Select Window ➤ Future Transactions
- Double-click on the Future Transactions icon (if it is visible)
- Press and hold Ctrl while you press Esc once or twice

CHANGING THE WINDOW DISPLAY

You can view this window in Top Line View, which shows only the first line of each transaction, or Entire Transaction View, which displays every line of each transaction.

You can change the view mode by selecting Options ➤ Entire Transaction View or Options ➤ Top Line View, or by pressing Ctrl-T to toggle between the two views. The various components of the window are:

View drop-down list box	Lets you select whether to display the transactions in chronological order or grouped according to the payee
Toolbar icon buttons	Shortcut buttons that duplicate several menu options
Date	The next date of the transaction; the field may be left blank
Freq/Acct	The frequency of the transaction (Weekly, Monthly, Only Once, etc.), and the account to which the transaction should be posted; the field may be left blank
Num	This field is either blank or contains the word **print** to indicate that the transaction should be printed; you cannot enter a code indicating the transaction type or an actual check number
Payee/Memo/Category	This column contains each transaction's payee, memo, category, and subcategory fields; if you have created classifications it also includes the classification item and sub-item fields
Payment	The amount of a payment transaction goes in this column
Deposit	The amount of a deposit transaction goes in this column

If you leave the Date field empty for a transaction, that transaction will be ignored by the Options ➤ Pay Bills command—you must use the Edit ➤ Enter from Schedule command to process the transaction.

SEE ALSO Lesson 6: Entering Future Transactions and Paying Bills; Account Drop-Down List Box; Edit ➤ Schedule in Future; Edit ➤ Enter from Schedule; Entering Transactions; Options ➤ Pay Bills; Toolbar Icon Buttons; View Drop-Down List Box; Window ➤ Account Book; Window ➤ Checks & Forms

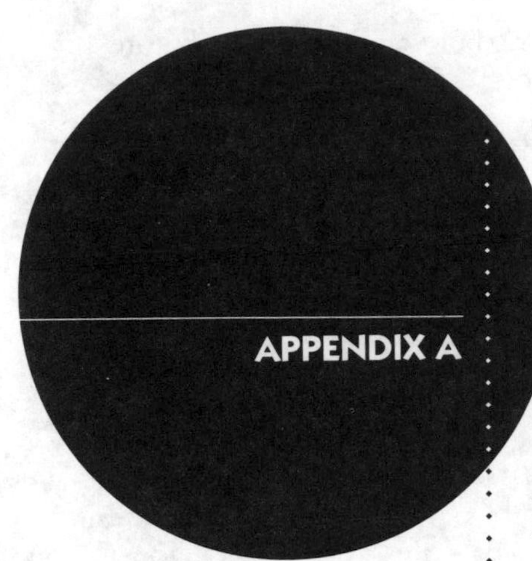

APPENDIX A

Setting Up Your Payroll

Money doesn't have a dedicated payroll system, but you can use the Future Transactions window to create a very simple system.

CREATING THE CATEGORIES

Money has a predefined Payroll category with the following subcategories:

Bonus

Commissions

Federal W/H

FICA W/H

Overtime

Salaries & Wages

State W/H

You may want to create your own categories though. If you have a single category for the Withholding subcategories, you will find it easier to produce a witholding Report later. You could even create two categories: **Payroll-To Employee** with the Salaries & Wages, Bonus, Commissions, and Overtime, and **Payroll-Withheld**, with the Federal, FICA, and State Withholding.

ENTERING THE FIRST PAYMENT

Enter the first payment into the Account Book window or the Checks & Forms window.

1. Place the highlight on the blank entry in the Account Window, or click on the Check button in the Checks & Forms window.
2. Press Ctrl-S to display the Split Transactions dialog box.
3. Enter the pay categories; select the categories, enter descriptions, and enter the full amount owed, *before* withholding.
4. Next, enter the withholding categories. Select the categories, enter descriptions, and enter the withholding amounts in parentheses as negative numbers. See Figure A.1 for an example.
5. Click on Done to close the Split Transactions dialog box.

FIGURE A.1:
Sample payroll entries in the Split Transaction dialog box

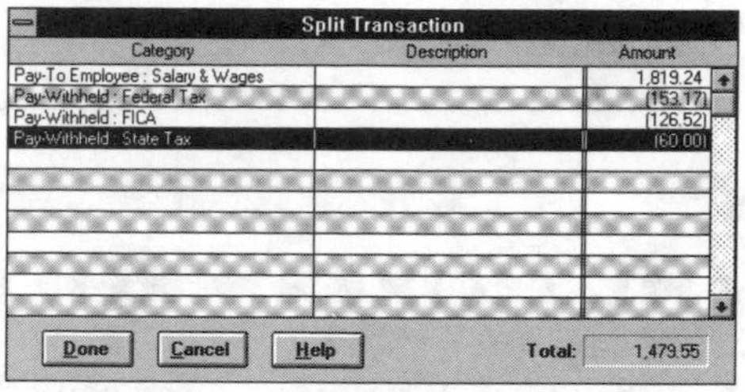

6. When the Spend or Receive dialog box appears, click on the Spend option button and click on OK. The amount of money that should be paid to the employee (the total pay minus the witholdings) is shown in the Payment column.

CREATING THE FUTURE PAYMENTS

You have just entered a payroll transaction. Now you can schedule this transaction and similar ones as future transactions.

1. With the highlight on the entry, press Ctrl-E. The Schedule Future Transaction dialog box appears.
2. Select the payment period, such as BiWeekly or Monthly.
3. Enter the date of the next transaction.
4. Click on OK. The transaction is entered as a future transaction.
5. Repeat steps 1 to 4 for each employee.
6. When you have finished, select Window ➤ Future Transactions. The Future Transactions window appears. Notice that all of the future transactions entries have the same name.
7. Change the names of the future transaction, so that you have one scheduled transaction for each employee.
8. Where necessary, edit the amounts in the Split Transaction dialog box for each employee.

PAYING YOUR EMPLOYEES

Now, each time you have to pay your employees, you can use the Options ➤ Pay Bills command. In some cases, you may have to modify the numbers slightly—when an employee has overtime or a bonus, for example. You can do this easily in the Enter Scheduled Transactions dialog box. See Lesson 6 and Options ➤ Pay Bills for more information about scheduling future transactions and paying bills.

PAYING THE GOVERNMENT

How does Money track your payroll? You could think of it this way: you paid the employee the entire salary amount, but the employee immediately repaid a portion of that amount in the form of withholding. The positive number in the Split Transaction dialog box was the amount owed to the employee by you. The negative numbers are the amount owed by the employee to the government, and that you, as the government's agent, must hold to pass on to the government at a later date.

Of course, the withheld money hasn't actually gone anywhere; it's still in your account. But the withholding categories will show negative numbers. Create a Summary Report and customize it so that each row shows a subcategory. Click on the Select Transactions option in the Customize Summary Report dialog box, and then select the payroll withholding categories only. Now, when you view the report, you will see the amounts that have been withheld from your employees and placed back into your account. Figure A.2 shows an example of a Summary report. The numbers in parentheses are, of course, negative.

You clear the totals for each category by writing a check to the various government bodies for an amount equal to the negative amount. When you write these checks, assign them to the same payroll withholding categories. The amounts will balance out the negative numbers created when you withheld the money from your employees.

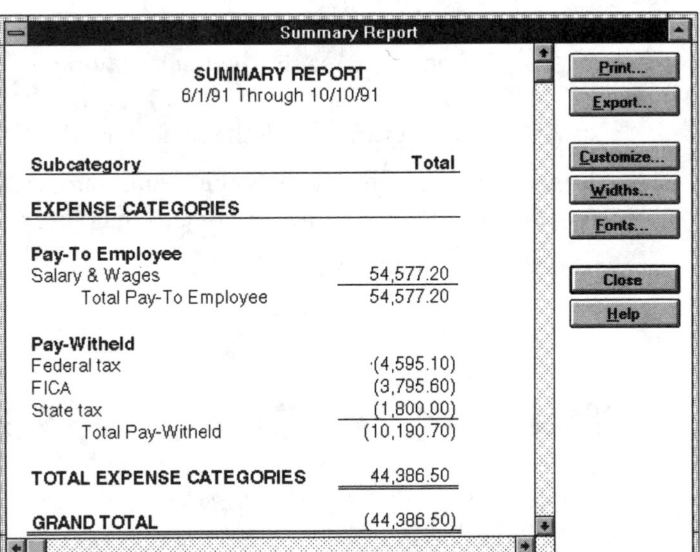

FIGURE A.2:

A Summary Report showing the payroll witholding categories

Doesn't this mean that "at the end of the day" your accounts will show that you haven't paid the government any withholding? Correct. But you didn't pay the government any withholding—your employees did, it was their money that you simply held for a while before passing it onto the government. The money will appear instead in the pay categories from which it was deducted—Salaries & Wages, Bonus, Commissions, and so on. Of course, you will still have the payments to those various government bodies recorded if you need to check the information—you can search for the payee name, or display the payee using the View drop-down list box.

Don't mix money **you** *owe to the government in the same categories as those recording withholdings. For example, if you have employees, you have to withhold FICA for them, but you also have to pay the government your own FICA amount. You should set up* **two** *categories for FICA—one for FICA withheld from your employees, and one for FICA paid by you.*

If you pay your employees twice a month, the check totals may vary slightly. Just enter two future transactions for each person and schedule each one monthly.

CREATING A PAYROLL REPORT

You can produce a payroll report showing the earnings and withholding for each employee. Use the Summary report; customize it to display a row for each Payee (the employees) and a column for each category. Then select only the relevant transactions—the transactions assigned to the payroll categories. The report will contain one line per employee, with columns showing each deduction and payment.

Questions and Answers

The questions in this section cover the following topics:

QUESTION	TOPIC
1	Removing old information from accounts
2	Payments to credit card accounts
3	Transferring transactions to another account
4	Merging categories and changing the category to which several transactions are assigned
5	Cash withdrawals
6	Bounced checks
7	Double-entry vs. Single-entry bookkeeping
8	Moving money between personal and business accounts
9	Single deposits from several sources
10	Categorizing paychecks
11	Tracking reimbursable business expenses
12	Merging files and accounts
13	Accounts Payable and Accounts Receivable
14	Checks from credit card accounts
15	Tracking car loans and mortgages
16	Debit cards
17	Printing reconciliation reports

1. It's January and I want to remove last year's information from the file. How do I do that?

Use the File ➤ Archive command to make a backup of the file you are currently working with and remove the transactions that occurred before a specified date. You may want to wait a couple of months until all of the previous year's transactions have been reconciled against your account statements; the archive process only removes reconciled transactions. However, the backup copy contains *all* of the transactions, not just reconciled ones. Remember that you will need the archived information for your tax returns and can restore the archived files when needed.

2. **How do I categorize a payment to my credit card account?**

   Categorize them as *transfers* to the credit card account. You should categorize the individual transactions in the credit card account according to the type of purchase, but the check you send to the credit card company is simply a transfer to your credit card account to reduce the account balance.

3. **I've just entered 15 transactions *in the wrong account*! What can I do?**

   Go to the Account Book window. Select Multiple Accounts from the Account drop-down list box. Select the account you entered the transactions into, and the account you *should have* entered them into. Turn on Options ➤ Entire Transaction View. Now click on the Account Name field in each of the incorrect entries, and select the other account name. The transaction is automatically transferred to that account. Or just select the account for the *first* transaction, and each time you place the cursor in the account field in subsequent transactions press Shift-" (quotation mark) to enter the same information.

   You can merge accounts and files using the File ➤ Import and File ➤ Export commands. See question 12 in this appendix.

4. **I assigned a number of transactions to the wrong categories. How do I move them to the correct ones?**

   You can use a similar method to the one just described for transferring transactions to other accounts. Start by displaying only the transactions you want to work on—select A Category from the View drop-down list box and select the category to which you mistakenly assigned the transactions. Then change the selected category for each one (after the first one use the Shift-" shortcut to copy the same information into subsequent fields).

   There's also a quicker method that you can use if you want to transfer *all* the transactions from one category into another. Display the Category list (List ➤ Category List), click on the category from which you want to move the transactions, and click on the Delete button. Money will warn you that you have transactions assigned to that category. Click on the OK button and Money will then let you transfer the transactions to another category. When you have finished you can recreate the deleted category if you still need it.

5. **How do I categorize a cash withdrawal, such as from a cash machine?**

   That depends what you plan to do with the money. If, for example, you have a petty cash account for your business—or a personal Cash account if the money is for personal use—categorize the transaction as a transfer to the Cash account. If you don't bother with Cash accounts and the money is for general use, maybe you should create a category called Cash. Or if the withdrawal is for a specific purpose—to buy a specific item—categorize the withdrawal according to the purpose you are going to make.

6. **I deposited a check in my account, and that check turned up on my statement the following month. But then the check was returned unpaid, and the next month my statement showed a charge to my account for that amount. How do I handle this?**

   Don't go back and change the original deposit—don't remove it, or change the value, or change its reconciliation status. This will mess up your account balance, and the next time you try to reconcile the account, you will have innumerable problems. Besides, if you remove the deposit, your account reports won't show correct information.

   Instead, enter a new Payment transaction for the returned check. Use the same payee name, and enter a memo indicating the purpose of the transaction as deducting the previous deposit amount. Assign the transaction to exactly the same category as the original check in order to keep category and budget information correct.

7. **I've heard about double-entry and single-entry bookkeeping. Which system does Money use?**

   Money uses a single-entry bookkeeping system. Double-entry bookkeeping is a process that requires an accounting course to understand. In double-entry bookkeeping, each transaction must be entered *twice*, once as a "debit" entry and once as a "credit" entry. It's a complicated system that is unnecessary for personal finances and for most small businesses. If you are using Money to keep your business's books, you probably don't need double-entry bookkeeping.

8. **I have a small business and have a separate bank account for the business. I take money out of that bank account for personal use, and must sometimes transfer money to the account for business use. How do I categorize these transactions?**

   If you are a sole proprietor—that is, if your business is not incorporated—you and the business are the same tax entity. Your business profit or loss is *your* profit or loss, and business assets and debts are *your* assets and debts. Money deducted from or added to your business is simply transferred from one account to another and should be categorized as such.

   If your business is incorporated, the story is very different. You and your business are different tax entities, and the finances of each must be kept separate. If you take money from the business, it must be categorized as a loan, a dividend, or some form of employee compensation. If you put money into the business, it must be categorized as a loan or as some type of stock purchase. Talk to an accountant or tax advisor.

9. **What do I do when I send several checks to my bank? They appear on my statement as one deposit, but I want to be able to break them down in my account.**

   Enter the deposit as a single transaction, but use the Split Transactions dialog box to categorize each check individually. You can use the Memo line in the Split Transactions dialog box to indicate the source of each of the checks.

10. **How can I categorize a paycheck? The money I'm paid goes several different places.**

    Enter the date, payee information, and deposit amount. Then press Ctrl-S or select Edit ➤ Split Transaction. On the first line of the Split Transaction box, select the Wages & Salary category and the Gross Pay subcategory. Then type the amount of your gross pay (that is, type the total pay *before* deductions for FICA, federal tax, savings plans, and so on) in the Deposit field. When you enter the Split Transactions dialog box, there will already be a number in this field, the amount you entered in the deposit. Type over this value with the gross pay amount.

    Then, on the next line, enter the first deduction. For example, select the Taxes category and Social Security Tax subcategory. Then enter the amount paid in the amount field, but enter the sum as a negative number by typing –100 or (100). Continue in this manner, entering all of the deductions. If some of the deductions are placed in a savings plan, enter that line as a transfer to an Asset account.

    Notice that after you enter your gross pay, the unassigned amount changes to show the gross pay minus your net pay. The unassigned amount must be 0 before you leave the Split Transactions dialog box.

11. **I have business-related expenses that I pay for in a variety of ways: cash, checks, credit cards. I can claim this money back from my employer, but I lose track of a lot of it. What's a good way to keep account of these expenses?**

    Set up an asset account for your expenses. Then, each time you spend money for your employer, enter the transaction as a transfer to the expense account. When your employer reimburses you, enter the sum in the account in which you deposit the check, but show it as a transfer *from* the expense account. As long as your employer owes you money, it will appear as an asset, a positive number in the asset account. When your employer pays you a check, the balance in the asset account will be reduced.

When your employer pays you, mark the appropriate expenses as reconciled (Shift-Ctrl-M). You can then use the View drop-down list box to see the unreconciled items in that account, that is, the expenses for which you have not yet been reimbursed. Or print a customized Register report to show only the unreconciled items.

12. I created two files, and now realize that I should have kept all the information in one. How can I merge the two?

Use the File ➤ Export command. You can only export one account at a time. So open the file with the fewest accounts and export each one into a separate .QIF file. Make sure that the Strict .QIF Compatibility check box is turned *off*, so that the payee and category names are not cut down to 15 characters. Then open the other file and create an account for each one that you intend to import. Import the .QIF files one by one, placing them in the new accounts you created. You can even use this method to merge two accounts in the same file, exporting one account and reimporting it into the same file, but placing it in the other account.

Some information is lost when you export, by the way. You will lose addresses, comments, budget amounts, bank names, account numbers, and shortcuts. If you use a lot of payee shortcuts, or print a lot of checks with addresses, that could cause a real problem. It's much easier to make sure you set up your files correctly in the first place, so you won't need to merge them.

13. What's the best way to handle Accounts Payable and Accounts Receivable for my small business?

Accounts Payable refers to money that you owe someone else. Accounts Receivable is the oppposite—money someone else owes you.

Create a liability account called Accounts Payable. Each time you make a purchase on credit, enter the transaction into the Accounts Payable account as an Increase, since your debt is increasing. Categorize the transaction according to its type, such as Office Supplies or Business Services. When you make a payment to your supplier, enter the transaction as a transfer from your checking account to the Accounts Payable account. The transfer will show up as a *decrease* in the Accounts Payable account.

Create an asset account called Accounts Receivable. When you sell someone something on credit, it should go into the account as an increase. When they pay you what they owe, enter the transaction as a transfer *from* the Accounts Receivable account into your checking account—a decrease in the Accounts Receivable.

One advantage of creating these accounts is that you can use the Summary report to produce a list of who you owe and who owes you. And if you want to find out about a particular creditor or lender, you can use the View drop-down list box to display just those transactions.

14. My credit card (or money market or loan account) provides me with checks. How do I enter transactions when I use them?

No matter what form you receive money in from these accounts, the transactions are entered in the same way. In a credit card account, you should still enter a check as a charge. In a money market account, it would be entered as a Decrease since you are taking money out of the account. In a loan account, a check would be entered as an Increase because you are increasing your debt. You *cannot* print checks from these accounts, by the way, only from checking accounts.

15. How can I track my car loan? How about tracking my mortgage?

Part of a loan payment pays principal, part pays interest. You could set up a loan account, beginning with the current loan balance. When you make a payment, split the transaction; assign part of it to a category such as Interest Expense:Personal Interest and assign the rest as a transfer to the car loan, reducing the balance. How do you know how much is interest and how much is principal? Your lender should give you a schedule showing each payment, or a monthly statement.

The mortgage payment should also be split. Categorize one part as interest expense, one part as a transfer to an escrow account, and another part as a transfer to your mortgage loan account. Remember to adjust the escrow account when you receive a statement from your lender to show the insurance and tax payments.

16. My checking account provides me with a credit card. When I make a purchase the money is removed from my checking account as soon as the bank receives the transaction. Do I have to create a separate credit card account for this card?

No, because it's not a *credit* card, but actually a *debit* card. A credit card is one which allows you to make purchases and pay the balance later, in one or many payments. The bank issuing the card pays for the purchases, based on the agreement that you will pay them later. Debit cards may look like credit cards, but if the money is removed from your account as soon as the transaction reaches your bank, *you* are paying for the purchases, not the bank. The debit card works like a plastic check. *Don't* create a credit card account for these cards; just enter the transaction like a check. You may want to type a code in the Num column, such as Dcard, so you can identify which transactions are related to the card.

17. I would like to print a reconciliation report each time I balance my checking account. How do I do this?

When you have finished balancing your account—but before you click the Finish button—select Report ➤ Register Report. The register report will only include the transactions that are displayed in the Balance window, and will have a C column to indicate the transactions that you marked as cleared. Money will make you postpone the balancing procedure when you print the report, so you should select Option ➤ Balance Account again to continue balancing the account.

INDEX

A

Account Balance dialog box, 98
Account Book window, 6, 8–9
  opening, 19–20
  transactions in, 21–26, 199–200
Account Didn't Balance dialog box, 102–103
Account List dialog box, 13–14, 80
Account List Report dialog box, 157
accounts
  account numbers for, 13–14, 154–155
  balancing, 98–105, 130, 167, 218
  creating, 4–6, 12–15, 27–29, 155–157
  deleting, 15, 29, 154, 156
  drop-down lists for, 9, 199, 201
  editing, 13–14, 157
  exporting, 146–148, 216
  for future transactions, 203
  importing, 148–150
  listing, 13–14, 80, 154–155, 157
  multiple, 26–27, 76, 177
  number of, 10
  printing, 76
  renaming, 15, 154, 156–157
  for reports, 85, 184–187, 189, 191, 193
  selecting, 21, 26–27, 76, 146, 176–177
  for transactions, 21, 135, 213
  types of, 13, 117–120
accounts payable and receivable, 216–217
addresses
  on checks, 50, 74
  for payees, 42, 164
Adjust Account Balance dialog box, 167
Adjust Split dialog box, 60
Alternate Register Navigation option, 122, 141
amounts
  for reports, 188
  with split transactions, 58–61
  SuperSmartFill for, 25
  viewing transactions by, 180
Archive dialog box, 142
archive files, 142–144, 212
arrow keys in fields, 136
ASCII files, 90–91, 146–148, 182, 194
asset accounts, 13, 55, 113, 118–119
automatic backups, 143–144
Automatically Drop Lists option, 24, 122

B

Backup dialog box, 11–12, 15, 142–143
backup files, 11, 142–143, 212
Balance Account dialog box, 99–100
Balance window, 100
balances
  in Check form, 52
  for credit cards, 14
  with transactions, 20, 71, 200
balancing checkbooks, 97–105, 130, 167, 218
bank accounts, 13, 54, 117
bank names for accounts, 13–14, 154–155
beeping, 141
braces ({ }) with printing, 75, 138
Budget Report dialog box, 110, 112, 183
budgets, 107
  for categories, 35, 108–110, 159, 161
  reports for, 80, 110–113, 183–184
  for subcategories, 38, 108–110
businesses
  accounts for, 214–215
  categories for, 33–34
  files for, 10

C

calculator, Windows', 61–62, 167–170
Calculator Entry option, 122, 137
cancelling transaction entries, 25, 141
car loans, 217
cash accounts, 13, 118
  forms for, 54
  transactions in, 18, 213–214
categories, 31
  budgets for, 35, 38, 108–110, 159, 161
  in Check form, 52
  creating, 28–29, 36–38, 140, 159–160
  deleting, 35–36, 158, 160
  editing, 35, 161
  listing, 32–34, 80, 82, 108, 158–159, 161, 193
  for payroll, 206
  printing, 38
  renaming, 34–35, 159–160
  for reports, 187–188
  selecting, 4, 47–50, 113, 140
  SuperSmartFill for, 25
  tax-related, 35, 37–38, 159, 161, 193–194
  for transactions, 20, 23–24, 57–62, 135, 199, 203
  viewing transactions by, 46, 178–179
Category List dialog box, 32, 80, 108, 193
Category List Report dialog box, 161
Check form, 51–52
check numbers
  in Check form, 51–52
  printing, 77
  for reports, 189
  for transactions, 19, 21, 71, 134, 137, 147, 199, 203
  in Transfer form, 54
  viewing transactions by, 46, 180
checkbooks, reconciling, 97–105, 130, 167, 218
checking accounts, creating, 5–6
checks
  addresses on, 50
  printing, 73–78, 151–152
  returned, 214
Checks & Forms window, 50–55, 201–202
Classification List dialog box, 40, 80, 162
Classification List Report dialog box, 163
classifications, 38–39
  in Check form, 52
  creating, 39–41, 140
  deleting, 40, 162
  editing, 40, 163
  listing, 40, 80, 162–163
  renaming, 40, 162–163
  for reports, 187–188
  selecting, 47–48, 50
  for transactions, 58, 135
  viewing transactions by, 47, 179
clipboard, 28, 127, 130
closing Money, 15, 145
collating reports, 90, 181
color settings, 122–123
columns for reports, 84–85, 87, 180, 183, 185, 190, 192
commands, icons for, 9, 197, 199, 201
comments
  for accounts, 13–14, 154–155
  for categories, 35, 158–159
  for payees, 42, 165
  for subcategories, 38
Confirm Printing dialog box, 77
Confirmation option, 123
confirmations
  for printing, 77
  for transactions, 123, 141
context-sensitive help, 153
Control menus, 6, 8
Control Panel, 75, 121
copies, report, 90, 181
copying
  calculator results, 62, 169–170
  text, 28, 127
  transaction information, 24–25, 139–140, 163
corporations, 214–215
Create First Account dialog box, 14
Create New Account dialog box, 4, 6, 27, 155, 157
Create New Category dialog box, 36–37, 159
Create New Subcategory dialog box, 160

creating
accounts, 4–6, 12–15, 27–29, 155–157
categories, 28–29, 36–38, 140, 159–160
classifications, 39–41, 140
files, 11–12, 150
credit card accounts, 13, 117–118
creating, 14
forms for, 54
transactions in, 18, 213, 215–217
currency formats, 125
cursor for transactions, 136
Custom Budget dialog box, 109
Customize Account List Report dialog box, 157
Customize Budget Report dialog box, 112, 183
Customize Category List Report dialog box, 161
Customize Classification List Report dialog box, 163
Customize Future Transaction Report dialog box, 189
Customize Income and Expense Report dialog box, 184
Customize Net Worth Report dialog box, 186
Customize Payee List dialog box, 165
Customize Register Report dialog box, 187
Customize Summary Report dialog box, 84, 190, 208
Customize Tax Report dialog box, 192
customizing, 121
budgets, 109
date and number formats, 124–126
reports, 84–85, 176–181, 183–194
Settings dialog box for, 122–124
cutting text, 28, 127

D

dates
in Check form, 51–52
formats for, 124–125
for reports, 85, 183, 185, 188, 191, 193
SuperSmartFill for, 25
for transactions, 19–22, 67–71, 134, 137–138, 147, 199, 203
viewing transactions by, 46, 179
debit cards, 217–218
decimal places and separators, 125, 137
Default Preferences dialog box, 92
default printer, 75, 89, 181
Delete Category dialog box, 35–36, 160
Delete Classification dialog box, 162
Delete Transaction dialog box, 36
deleting
accounts, 15, 29, 154, 156
categories, 35–36, 158, 160
classifications, 40, 162
payees, 42, 164–165
transactions, 28, 36, 127, 134
Deposit form, 53
deposits, 215
for reports, 189
for transactions, 20, 22, 135, 200, 203
Destination Path dialog box, 4
directories, 4, 11
Display-Type Size option, 123
document-window icons, 7
DOS, starting Money from, 195
double-entry bookkeeping, 214
drives for files, 11
drop-down lists, 9, 24, 41, 46, 122, 138–139, 198–199, 201

E

Edit/Copy command, 28, 62, 127, 133–134, 169–170
Edit/Cut command, 28, 127, 133–134
Edit/Delete Transaction command, 28, 127, 134
Edit/Enter from Schedule command, 127–128, 173, 202
Edit/Find command, 9, 128–129, 197
Edit/Mark as Cleared command, 129–130
Edit/Mark as Uncleared command, 130
Edit/Mark as Unreconciled command, 130
Edit/Paste command, 28, 62, 130–131, 133–134, 170

Edit/Schedule in Future command, 9, 67, 131, 197
Edit/Split Transaction command, 9, 58, 131–132, 197
Edit/Undo command, 28, 132–134, 141
Edit/Unvoid Transaction command, 132–133
Edit/Void Transaction command, 28, 133
editing
  accounts, 13–14, 157
  budget reports, 111–112, 183–184
  categories, 35, 161
  classifications, 40, 163
  payees, 165
  transactions, 28, 60, 133–134
End key, 23, 136, 139
Enter key, 23, 139, 141
Enter Scheduled Transactions dialog box, 70
entering transactions, 21–26, 134–141
Entire Transaction View, 20, 23, 170
Esc key, 25, 141
exiting Money, 145
expenses
  categories for, 32–33
  in reports, 80–81, 184–186
Export dialog box, 146, 182
exporting
  accounts, 146–148, 216
  reports, 90–91, 182

F

fields for transactions, 22–23, 134–136
File/Archive command, 142–143, 212
File/Backup command, 143–144
File/Exit command, 15, 145
File/Export command, 146–148, 216
File/Import command, 148–150
File/New command, 11, 150
File/Open command, 12, 144, 150–151
File/Print Checks command, 76, 151
File/Print Setup command, 75, 151–152
File/Run command, 4, 91, 196
File/Save command, 94
files, 10
  backup, 11, 142–144, 212
  creating, 11–12, 150
  importing and exporting, 146–150, 216
  merging, 148, 150, 216
  names for, 11, 94
  opening, 12, 144, 150–151
fonts, 88, 180–181
formats
  for dates, numbers, and currency, 124–126
  printer, 74
  Quicken, 146–150
future transactions, 202–204
  entering, 65–67, 172–173
  reports for, 80, 189–190
  scheduling, 67–71, 127, 131
Future Transactions window, 68–70, 172, 202–204

H

Help menu, 5, 153
Home key, 23, 136, 139

I

icons
  for commands, 9, 197, 199, 201
  document-window, 7
Import dialog box, 149
importing files, 148–150
income and expense reports, 80–81, 184–186
income categories, 32–33
installation, 3–4
International dialog box, 124
International option, 121
irregular transactions, 66

K

keyboard for transactions, 22–23

L

landscape orientation, 89, 181
laser printers, 74, 77
leading zeros, 125
liability accounts, 13, 55, 119–120
List/Account List command, 13, 154–157
List/Category List command, 32, 108, 158–161
List/Other Classification command, 39, 162–163
List/Payee List command, 41, 74, 163–166
listing
- accounts, 13–14, 80, 154–155, 157
- categories, 32–34, 80, 82, 108, 158–159, 161, 193
- classifications, 40, 80, 162–163
- payees, 41, 74, 163–166

loans, 217

M

Macro/Record command, 93
macros for reports, 91–95
marking transactions, 100–101, 129–130
maximize buttons, 7–8
memos
- in Check form, 51–52
- for reports, 187
- SuperSmartFill for, 25
- for transactions, 20, 135, 138, 147, 199, 203

merging files, 148, 150, 216
message bars, 7–8
minimize buttons, 7–8
minus signs (–), 25, 132, 137
Modify Classification Scheme dialog box, 163
Money window, 6–8
monthly budgets, 108
mortgages, 217
mouse
- with macros, 92, 94
- settings for, 122

MS Solution Series group window, 18
MSMONEY directory, 4, 145
MSMONEY.INI file, 145, 151
MSMONEY.MNY file, 10, 150
multiple accounts, 26–27, 76, 177
multiple categories, 49–50
multiple classifications, 50

N

names
- for accounts, 5, 15, 154–157
- for categories, 34–35, 159–160
- for classifications, 40, 162–163
- for files, 11, 94
- for macros, 93
- for payees, 22, 42, 164
- in title bars, 6

negative numbers, 125, 131–132
net worth reports, 80–82, 186
New Classification dialog box, 39–41
New dialog box, 11
New Password dialog box, 171
numbers
- formats for, 125
- in transactions, 137

O

on-line help, 153
Open dialog box, 12, 144, 150–151
opening
- Account Book window, 19–20
- files, 12, 144, 150–151
- Money, 4–6

Opening Balance dialog box, 14, 155
opening balances for accounts, 5, 13–14, 154–157
Options/Balance Account command, 9, 98, 130, 167, 197, 218
Options/Calculator command, 9, 61, 167–170, 197

Options/Enter from Schedule command, 9, 197
Options/Entire Transaction View command, 9, 23, 170, 197, 203
Options/Password command, 171–172
Options/Pay Bills command, 70, 172–173, 202, 207
Options/Preferences command, 92
Options/Settings command, 69, 122, 173
Options/Top Line View command, 9, 20, 173–174, 197, 203
orientation, printer, 89, 181
Other Classification dialog box, 39–41
Other View dialog box, 48–49

P

paper, 75, 89, 181
parentheses (), 125, 132
Password dialog box, 171–172
pasting text, 28, 130
paychecks, 215
Payee List, 41–43, 163–166
Payee List dialog box, 41–42, 80, 165
payees
- in Check form, 51–52
- listing, 41–43, 74, 80, 163–166
- renaming, 42, 164
- in reports, 94
- selecting, 47
- SmartFill for, 24–25, 139, 163
- for transactions, 20, 22, 135, 138, 147, 199, 203
- viewing transactions by, 46, 178

Payment form, 53
payments
- for reports, 189
- for transactions, 20, 22, 135, 200, 203

payroll reports, 206–209
phone numbers for payees, 42, 164–165
plus signs (+), 25, 137
portrait orientation, 89, 181
Possible Error dialog box, 103
Print Checks dialog box, 76–77
Print Report dialog box, 89, 181
Print Setup dialog box, 75, 89, 181
printing
- categories, 38
- checks, 73–78, 151–152
- fonts for, 88
- reports, 89–90, 152, 181–182
- scheduled transactions, 70–71
- setup for, 75, 89, 151–152

program groups, 18

Q

.QIF files, 146–148, 216
quality of printing, 90, 182
questions and answers, 212–218
Quicken format, 146–150

R

reconciling checkbooks, 97–105, 167, 218
Record Due Transactions dialog box, 69–70
Recorder, 91–95
register reports, 80–81, 187–190
regular transactions, 65
Reminder dialog box, 69–70
Reminder to Backup option, 123, 143, 145
Rename Category dialog box, 35, 160
renaming
- accounts, 15, 154, 156–167
- categories, 34–35, 159–160
- classifications, 40, 162–163
- payees, 42, 164

replacing transaction information, 133
Report Column Width dialog box, 87, 180
Report dialog box, 94
Report/Budget command, 110, 183–184
Report/Income and Expense Report command, 184–186
Report/Net Worth Report command, 186
Report/Register Report command, 187–190, 218

Report/Summary Report command, 41, 83, 86, 190–191
Report/Tax Report command, 192–194
reports, 41, 79–82, 175
account list, 157
for budgets, 110–113, 183–184
buttons for, 176
for categories, 161
customizing, 84–85, 176–181, 183–194
displaying, 83, 95
exporting, 90–91, 182
income and expense, 184–186
net worth, 186
payroll, 206–209
printing, 89–90, 152, 181–182
reconciliation, 218
Recorder for saving, 91–95
register, 187–190
summary, 175–176, 190–191
tax, 192–194
viewing, 86–88
Restore Backup dialog box, 144
restoring archive files, 142–144
returned checks, 214
rows for reports, 84, 183, 185, 190, 192
Run dialog box, 4, 91

S

sample checks, 76–77
Schedule Future Transaction dialog box, 67, 207
scheduled transactions, 66–71, 124, 172–173, 207
screen fonts, 88
Search/Find command, 196
searches for transactions, 128–129
Select Account dialog box, 76
Select Accounts dialog box, 26–27, 177
Select Category dialog box, 47–49, 113
Select Checks dialog box, 77
Select Checks to Reprint dialog box, 77
Select Classification dialog box, 48, 50
Select Export Account dialog box, 146
Select Fonts dialog box, 88, 180
Select Payee dialog box, 47
Select Transactions dialog box, 85, 87, 113, 177–180
selecting
accounts, 21, 26–27, 76, 146, 176–177
categories, 4, 47–50, 113, 140
classifications, 47–48, 50
fonts, 88, 180
payees, 47
text, 137
transactions, 46–50, 85, 87, 113, 177–180
separators for dates and numbers, 125
Settings dialog box, 69, 122–124, 173
setup command, 4
Setup New File dialog box, 4–5, 12
Shift-" keys, 25–26, 138
shortcuts
for accounts, 154–155, 157
for categories, 24, 35, 38, 158–159, 161
in Checks & Forms window, 51
for classifications, 163
for macros, 93
for payees, 42, 140, 164–165
for reports, 190, 192
for subcategories, 38
Show Message Bar option, 123
single-entry bookkeeping, 214
SmartFill, 24–25, 123–124, 139, 163
SmartFill On option, 123–124
SmartReconcile, 102–103
Split Transaction dialog box, 58–60, 71
split transactions
entering, 57–62, 71, 131–132
for loans, 120, 217
for paychecks, 208, 215
in reports, 188
Starting Balance Adjustment dialog box, 103–104
Starting Balance Warning dialog box, 99–100
starting Money, 18, 195–196
subcategories, 32, 158
budgets for, 38, 108–110

creating, 37–38, 160–161
deleting, 35–36, 160
renaming, 160
subclassifications, 40
Summary Report dialog box, 83, 86, 91, 175–176
summary reports, 41, 80–81, 83, 86, 91, 175–176, 190–191
SuperSmartFill, 25–26, 139–140, 163

T

tab-delimited text files, 90, 182
Tab key for transactions, 21–23, 136
Task List dialog box, 93–94, 170
tax reports, 80, 192–194
and categories, 35, 37–38, 159, 161, 193–194
and subcategories, 38
text
editing, 28, 127
selecting, 137
thousands separator, 125
title bars, 6
titles for reports, 183, 185–187, 190, 192
Toolbar, 9, 197, 199
Top Line View, 20, 173–174
totals
for reports, 188
with split transactions, 58–61
transactions, 17–18
accounts for, 21, 135, 213
categories for, 20, 23–24, 57–62, 135, 199, 203
Checks & Forms window for, 50–55
classifying, 38–39, 58, 162–163
creating accounts and categories in, 28–29, 37, 140, 159
cursor for, 136
deleting, 28, 36, 127, 134
editing, 28, 133–134
entering, 21–26, 134–141
exporting, 147–148
fields for, 22–23, 134–136
future. *See* future transactions
marking, 100–101, 129–130
multiple accounts with, 26–27
opening Account Book window for, 19–20
for reports, 85, 184–185, 189, 191–193
searching for, 128–129
selecting, 46–50, 85, 87, 113, 177–180
SmartFill for, 24–25, 123–124, 139–140, 163
split. *See* split transactions
SuperSmartFill for, 25–26
transfers, 29, 54, 213
views for, 20–21
workspace for, 9–10
Transactions Due Reminder option, 124
Transfer category, 29
Transfer form, 54
transfers, 29, 54, 213
with asset accounts, 119
importing, 149
for reports, 186
type, viewing transactions by, 178

U

undoing commands, 28, 132, 141

V

view drop-down lists, 9, 42, 46, 198–199, 201
View/Other command, 48–49
View/Scientific command, 168
View/Standard command, 168
viewing, 45
reports, 86–88
transactions, 20–21, 46–50, 178–180
VOID checks and transactions, 28, 77, 132–133
vouchers, 74

width of reports, 87, 180
WIN.INI file, 195
Window/Account Book command, 6, 199–200
Window/Checks & Forms command, 50, 201–202
Window/Future Transactions command, 67–68, 202–204, 207
Windows' calculator, 61–62, 167–170
Windows fonts, 88, 180
Windows Recorder, 91–95
withholding payroll taxes, 208–209
workspace, transaction, 9–10

yearly budgets, 108

zeros, 125

Selections from The SYBEX Library

HOME MONEY MANAGEMENT

Understanding Managing Your Money
Gerry Litton
372pp. Ref. 751-7
A complete guide to the principal features of this practical software package. Replete with valuable examples and useful illustrations. Learn how various screens should be handled, and how to avoid trouble spots. Topics include: using the word processor and the calculator; managing a budget; maintaining a checkbook; estimating tax liabilities; calculating net worth; and more.

ACCOUNTING

Mastering DacEasy Accounting (Second Edition)
Darleen Hartley Yourzek
463pp. Ref. 679-0
This new edition focuses on version 4.0 (with notes on using 3.0), and includes an introduction to DacEasy Payroll. Packed with real-world accounting examples, it covers everything from installing DacEasy to converting data, setting up applications, processing work and printing custom reports.

Mastering DacEasy Accounting (Third Edition)
Darleen Hartley Yourzek
480pp; Ref. 876-9
This newly revised edition is updated to cover versions 3.1 and 4.1. Turn here for a systematic approach to setting up, managing and maintaining an efficient, easy-to-use accounting system. Practical, business-minded examples help you apply DacEasy, and to master the ins and outs of routine accounting procedures.

Mastering Peachtree Complete III
Darleen Hartley Yourzek
601pp. Ref. 723-1
Presented from the business user's perspective, this practical, task-oriented guide can be used as a step-by-step tutorial or an easy reference guide. Detailed topics include: preparing your records for computer conversion; setting up and maintaining files; managing accounts payable and receivable; tracking inventory, and more. With a glossary of accounting and computer terms.

Up & Running with Quicken 4
Darleen Hartley Yourzek
139pp. Ref. 783-5
Enjoy a fast-paced introduction to this popular financial management program. In just 20 steps—each taking only 15 minutes to an hour—you can begin computerized management of all your financial transactions. Includes a special chapter for small business.

Understanding Quicken 4
Steve Cummings
506pp. Ref. 787-8
A practical guide to managing personal and business finances. Readers build a solid financial recordkeeping system, as they learn the ins and outs of using Quicken 4 to print checks; manage monthly bills; keep tax records; track credit cards, investments, and loans; produce financial statements, and much more.

SPREADSHEETS AND INTEGRATED SOFTWARE

1-2-3 for Scientists and Engineers
William J. Orvis
371pp. Ref. 733-9

This up-to-date edition offers fast, elegant solutions to common problems in science and engineering. Complete, carefully explained techniques for plotting, curve fitting, statistics, derivatives, integrals and differentials, solving systems of equations, and more; plus useful Lotus add-ins.

The ABC's of 1-2-3 (Second Edition)

Chris Gilbert
Laurie Williams

245pp. Ref. 355-4

Online Today recommends it as "an easy and comfortable way to get started with the program." An essential tutorial for novices, it will remain on your desk as a valuable source of ongoing reference and support. For Release 2.

The ABC's of 1-2-3 Release 2.2

Chris Gilbert
Laurie Williams

340pp. Ref. 623-5

New Lotus 1-2-3 users delight in this book's step-by-step approach to building trouble-free spreadsheets, displaying graphs, and efficiently building databases. The authors cover the ins and outs of the latest version including easier calculations, file linking, and better graphic presentation.

The ABC's of 1-2-3 Release 2.3

Chris Gilbert
Laurie Williams

350pp. Ref. 837-8

Computer Currents called it "one of the best tutorials available." This new edition provides easy-to-follow, hands-on lessons tailored specifically for computer and spreadsheet newcomers—or for anyone seeking a quick and easy guide to the basics. Covers everything from switching on the computer to charts, functions, macros, and important new features.

The ABC's of 1-2-3 Release 3

Judd Robbins

290pp. Ref. 519-0

The ideal book for beginners who are new to Lotus or new to Release 3. This step-by-step approach to the 1-2-3 spreadsheet software gets the reader up and running with spreadsheet, database, graphics, and macro functions.

The ABC's of 1-2-3 for Windows

Robert Cowart

300pp; Ref. 682-0

This friendly introduction covers the new Windows-compatible 1-2-3 speadsheet, with tutorials suitable for Windows newcomers—even those using a computer for the first time. Easy-to-follow lessons show how to build business spreadsheets, create graphs to illustrate the numbers, print worksheets and graphs, use the database manager, and more.

The ABC's of Excel on the IBM PC

Douglas Hergert

326pp. Ref. 567-0

This book is a brisk and friendly introduction to the most important features of Microsoft Excel for PC's. This beginner's book discusses worksheets, charts, database operations, and macros, all with hands-on examples. Written for all versions through Version 2.

The ABC's of Quattro Pro 3

Alan Simpson
Douglas Wolf

338pp. Ref. 836-6

This popular beginner's tutorial on Quattro Pro 2 shows first-time computer and spreadsheet users the essentials of electronic number-crunching. Topics range from business spreadsheet design to error-free formulas, presentation slide shows, the database, macros, more.

The Complete Lotus 1-2-3 Release 3 Handbook

Greg Harvey

700pp. Ref. 600-6

Everything you ever wanted to know about 1-2-3 is in this definitive handbook. As a Release 3 guide, it features the design and use of 3D worksheets, and improved graphics, along with using Lotus under DOS or OS/2. Problems, exercises, and helpful insights are included.

Lotus 1-2-3 Instant Reference Release 2.2 SYBEX Prompter Series

Greg Harvey
Kay Yarborough Nelson

254pp. Ref. 635-9

The reader gets quick and easy access to any operation in 1-2-3 Version 2.2 in this handy pocket-sized encyclopedia. Organized by menu function, each command and function has a summary description, the exact key sequence, and a discussion of the options.

Lotus 1-2-3 Release 2.3 Instant Reference

Judd Robbins

175pp; Ref. 658-8

The concise guide to 1-2-3 commands, functions, and options covers all versions of release 2—offering on-the-job help and quick reminders in a compact, easy-to-use format. Entries are organized alphabetically and provide a summary description, exact syntax, complete options, a brief discussion with examples, and valuable tips.

Lotus 1-2-3 for Windows Instant Reference

Gerald E. Jones

175pp; Ref. 864-5

This complete quick-reference guide to 1-2-3 for Windows includes an overview of new features, and a special section on Windows. Concise, alphabetized entries present and briefly explain every feature and function of the software—for a quick reminder, or fast help with new options. Each entry provides a summary, exact syntax, complete options, and examples.

Mastering Enable/OA

Christopher Van Buren
Robert Bixby

540pp. Ref 637-5

This is a structured, hands-on guide to integrated business computing, for users who want to achieve productivity in the shortest possible time. Separate in-depth sections cover word processing, spreadsheets, databases, telecommunications, task integration and macros.

Mastering Excel 3 on the Macintosh

Marvin Bryan

586pp; Ref. 800-9

Turn here for in-depth coverage of today's Excel, and how to make the most of its enhanced capabilities—including those applicable to System 7. For all user levels: clear, jargon-free explanations and exercises for the beginner are complemented by advanced information and tips for the power user.

Mastering Excel 3 for Windows

Carl Townsend

625pp. Ref. 643-X

A new edition of SYBEX's highly praised guide to the Excel super spreadsheet, under Windows 3.0. Includes full coverage of new features; dozens of tips and examples; in-depth treatment of specialized topics, including presentation graphics and macros; and sample applications for inventory control, financial management, trend analysis, and more.

Mastering Framework III

Douglas Hergert
Jonathan Kamin

613pp. Ref. 513-1

Thorough, hands-on treatment of the latest Framework release. An outstanding introduction to integrated software applications, with examples for outlining, spreadsheets, word processing, databases, and more; plus an introduction to FRED programming.

Mastering Freelance Plus

Donald Richard Read

411pp. Ref. 701-0

A detailed guide to high-powered graphing and charting with Freelance Plus. Part I is a practical overview of the software. Part II offers concise tutorials on creating specific chart types. Part III covers drawing functions in depth. Part IV shows how to organize and generate output, including printing and on-screen shows.

Mastering Quattro Pro 3

Gene Weisskopf

618pp. Ref. 841-6

A complete hands-on guide and on-the-job reference, offering practical tutorials on the basics; up-to-date treatment of advanced capabilities; highlighted coverage of new software features, and expert advice from author Gene Weisskopf, a seasoned spreadsheet specialist.

Mastering SuperCalc5

Greg Harvey
Mary Beth Andrasak

500pp. Ref. 624-3

This book offers a complete and unintimidating guided tour through each feature. With step-by-step lessons, readers learn about the full capabilities of spreadsheet, graphics, and data management functions. Multiple spreadsheets, linked spreadsheets, 3D graphics, and macros are also discussed.

Quattro Pro 3 Instant Reference

Gene Weisskopf

225pp; Ref. 822-X

A superb quick reference for anyone using Quattro Pro 3. This pocket guide offers quick access to instructions on all menu commands, @ functions, and macro keywords. Beginners will use this book to pick up the basics, while more experienced users will find it a handy place to check unusual or specialized commands.

Teach Yourself Lotus 1-2-3 Release 2.2

Jeff Woodward

250pp. Ref. 641-3

Readers match what they see on the screen with the book's screen-by-screen action sequences. For new Lotus users, topics include computer fundamentals, opening and editing a worksheet, using graphs, macros, and printing typeset-quality reports. For Release 2.2.

Understanding 1-2-3 Release 2.3

Rebecca Bridge Altman

700pp. Ref. 856-4

This comprehensive guide to 1-2-3 spreadsheet power covers everything from basic concepts to sophisticated business applications. New users will build a solid foundation; intermediate and experienced users will learn how to refine their spreadsheets, manage large projects, create effective graphics, analyze databases, master graphics, more.

Understanding 1-2-3 for Windows

Douglas Hergert

700pp; Ref. 845-9

This all-new guide to 1-2-3 is written especially for the new Windows version. There are self-contained chapters for beginning, intermediate and advanced users, with business-oriented coverage of such topics as the Windows environment, worksheet development, charting, functions, database management, macro programming, and data sharing.

Understanding PFS: First Choice

Gerry Litton

489pp. Ref. 568-9

From basic commands to complex features, this complete guide to the popular integrated package is loaded with step-by-step instructions. Lessons cover creating attractive documents, setting up easy-to-use databases, working with spreadsheets and graphics, and smoothly integrating tasks from different First Choice modules. For Version 3.0.

Up & Running with Excel for Windows

D.F. Scott

140pp; Ref. 880-7

In just 20 easy steps, you can learn the fundamentals of Excel for Windows. This concise, no-nonsense approach is ideal for computer-literate users who are upgrading from an earlier version of Excel, or migrating from another spreadsheet program.

Up & Running with Lotus 1-2-3 Release 2.2

Rainer Bartel

139pp. Ref 748-7

Start using 1-2-3 in the shortest time possible with this concise 20-step guide to the major features of the software. Each "step" is a self-contained, time-coded lesson (taking 15, 30, 45 or 60 minutes to complete) focused on a single aspect of 1-2-3 operations.

Up & Running with 1-2-3 Release 2.3

Robert M. Thomas

140pp. Ref. 872-6

Get a fast start with this 20-step guide to 1-2-3 release 2.3. Each step takes just 15 minutes to an hour, and is preceded by a clock icon, so you know how much time to budget for each lesson. This book is great for people who want to start using the program right away, as well as for potential 1-2-3 users who want to evaluate the program before purchase.

Up & Running with Lotus 1-2-3 Release 3.1

Kris Jamsa

141pp. Ref. 813-0

A 20-step overview of the new 3.1 version of 1-2-3. The first twelve steps take you through the fundamentals of creating, using and graphing worksheets. Steps 13 through 15 explain the database, and the balance of the book is dedicated to 3.1's powerful WYSIWYG capabilities.

Up & Running with Lotus 1-2-3 for Windows

Robert M. Thomas

140pp; Ref. 73-4

The ideal book for computer-literate users who are new to spreadsheets, upgrading from a previous version of 1-2-3, or migrating from another spreadsheet program. In just 20 concise lessons, you learn the essentials of the new 1-2-3 for Windows, with no time wasted on necessary detail.

Up & Running with Quattro Pro 3

Peter Aitken

140pp. Ref.857-2

Get a fast start with this 20-step guide to Quattro Pro 3. Each step takes just 15 minutes to an hour, and is preceded by a clock icon, so you know how much time to budget for each lesson. This book is great for people who want to start using the program right away, as well as for potential Quattro Pro 3 users who want to evaluate the program before purchase.

WORD PROCESSING

The ABC's of Microsoft Word (Third Edition)

Alan R. Neibauer

461pp. Ref. 604-9

This is for the novice WORD user who wants to begin producing documents in the shortest time possible. Each chapter has short, easy-to-follow lessons for both keyboard and mouse, including all the basic editing, formatting and printing functions. Version 5.0.

The ABC's of Microsoft Word for Windows

Alan R. Neibauer

334pp. Ref. 784-6

Designed for beginning Word for Windows users, as well as for experienced Word users who are changing from DOS to the Windows version. Covers everything from typing, saving, and printing your first document, to creating tables, equations, and graphics.

The ABC's of WordPerfect 5

Alan R. Neibauer

283pp. Ref. 504-2

This introduction explains the basics of desktop publishing with WordPerfect 5: editing, layout, formatting, printing, sorting, merging, and more. Readers are shown how to use WordPerfect 5's new features to produce great-looking reports.

The ABC's of WordPerfect 5.1 for Windows

Alan R. Neibauer

350pp; Ref. 803-3

This highly praised beginner's tutorial is now in a special new edition for WordPerfect 5.1 for Windows—featuring WYSIWYG graphics, font preview, the button bar, and more. It covers all the essentials of word processing, from basic editing to simple desktop publishing, in short, easy-to-follow lessons. Suitable for first-time computer users.

The ABC's of WordPerfect 5.1

Alan R. Neibauer

352pp. Ref. 672-3

Neibauer's delightful writing style makes this clear tutorial an especially effective learning tool. Learn all about 5.1's new drop-down menus and mouse capabilities that reduce the tedious memorization of function keys.

The Complete Guide to MultiMate

Carol Holcomb Dreger

208pp. Ref. 229-9

This step-by-step tutorial is also an excellent reference guide to MultiMate features and uses. Topics include search/replace, library and merge functions, repagination, document defaults and more.

Encyclopedia WordPerfect 5.1

Greg Harvey
Kay Yarborough Nelson

1100pp. Ref. 676-6

This comprehensive, up-to-date WordPerfect reference is a must for beginning and experienced users alike. With complete, easy-to-find information on every WordPerfect feature and command—and it's organized by practical functions, with business users in mind.

Mastering Microsoft Word on the IBM PC (Fourth Edition)

Matthew Holtz

680pp. Ref. 597-2

This comprehensive, step-by-step guide details all the new desktop publishing developments in this versatile word processor, including details on editing, formatting, printing, and laser printing. Holtz uses sample business documents to demonstrate the use of different fonts, graphics, and complex documents. Includes Fast Track speed notes. For Versions 4 and 5.

Mastering Microsoft Word 5.5 (Fifth Edition)
Matthew Holtz
650pp; Ref. 836-X
This up-to-date edition is a comprehensive guide to productivity with Word 5.5—from basic tutorials for beginners to hands-on treatment of Word's extensive desktop publishing capabilities. Special topics include style sheets, form letters and labels, spreadsheets and tables, graphics, and macros.

Mastering Microsoft Word for Windows
Michael J. Young
540pp. Ref. 619-7
A practical introduction to Word for Windows, with a quick-start tutorial for newcomers. Subsequent chapters explore editing, formatting, and printing, and cover such advanced topics as page design, Style Sheets, the Outliner, Glossaries, automatic indexing, using graphics, and desktop publishing.

Mastering Microsoft Word for Windows (Second Edition)
Michael J. Young
550pp; Ref. 1012-6
Here is an up-to-date new edition of our complete guide to Word for Windows, featuring the latest software release. It offers a tutorial for newcomers, and hands-on coverage of intermediate to advanced topics, with an emphasis on desktop publishing skills. Special topics include tables and columns, fonts, graphics, Styles and Templates, macros, and multiple windows.

Mastering Microsoft Works on the IBM PC
Rebecca Bridges Altman
536pp. Ref. 690-1
Written especially for small business and home office users. Practical tutorials cover every aspect of word processing, spreadsheets, business graphics, database management and reporting, and basic telecommunications under Microsoft Works.

Mastering MultiMate 4.0
Paula B. Hottin
404pp. Ref. 697-9
Get thorough coverage from a practical perspective. Tutorials and real-life examples cover everything from first startup to basic editing, formatting, and printing; advanced editing and document management; enhanced page design, graphics, laser printing; merge-printing; and macros.

Mastering WordPerfect 5
Susan Baake Kelly
709pp. Ref. 500-X
The revised and expanded version of this definitive guide is now on WordPerfect 5 and covers wordprocessing and basic desktop publishing. As more than 200,000 readers of the original edition can attest, no tutorial approaches it for clarity and depth of treatment. Sorting, line drawing, and laser printing included.

Mastering WordPerfect 5.1
Alan Simpson
1050pp. Ref. 670-7
The ultimate guide for the WordPerfect user. Alan Simpson, the "master communicator," puts you in charge of the latest features of 5.1: new dropdown menus and mouse capabilities, along with the desktop publishing, macro programming, and file conversion functions that have made WordPerfect the most popular word processing program on the market.

Mastering WordPerfect 5.1 for Windows
Alan Simpson
1100pp. Ref. 806-8
The complete guide to learning, using, and making the most of WordPerfect for Windows. Working with a mouse and the Windows graphical user interface, readers explore every software feature, build practical examples, and learn dozens of special techniques—for macros, data management, desktop publishing, and more.

Microsoft Word Instant Reference for the IBM PC
Matthew Holtz
266pp. Ref. 692-8
Turn here for fast, easy access to concise information on every command and feature of Microsoft Word version 5.0—for editing, formatting, merging, style sheets, macros, and more. With exact keystroke sequences, discussion of command options, and commonly-performed tasks.

Microsoft Word for the Macintosh Instant Reference

Louis Columbus

200pp; Ref. 859-9

Turn here for fast, easy access to precise information on every command and feature of Word version 4.0 for the Mac. Alphabetized entries provide exact mouse or key sequences, discussion of command options, and step-by-step instructions for commonly performed tasks.

Teach Yourself WordPerfect 5.1

Jeff Woodward

444pp. Ref. 684-7

Key-by-key instructions, matched with screen-by-screen illustrations, make it possible to get right to work with WordPerfect 5.1. Learn WordPerfect as quickly as you like, from basic editing to merge-printing, desktop publishing, using graphics, and macros.

WordPerfect 5.1 On-Line Advisor Version 1.1

SYBAR, Software Division of SYBEX, Inc.

Ref. 934-X

Now there's no more need to thumb through lengthy manuals. The On-Line Advisor brings you answers to your WordPerfect questions on-screen, right where you need them. For easy reference, this comprehensive on-line help system divides up each topic by key sequence, syntax, usage and examples. Covers versions 5.0 and 5.1. Software package comes with 3½" and 5¼" disks. **System Requirements:** IBM compatible with DOS 2.0 or higher, runs with Windows 3.0, uses 90K of RAM.

Understanding Professional Write

Gerry Litton

400pp. Ref. 656-1

A complete guide to Professional Write that takes you from creating your first simple document, into a detailed description of all major aspects of the software. Special features place an emphasis on the use of different typestyles to create attractive documents as well as potential problems and suggestions on how to get around them.

Understanding WordStar 2000

David Kolodney
Thomas Blackadar

275pp. Ref. 554-9

This engaging, fast-paced series of tutorials covers everything from moving the cursor to print enhancements, format files, key glossaries, windows and MailMerge. With practical examples, and notes for former WordStar users.

Up & Running with Grammatik 2.0

David J. Clark

133pp. Ref. 818-1

Learn to use this sleek new grammar- and style-checking program in just 20 steps. In short order, you'll be navigating the user interface, able to check and edit your documents, customizing the program to suit your preferences, and rating the readability of your work.

Up & Running with WordPerfect Office/Library PC

Jeff Woodward

142pp. Ref. 717-7

A concise tutorial and software overview in 20 "steps" (lessons of 15 to 60 minutes each). Perfect for evaluating the software, or getting a basic grasp of its features. Learn to use the Office PC shell; use the calculator, calendar, file manager, and notebooks; create macros; and more.

Up & Running with WordPerfect 5.1

Rita Belserene

164pp. Ref. 828-9

Get a fast-paced overview of telecommunications with PROCOMM PLUS, in just 20 steps. Each step takes only 15 minutes to an hour to complete, covering the essentials of creating, editing, saving and printing documents; formatting text; creating multiple-page documents; working with fonts; importing graphic images, and more.

Up & Running with WordPerfect 5.1 for Windows

Rita Belserene

140pp; Ref. 827-0

In only 20 lessons, you can start making productive use of the new WordPerfect 5.1 for Windows. Each lesson is pre-timed to take just 15 minutes to an hour to complete. As you work through the book, you'll pick up all the skills you need to create, edit, and print your first document—plus some intermediate and advanced skills for a more professional look.

SYBEX

FREE BROCHURE!

Complete this form today, and we'll send you a full-color brochure of Sybex bestsellers.

Please supply the name of the Sybex book purchased.

____

How would you rate it?

____ Excellent　____ Very Good　____ Average　____ Poor

Why did you select this particular book?

- ____ Recommended to me by a friend
- ____ Recommended to me by store personnel
- ____ Saw an advertisement in ______________________
- ____ Author's reputation
- ____ Saw in Sybex catalog
- ____ Required textbook
- ____ Sybex reputation
- ____ Read book review in ______________________
- ____ In-store display
- ____ Other ______________________

Where did you buy it?

- ____ Bookstore
- ____ Computer Store or Software Store
- ____ Catalog (name: ______________________)
- ____ Direct from Sybex
- ____ Other: ______________________

Did you buy this book with your personal funds?

____Yes　____No

About how many computer books do you buy each year?

____ 1-3　____ 3-5　____ 5-7　____ 7-9　____ 10+

About how many Sybex books do you own?

____ 1-3　____ 3-5　____ 5-7　____ 7-9　____ 10+

Please indicate your level of experience with the software covered in this book:

____ Beginner　____ Intermediate　____ Advanced

Which types of software packages do you use regularly?

____ Accounting	____ Databases	____ Networks
____ Amiga	____ Desktop Publishing	____ Operating Systems
____ Apple/Mac	____ File Utilities	____ Spreadsheets
____ CAD	____ Money Management	____ Word Processing
____ Communications	____ Languages	____ Other ______________ (please specify)

Which of the following best describes your job title?

____ Administrative/Secretarial ____ President/CEO

____ Director ____ Manager/Supervisor

____ Engineer/Technician ____ Other ______________________
(please specify)

Comments on the weaknesses/strengths of this book: ______________________

____

____

____

____

Name ______________________

Street ______________________

City/State/Zip ______________________

Phone ______________________

PLEASE FOLD, SEAL, AND MAIL TO SYBEX

-- --

SYBEX, INC.
Department M
2021 CHALLENGER DR.
ALAMEDA, CALIFORNIA USA
94501

SEAL

EDITING A FIELD

TO	PRESS
Undo last change	Alt-Backspace or Ctrl-Z
Extend selection	Shift-Arrow Keys
Delete selection	Del
Delete selection without being asked to confirm the deletion	Ctrl-Del
Cut to clipboard	Ctrl-X or Shift-Del
Copy to clipboard	Ctrl-C or Ctrl-Ins
Paste from clipboard	Ctrl-V or Shift-Ins

SPECIAL COMMANDS

TO	PRESS
Schedule a future transaction or enter a scheduled transaction into an account	Ctrl-E
Pay bills	Ctrl-P
Balance (reconcile) an account against a statement	F9
Display calculator	Ctrl-K
Switch between Top Line and Entire Transaction Views	Ctrl-T
Create a custom view (the Other option from the View drop-down menu)	Ctrl-O
Find	Ctrl-F
Repeat last Find	F7
Help	F1